SELLING THE FREE MARKET

Selling the Free Market

The Rhetoric of Economic Correctness

JAMES ARNT AUNE

THE GUILFORD PRESS
New York   London

© 2001 The Guilford Press
A Division of Guilford Publications, Inc.
72 Spring Street, New York, NY 10012
www.guilford.com

Printed in the United States of America

This book is printed on acid-free paper.

Last digit is print number: 9 8 7 6 5 4 3 2 1

Library of Congress Cataloging-in-Publication Data

Aune, James Arnt.
   Selling the free market : the rhetoric of economic correctness / by James
Arnt Aune.
      p. cm. (Revisioning rhetoric)
   Includes bibliographical references and index.
   ISBN 1-57230-598-3
      1. Free enterprise—United States.   2. Social choice—United States.
   3. Libertarianism—United States.   I. Title.   II. Series.

   HB95.A94 2001
   330.12′2′0973—dc21   00-061696

Selling the Free Market is the latest volume in the Guilford series
"Revisioning Rhetoric," edited by Karlyn Kohrs Campbell and
Celeste Michelle Condit.

For James W. Pratt,
Michael L. Tillmann,
and Kenneth G. Wilkens

Good men speaking well

I hope our generation may have learned that it is perfectionism of one kind or another that has often destroyed whatever degree of decency societies have achieved.

—FRIEDRICH HAYEK, *The Constitution of Liberty*

Economic studies call for and develop the faculty of sympathy, and especially that rare sympathy which enables people to put themselves in the place, not only of their comrades, but also of other classes.

—ALFRED MARSHALL, *Principles of Economics*

A commonwealth is the property of a people. But a people is not any collection of human beings brought together in any sort of way, but an assemblage of people in large numbers associated in an agreement with respect to justice and a partnership for the common good.

—CICERO, *De republica*

Contents

PART III. The Struggle over Reagan's Free-Market Legacy

Acknowledgments

I will dispense with the usual academic convention of placing family members last in the list of acknowledgments. Miriam Ruth Aune read successive versions of the manuscript and helped me keep my life and values in perspective. My sons, Nick and Daniel, both of whom have autism, provided useful distractions from writing. They will no doubt be among the first casualties of the free marketeers' assault on public education. Only the care of several public school employees, in both Minnesota and Texas, have kept them (and, perhaps, me) from being institutionalized: Kathy Holden, Judy Code, Jacky Meyer, Doreen Wentrcek, and Sue Calhoun.

For encouragement at crucial stages of the project, I especially want to thank Charles Conrad and Dana Cloud. Melissa Rector and Katherine DeMaria were extraordinarily helpful research assistants. The Office of the Vice President for Research at Texas A&M University awarded me a Scholarly and Creative Activities Grant that enabled me to do research for this volume. Ron Aronson invited me to present a portion of it at the 1997 "Arguing with the Right" conference sponsored by Democratic Socialists of America and helped me develop my arguments for an activist audience. Eileen Scallen introduced me to the world of legal scholarship and otherwise provided friendship and inspiration. My department heads at Texas A&M, Linda Putnam and Rick Street, helped provide the best possible environment for productive work, as did Marty Medhurst—my favorite conservative.

I am grateful to Deirdre McCloskey, Karlyn Kohrs Campbell, and Celeste Condit for their gracious and perceptive prepublication reviews. Peter Wissoker of The Guilford Press has been the ideal editor, patiently tolerating my precapitalist sense of deadlines. I have tried to shape this volume both for academic students of rhetoric and for a general audience. If I have succeeded at all in reaching a general audience, it is owing to the extraordinarily helpful work of Karen Verde, Kelly Waering, and Laura Specht Patchkofsky, my other editors.

Finally, I want to thank the three men who introduced me to the art of rhetoric: James W. Pratt, Michael L. Tillmann, and Kenneth G. Wilkens. Good teachers always know that there are higher values than the market.

Preface

When undertaking a work that covers such a wide range of theories and concepts, convention dictates a brief discussion of the author's commitments and limitations. For a time I felt rather nervous about poaching in the preserve of economists, but it eventually struck me that, however difficult the technical vocabulary often is, economists are actually more responsible about writing for a larger public than many academics, especially in the humanities, are. And it is the *public* aspects of economic argument with which I concern myself in this volume—the way in which technical economic rhetoric has been allowed to trump the moral and cultural *meanings* of community, nature, work, and the market. I am interested in helping readers develop ways of talking about economic policy issues publicly. U.S. citizens for some time have lacked the ability to deliberate publicly about the meaning of the market and its increasing invasion of every aspect of their daily lives. I am interested in contributing to the project John Dewey defined in 1929 in *The Public and Its Problems*, namely, "the improvement of the methods and conditions of debate, discussion, and persuasion" (1980: 208)—and in applying it to contemporary public discussion of economic policy.

This volume is written by an old-fashioned socialist. I have learned as much, however, from traditionalist conservative critics of market rhetoric as I have from those on the left. In fact, this book developed out of my first book, *Rhetoric and Marxism*, in which I took seriously (much to the dismay of some leftist comrades) the critique of Marxism by cultural conservatives. I began to realize that the same arguments traditionalists made against communism are equally applicable to libertarianism:

1. There is a problem with the "rationalist" desire to radically transform traditional institutions and human nature on the basis of an intellectual plan (see Oakeshott 1962).
2. There is a need to maintain a strong commitment to "mediating institutions," or "seedbeds of virtue" (such as the family, the neighborhood, the union, the church or synagogue) that stand between the individual and the market, just as they stand between the individual and the state (see Berger and Neuhaus 1977; Glendon and Blankenhorn 1995; for a perceptive critique of Berger and Neuhaus's approach to mediating institutions, see Schwartz 1998: 125–126).
3. Human *motivation* cannot be reduced solely to economic terms (regardless of whether the economic is framed in terms of class struggle or utility maximization).
4. Those who revolt so intensely against the real world as to scorn such accomplishments and well-established institutions as representative democracy, unions, welfare, and public education are mentally at odds with themselves and the real world.

I have written this book with considerable optimism largely in the hope that a coalition can be created to temper the depredations wrought by the latest incarnation of the free market—that is, globalized laissez-faire capitalism. It is my view that the *extreme consequences* of much free-market thinking have been insufficiently appreciated. The study of rhetoric, among other things, is a way of overcoming the recent fragmentation of left-leaning coalitions. We can begin overcoming this fragmentation by understanding the intellectual limits of a free-market rhetoric that proposes to turn us all into lonely, utility-maximizing monads with no *place* of our own, that is, no ties to a wider social and political community based on time-tested practices and thought.

Introduction

How the Right Triumphed

Selling the Free Market investigates the strategies used to promote the "market revolution" that appears to have triumphed around the world since the fall of the Berlin Wall in 1989. As president, Bill Clinton proclaimed in 1996 that "the era of big government is over"—even if in private he had also complained about being turned into an "Eisenhower Republican" in order to satisfy "a bunch of f——ing bond traders" (Woodward 1994: 84).

The most puzzling thing about this apparent triumph of free-market arguments in politics and economics is how remarkably unsuccessful the application of radical free-market policies has actually been. Until fairly recently, the economic growth since 1991 had been at the slowest pace experienced during any post-World War II business cycle (Henning 1998: 8; Krugman 1994: 107–129). During the Reagan and Bush years, the monetarism of Milton Friedman and the Chicago school pushed the United States and Great Britain into recession and yet did not cure inflation (Henning 1998: 200–202). The shortcomings of airline deregulation are apparent to most consumers, who continue to experience frequent delays, substandard meals, and cramped and stuffy cabins; small-town travelers, in particular, suffer from increased fares and limited access (see Harrison and Bluestone 1991: 160). Although long-distance telephone rates dropped after deregula-

1

tion, basic local telephone service costs rose 50–60 percent nationwide, most significantly affecting low-income families (Phillips 1990:
99). However, the most spectacular fiasco of deregulation resulted
from the removal of interest-rate ceilings in 1980 and the 1983 act
that effectively permitted savings-and-loan associations to get out of
the home mortgage business. The resulting S&L bailout ended up
costing taxpayers about $200 billion (Krugman 1994: 161–164; Hen-
ning 1998: 86–92).

Not only did free-market "solutions" fail to attain stated goals,
they also dramatically increased income inequality in the United
States. In 1994 the average income of the top 5 percent of families was
more than 19 times that of the bottom 20 percent of families, as compared with "only" 11.5 times as much in 1970. The income share of
the middle 20 percent of families also fell during this same period
(Krugman 1994: 130–150). Despite President Ronald Reagan's oft-
stated concern for the "truly needy," the average supplemental social
security (SSI) recipient (the physically and mentally disabled) by the
mid-1990s received 50 percent less in constant dollars than in 1970
(Peterson 1995: 114). Interestingly, the decline in SSI and other welfare
benefits probably is explainable in market terms, since the decreasing
commitment of the federal government to either income redistribution or block grants to the states has created a powerful incentive for
the states to engage in a "race to the bottom," further beggaring welfare recipients in the process (Peterson 1995: 114). States "rationally"
cut welfare expenses in order to avoid becoming "welfare magnets."

Despite this record of failure, proposals to extend the "discipline"
of the market to social security (by privatizing the system or linking it
more closely to the stock market), the public schools (through a
voucher system), and the delivery of social services (through government grants to churches) are now gaining in popularity. Certainly part
of the free-marketeers' popularity can be attributed to a failure of
nerve by liberal Democrats to propound meaningful alternative solutions. The primary focus of this book, however, is on the arguments for
radical free-market principles. Albert O. Hirschman (1991), in his
pathbreaking book *The Rhetoric of Reaction*, was puzzled by the ascendancy of conservatism. He decided to avoid an in-depth attack on
conservatives, especially through an inquiry into the conservative
mind or personality, and sought instead to focus on the "cooler" matters of the "surface phenomena" of "discourse, arguments, rhetoric"

(x). Although I have been inspired by Hirschman's work, I cannot share his detachment. Rhetoric is not solely a surface phenomenon. Rhetorical practice constantly reconstitutes our collective notions of character and community. This volume is an attempt to begin to come to terms with the destructive impact that free-market economics has had on character and community in the United States.

THE "NONEXECUTIVE" SUMMARY

At some point during the mid-1990s I began noticing "executive summaries" attached to official documents of various kinds. As the actual costs of distributing information have declined dramatically, owing to computing advances and improved communications technology, the cost of the executive reader's time has increased equally dramatically, encouraging heightened efficiency in business prose and public speech. The "bulleted" list, the seamless PowerPoint presentation with its preset organizational devices, and the software templates for constructing pie charts, graphs, and spreadsheets have become normal features of everyday communication in business and the corporate world.

The business of communicative efficiency and its relation to serious thought is not a new preoccupation. G. W. F. Hegel's (1967) preface to *The Phenomenology of Mind* reflects on the problem of writing a "preface" that somehow supplements the hard reflective work of slogging through philosophic rhetoric.[1] Richard Rorty (1982) points out that the great dream of Western thought has always been to "write up the results" of an investigation as clearly as possible. Truth itself would best be expressed in that moment when one "sees" these results in an intuitive flash, requiring no further conversation.[2]

Armed with the insights of Hegel and Rorty, many contemporary humanities scholars have prescribed a radical slowing down of the reading process to prevent the dire ideological consequences of too much clarity. The result has been an increased distancing of the general reader from much advanced work in the humanities and qualitative social sciences—leading to such effective parodies as the "Bad Writing Contest" sponsored by the journal *Philosophy and Literature* (see Cohen 1997). In much the same way that Republicans expropriated the language of "class" from Democrats during the 1980s—accusing them of being Brie-eating, Volvo-driving elitists who despised

ordinary working folks, for example—traditional humanists have in effect depicted newer methods of scholarly inquiry as undermining the
very possibility of communication.

Rhetorical studies—my disciplinary "home"—occupies a peculiar
contradictory cultural and institutional space in the two trends I have
identified. The shift in the nature of work from producing *things* to
producing *texts* means that there is great demand nowadays for skilled
communicators–whether in written, spoken, or graphic modes. Yet,
the special insight of classical rhetoricians into the strategic character
and radical contingency of all forms of human symbolic action seems
to disappear as "communication" becomes increasingly synonymous
with "information."

Lost somewhere along the way has been the insight that rhetoric
is the process of justifying decisions under conditions of uncertainty,
an insight shared by great figures of the rhetorical tradition, from Aristotle and Cicero down to Chaim Perelman and Richard McKeon.

So now I embark upon an examination of the rhetoric of academic defenders of the free market, a form of rhetoric I prefer to call
"economic correctness."[3] I also examine the ways in which free-
market rhetoric has been used in more workaday political rhetoric.
Such is the way that rhetoricians have proceeded at least since Aristotle, carefully cataloging strategies and their impact on audiences in
the hope of achieving a reasoned perspective on how human beings
justify decisions under conditions of uncertainty (Zarefsky 1995). But I
combine this procedure with what I believe was Karl Marx's greatest
contribution to the human sciences, namely, his unmasking of the
strategies used by apologists for capitalism to obscure alternative ways
of seeing both the nature of work and the possibilities of justice.

There has been much talk in recent years about the demoraliza-
tion of the left and its fraying into various subgroups characterized by
"identity politics." I believe that a clearly communicated moral and
practical assault on the dominance of free-market rhetoric could be a
unifying political force, one that would appeal to broad constituencies
across the left as well as to the center and to social conservatives, some
of whom have been the most powerful critics of global capitalism. The
right has been very successful in promoting the myth of a "political
correctness" movement (that supposedly erases all distinctions between groups, lest anyone be "offended"), so it is now necessary to
communicate to the public the right's promotion of "economic correctness"—at the expense of families, jobs, neighborhoods, and the

traditional "liberal arts" education. The unapologetically atomistic quality of free-market rhetoric deserves much wider public discussion—at least as much discussion as "speech codes" and other purported "PC" outrages actually warrant.

HOW THE RIGHT TRIUMPHED

Although the triumph of free-market rhetoric does not require an elaborate theoretical explanation, the analysis and refutation of free-market rhetoric does. The seemingly universal (though not necessarily irreversible) triumph of the market comes down to money, public relations skills, and the mobilization of the energies of a dedicated cadre of libertarians. Just when the left began to abandon class-interest-based forms of political and cultural explanation, the right upgraded its efforts to purchase a bit of intellectual respectability.

In July 1997 the National Committee for Responsive Philanthropy (NCRP) published a report titled *Moving a Public Policy Agenda: The Strategic Philanthropy of Conservative Foundations*. Thanks to an unusually skillful publicity effort, the report was widely covered in the mainstream press and eventually came to contribute to the argument (albeit uniquely) that a "vast right-wing conspiracy" against President Clinton underlay press treatment of the Monica Lewinsky scandal that broke in January 1998. Many of the details of the report had been familiar to left-leaning activists for some time, but with the report's publication the sheer enormity of the right-wing ideological offensive on universities, mainline churches, and the government became clear for the first time. Among the NCRP's many findings, the report disclosed that twelve conservative foundations contributed $210 million from 1995 to 1997 to fund free-market-oriented programs at universities and to subsidize the research of right-wing "public intellectuals."

In contrast, such traditionally liberal foundations as the Ford and Rockefeller foundations have deliberately eschewed coordinating their policy agendas, preferring instead to be more localized and community-based. It is hard to escape the conclusion that, ironically, during the past twenty years right-wing advocates have been the only people to take seriously Antonio Gramsci's injunction to create "organic" intellectuals.

In addition to better financing its intellectuals, the right has lately been honing its communications skills more assiduously and adeptly than liberals, or the left. Right-wing advocates nowadays have a much enlarged network in which well-crafted speeches, public relations campaigns, and mass media strategies are highly valued. In the spring of 1998, according to Conrad Martin, director of the Fund for Constitutional Government and the Charles Stewart Mott Fund, there was only one full-time progressive publicist working in Washington, DC.[4] It was not always so. The left used to be known for its oratory—emancipationist Frederick Douglass, socialist Eugene Debs, and Marxist revolutionary Rosa Luxemburg all were known as formidable public speakers.[5] Socialist leaders often developed oratorical skills in local debating societies organized by unions and other progressive groups, but obviously there is no modern-day equivalent.

The Origins of the American Right

It would be pointless, however, to overemphasize the power of conservative foundations and think tanks. In part they have been successful precisely because of the left's ineptness at communication and persuasion. The good news is that the conservative coalition, long held together by anticommunism and the sheer force of Ronald Reagan's rhetoric, has begun to split into factions. The focus of this book is on the emergence of a distinctive "free-market" strain in conservative thought, but this strain can best be defined "dialectically," that is, in terms of its relationship to other forms of conservativism. The major historians of American conservatism—George Nash (1996), and Paul Gottfried and Thomas Fleming (1988)—have identified four strains in post-World War II American conservative thought (see also Diamond 1995).

First is the traditionalist wing (now sometimes called the "paleocons"), represented above all by the late Russell Kirk, southern regionalists such as Richard Weaver and M. E. Bradford, and the Rockford Institute and its magazine, *Chronicles of Culture*. The recent revival of southern nationalism by the League of the South (formerly the Southern League) has also increased traditionalist ranks considerably.

A second tradition is libertarianism. The roots of American libertarianism lie in the thought of Albert Jay Nock and Frank Chodorow.

Libertarianism is defined by its obsessive emphasis on the market as a solution to all human problems.

Third, the "fusionist" wing, so called because of the desire to fuse cultural conservatism with a celebration of capitalism, is associated with Frank S. Meyer and William F. Buckley, Jr., both of *National Review*. Ronald Reagan is the patron saint of the fusionist approach, although his presidency came to be criticized by traditionalists for neglecting their "social" agenda. Reagan's staunch anticommunism was the ideological cement that unified the warring wings of the conservative movement.

Conservatives' anticommunist efforts have largely been directed by the fourth designated group, the neoconservatives. The "neocons" can be distinguished from the other wings by their more social-scientific focus, their secular outlook, their internationalism, and their acceptance of modest forms of social insurance. Irving Kristol, his son William (who wrote the infamous "Murphy Brown" speech for Dan Quayle), Norman Podhoretz, James Q. Wilson, and the journals *Commentary*, *The Weekly Standard*, and *The Public Interest* are all associated with neoconservatism. The Rupert Murdoch-financed *The Weekly Standard* (referred to unkindly by paleocons as "My Weekly Reader") is bidding to replace *National Review* as the most influential conservative journal of opinion.

In day-to-day Republican Party politics, the divisions I have described here are sublimated or often entirely ignored, especially where there are candidates who are able rhetorically to bridge differences and unite the factions. For example, Governor George W. Bush, Jr., of Texas has strong Christian Right support, but his own policies are more closely allied with traditional country-club Republicanism. Still, the ever present threat of Gary Bauer of the Family Research Council and Charles Dobson of Focus on the Family to bolt from the Republican Party over its only "lukewarm" opposition to abortion represents a serious threat to party unity (Tackett 1998). Were the stock market to crash, 1929-style, or were a major foreign policy crisis to require substantial troop commitments, Patrick Buchanan—by appealing to anxieties about the globalization of the economy—might be able to forge a new Reagan-like coalition of blue-collar workers, the Christian Right, militia types, and other radical populists. This emerging contradictory relationship between free-market rhetoric and free-trade realities that

send jobs elsewhere is the single most important development in contemporary politics.

AN OVERVIEW OF FREE-MARKET RHETORIC

Again, the good news from the early 1990s onward is that, after its apparent worldwide triumph during the 1980s, the right is seriously at
war with itself. Mainstream Republicans used the energies of the
Christian Right to mobilize voters, and they used the policy ideas of
the libertarians to attack government intervention in the economy,
but now the differences and tensions among various cultural, economic, and military definitions of conservatism are increasingly becoming evident. On issues such as Chinese religious persecution and
free trade, the left has an opportunity to exploit divisions among economic and cultural conservatives. Although this volume is addressed
to academic analysis more than practical politics, I cannot deny an
occasional pang of sympathy for the traditionalists. Most recent left-
academic critiques of conservatism have emphasized the Christian
Right. My conviction, however, is that by far the greatest danger emanates
from unreconstructed libertarianism. Unfortunately, much of the agenda
of the postmodernist academic left is quite congenial to libertarianism.
Postmodernists and libertarians appeal to the same audience of highly
educated young people, especially those in technology- and culture-
related enterprises. Yet, libertarianism's intensely intellectual appeal
makes it unlikely to develop into a serious political movement. During
the 1980s in England, the Tories were extremely successful in promoting the image of a Labour Party in thrall to the "loony left." Similarly,
in the United States today, the libertarian movement's most offbeat
beliefs and policy prescriptions—ranging from drug legalization, to
Federal Reserve-free banking, to the creation of markets for babies and
organ transplants—definitely deserve greater exposure by journalists
and a more intensified public discussion of their practical merits.

Libertarian policy prescriptions are based on just a few principles,
outwordly appealing in their seeming simplicity. They are, as the libertarian legal scholar Richard Epstein (1995) puts it, "simple rules for a
complex world." The first of these principles is that *social problems can
be solved by creating a market.* Are schools failing? Create a free market
in education. Is there pollution or waste of resources? Create a market

in the resource or sell the right to pollute. Above all, do not *conserve* any resources—because conservation will destroy incentives to find new resources. Is there a shortage of human organs for transplants? Let people sell their body parts. Not enough babies for adoption? Allow people to sell their babies.[6] Angered by vulgar displays of wealth when people are starving? Realize that "what today may seem extravagance or even waste, because it is enjoyed by the few and even undreamed of by the masses, is payment for the experimentation with a style of living that will eventually be average to many" (Hayek 1960: 44).

As Kenneth Burke wrote, human beings are "rotten with perfection" (1966: 19). There is a drive to give our lives and our beliefs a certain formal completeness, taking the consequences of a given vocabulary "to the end of the line." Sometimes we conceive of a "perfect" enemy, projecting onto that enemy "any troublesome traits of our own that we would negate" (Burke 1966: 18). Henry Adams once wrote that politics is the systematic organization of hatreds. One reason for the increased popularity of libertarianism could be that the traditional candidates for scapegoating have either disappeared (in the case of communism) or have become unacceptable (particular races or ethnic groups). Nowadays, "government" serves as the scapegoating device for all the ills in the body politic. And in the romantic drama spun by libertarians, the market assumes the role of hero in vanquishing government.

An analysis of libertarian rhetoric reveals that there is no principled way to stop the marketization of everything, including the most intimate spheres of family and cultural life. The most extreme libertarians, such as Murray Rothbard, even propose the replacement of government (which is, after all, simply a force that holds a monopoly on coercion) by private protection agencies. "The nation-state," writes Robert Bartley, editor of *The Wall Street Journal*, "is finished" (Brimelow 1996: 293).

The second principle of libertarianism states that *the transition to an information society is inevitable*. No sooner had Marxists given up on the idea of historical determinism than the free-marketeers reinvented it with a vengeance. Bill Gates's "frictionless capitalism" (which in practice may equate to getting screwed without noticing it) will be brought into being by the Net. Libertarians assert that no criticism or attempt to regulate the new communication technologies should be allowed—despite the fact that in some cases corporations' access to the airwaves and even the Internet was underwritten by American taxpayers. It is widely argued in libertarian and even more mainstream business journals that the Internet not only will create an integrated global market but also will radically reduce taxation and social services, eventually making government itself obsolete (see Huber 1996). It is precisely with this idea that free-marketeers part company once and for all with the conservatism of Presidents Reagan and Bush. It is not possible to promote *both* the need for patriotic sacrifice *and* the idea that the nation-state is finished.

Certain core ideas espoused by the right appear increasingly contradictory as libertarian perspectives come to the fore. As we have suggested, the market may conflict with family values, Third Wave developments may trump individual liberty, and the end of the nation-state as we know it may run counter to traditional patriotism. As Nietzsche said, if you see something slipping, give it a shove. The increased visibility of radical libertarian rhetoric in American politics may represent an irrepressible opportunity to give the right a much-deserved shove.

These principles of "economic correctness" are increasingly mouthed in the universities and especially in conservative think tanks, but their obvious long-term implications may strike ordinary Americans as horribly cruel. They need to hear this economic gibberish firsthand, and the left (as well as traditional conservatives) needs to make sure that they hear it. Free-market rhetoric is powerfully persuasive only to a certain kind of elite audience; uncoupled from nationalist appeals, as it has become in its drive for "perfection," it begins to lose its power to motivate general audiences in a positive way.

THE OUTLINE OF THIS VOLUME

In Part I, I develop an alternative formulation of the rhetoric of economics. Chapter 1 discusses the historical relationship between rhetoric and economics and provides an overview of the ideological uses of traditional economic analysis. I then examine three political issues on which free-market thinkers have promoted "economically correct" views: the farm crisis, the minimum wage, and the role of trade unions. Chapter 2 develops a "pure" model of free-market rhetoric in terms of its displacement of politics with economics. Drawing on Robert Hariman's work in *Political Style*, I contend that free-market rhetoric has been persuasive because of its skillful use of a "realist style" that denies its own discursiveness. Academically inclined readers may wish to turn at this point to the appendix, which discusses Deirdre McCloskey's proposal for a rhetoric of economics. I criticize McCloskey's neglect of the institutional basis of economic rhetoric, a neglect most apparent in her praise of the "bourgeois virtues."

In Part II, I present rhetorical criticism of three key intellectual defenses of the free market by examining the way in which Ayn Rand (Chapter 3), Robert Nozick (Chapter 4), and Murray Rothbard and Charles Murray (Chapter 5) portray character, community, and communication in their rhetoric.

In Part III, I examine the rhetoric of the market as applied in practical politics. Chapters 6 and 7 discuss the role of the market in Ronald Reagan's rhetoric and the efforts of Pat Buchanan and Newt Gingrich to resolve the inherent frictions between free trade and the free market that Ronald Reagan successfully sublimated during his presidency. The Conclusion sets forth certain "political lessons" that mindful readers, I hope, will have internalized by taking this text to heart.

PART I

Rhetoric, Economics, and Problems of Method

CHAPTER ONE

The Rhetoric–
Economics Connection

Rhetorical Strategies of Economic Analysis

There is nothing new about the connection between rhetoric and economics. Adam Smith, the father of modern economics, taught rhetoric and moral philosophy as well as political economy.[1] David Ricardo, author of *Principles of Political Economy and Taxation* (1817/ 1996), a still influential defense of free trade, was a skilled parliamentary speaker.[2] Thomas DeQuincey wrote on literature, rhetoric, and economics—in fact, he claimed to have been cured of his opium addiction by reading David Ricardo![3] Richard Whately, Anglican Archbishop of Dublin, wrote the only significant treatise on rhetorical theory in the nineteenth century and also held a chair in political economy at Oxford.[4]

One way to delve into the connection between rhetoric and economics is to examine economic *writing*: What does it mean to write a treatise on economics? The writings of Smith, Ricardo, and to some extent even Alfred Marshall read more like a philosophical treatise than a present-day textbook or scholarly paper in economics. Economics originally was taught as part of moral philosophy at Cambridge and gradually developed into a "science," taking on more and more aspects of the scientific method and emphasizing value-free inquiry, heavy use of mathematics and formal models, the devaluing of history, a belief that knowledge progresses, and so on.[5] But by the 1980s, economists became concerned about their seeming irrelevance to public policy, their inability to talk to the rest of the academy, the general ignorance of history among graduate students in economics, and, perhaps above all, the fact that if economics were really a science it should have developed more consensus by now.

The concern about economics as a discipline was galvanized by Deirdre N. McCloskey in a series of articles and books on the "rhetoric of economics," beginning in 1983, prior to her sex change operation (Donald McCloskey 1983, 1984, 1985). The notion that McCloskey, a prominent economist—and an economist of the *Chicago School* no less (the Chicago School being known for its scientism)—would be mucking around not just with the humanities, but with the oldest and least respectable part of the humanities, was something of a *succès de scandale*.

As McCloskey's work has developed, however, it is apparent that she is far more willing to let rhetoric trump the scientific pretensions of rational choice theory than to let any doubt be cast on the virtues of the free market. McCloskey has neglected the *institutional* foundations of economic inquiry. She frequently criticizes the "angry and distracted people of the academy" but never acknowledges in her writings that some economic ideas gain greater visibility because powerful persons and groups pay to make sure they are visible. In *Knowledge and Persuasion in Economics*, she combines Habermas's insights into communicative ethics with her view of rhetoric, proposing a *Sprachethik* (ethics of speech): "Don't lie; pay attention; don't sneer; cooperate; don't shout; let other people talk; be open-minded; explain yourself when asked; don't resort to violence or conspiracy in aid of your ideas. These are the rules adopted by joining a good conversation" (McCloskey 1994: 99).

But who pays for the room? For the transportation of the conversation partners? Such questions commit the sin of motivism, but they are not idle ones in the "angry and distracted" academic marketplace. As noted earlier, thanks to the National Committee for Responsive Philanthropy, we are now getting a clearer picture of who pays for the room. The NCRP's 1997 report (authored by Sally Covington) detailed how twelve foundations, including the Olin and Scaife foundations, contributed $210 million between 1995 and 1997 to create conservative academic programs at such esteemed institutions as the University of Chicago, Harvard, George Mason, Yale, and Claremont McKenna.[6]

These foundations also paid to support certain conservative regional and Washington-based think tanks that coordinate their policy agendas. The website of the regional "Heartland Institute" lists nearly 150 of these organizations, many devoted to coordinating an assault on public education and public support for the poor, homeless, and handicapped (see http://www.heartland.org).[7]

The foundations and think tanks also paid "public intellectuals" for their output. Dinesh D'Souza received a fellowship through the American Enterprise Institute, for example, and Robert Bork received one through the Heritage Foundation. Many influential books, from Christina Hoff Summers's *Who Stole Feminism?* (1994) to Richard Herrnstein and Charles Murray's *The Bell Curve* (1994), have been funded by right-wing foundations. Journals such as *First Things* (devoted to promoting political and theological conservatism) and *The New Criterion* (devoted to a defense of high modernism in the arts and an assault on new approaches to arts and humanities education) have received hundreds of thousands of dollars of start-up money and continuing support from the same foundations. To be fair, centrist and liberal think tanks also support academic scholarship, but they do not coordinate their public policy agendas as successfully as the right-wing groups do.

Particularly threatening to academic freedom is the foundations' willingness to pay students to take classes in law and economics, courses that inevitably promote a party line on the role of markets in solving all social problems. UCLA actually canceled such a program because administrators believed it unfairly exploited the financial need of students for ideological ends—a cancellation that received virtually no press coverage (Wilson 1995: 26–30).

An example of the sort of research such centers promote can be found in the website for the Private Enterprise Research Center at Texas A&M University.[8] The center was founded as part of a mandate from the Texas Senate in 1978 requiring education in the free-enterprise system in the public schools of Texas. The center issues working papers and press releases on such questions as executive compensation, the privatization of public lands, unionization, and the minimum wage, all from a radical libertarian economic perspective; it has close ties to the Olin-funded American Enterprise Institute.

The draft description of the economic component of the curriculum for the master's degree in public administration at the new George Bush School of Government and Public Service displayed a similar bias. The course in economic analysis is to be taught as two-thirds microeconomic analysis (itself an ideological choice), and "it is argued" (the passive voice, naturally) "that the government has a potential role [in the economy] when (i) property rights are ill-defined, and (ii) markets are not competitive."[9]

Not long after I wrote the first draft of this chapter, I found myself embroiled in a controversy at the Bush School. In October 1998 I received a telephone call from a political reporter at the *Dallas Morning News*, who asked me if I would be willing to comment on the gubernatorial debate between Democrat Gerry Mauro and Republican incumbent George W. Bush. Since I teach courses in argumentation and debate, I believed I was competent to make some observations. I told the reporter that neither candidate made any glaring mistakes, that Governor Bush looked presidential and that he was an excellent public speaker, unlike his father, whose rhetorical skills I characterized as "inept."

I found out a month later that my comments had angered someone in the Bush family. The full story emerged only in July 1999 when an intrepid local reporter named John Kirsch uncovered a series of Bush School memos through a Freedom of Information Act request. Dale Laine, a top aide to Governor Bush, complained directly to the head of the Bush School about my comments. The director of the school drafted guidelines prohibiting professors from claiming an affiliation with the Bush School when offering opinions or "undocumented material" about the Bush family. In a later interview Mr. Laine denied he was trying to stifle my academic freedom, but was merely accusing me of offering only a personal opinion not grounded in a "scientific" study. The only reason I even made the comment about former President Bush's rhetorical difficulties was that he had made the point himself in a public presentation at Texas A&M in the fall of 1997. President Bush disparaged his own rhetorical skills, contending that it is more important for a president to have managerial abilities.

It turned out that I was not the only faculty member with a Bush School connection who had been the victim of attempted intimidation by the governor's aides. George Edwards, who holds an endowed chair in political science, also was criticized for having projected Republican Senator Bob Dole's loss in the 1996 presidential election. Neither Edwards nor I really suffered any direct injury, but I experienced a few sleepless nights wondering if I had injured the reputation of my department. Thus far, articles about political influence in the Bush School have appeared in local Texas papers, the Associated Press wire, the *Chronicle of Higher Education, Editor and Publisher,* the *Nation,* and *Lingua Franca* (see Soskis 2000). Sources at the Bush School who wish to remain anonymous have confirmed that Governor Bush himself was involved in the efforts to regulate professorial speech. The irony is that if I were a conservative academic who had received similar treatment from a Democratic governor, I would have become a poster child for "political correctness."

Another disturbing trend is the pervasiveness of direct corporate influence on universities. Changes in patent law and tax law in the early 1980s permitted greater corporate contributions to universities in exchange for the right to purchase the results of university research. Corporations were thus able to shift part of their research and development costs to universities at a time when the college work–study program was cut by 26.5 percent (after adjusting for inflation), tuition rates at public universities increased 170 percent, and the funding of meritorious proposals before the National Institutes of Health (NIH) dropped from 50 percent to 20 percent (Soley 1995: 9–10).

Professors who largely turned a blind eye to the gutting of U.S. labor law under the Reagan-appointed National Labor Relations Board (NLRB) and the unwillingness of President Clinton to address the issue of labor law reform while he had Democratic majorities in both houses of Congress now find themselves in a position comparable to that of industrial workers in the early 1980s.[10] The assault on tenure as well as the pressure to quantify educational outcomes and increase teaching loads are part of the same triumph of the market that, as Habermas (1991) writes, blinds itself to every value that cannot be expressed in the form of a price (32).

THE PRINCIPLES OF RATIONAL CHOICE

Economics rests on "microfoundations": *Homo economicus*, the rational actor calculating utility in the given case. Arjo Klamer and Donald McCloskey (1988) write that the "rational choice model is the master metaphor, enticing one to think 'as if' people really made decisions in this way" (14).[11] Methodological individualism and rational choice have been transposed from the theory of pricing in microeconomics to economics as a whole, and thence to sociology, political science, and law. Under the various labels of rational choice, social choice, public choice, and law-and-economics, this view of human reasoning has settled into major law schools and university departments (although not without some subsidization from right-wing foundations). It has even spawned a school of rational choice Marxism, of whom the outstanding practitioners are Erik Olin Wright (1985), Jon Elster (1985), and G. A. Cohen (1978).

The economic analysis of human behavior derives from a basic definition of human behavior as "involving participants who maximize their utility from a stable set of preferences and accumulate an optimal amount of information and other inputs in a variety of markets" (Becker 1976: 14). People weigh costs and benefits based on their subjective tastes and their available information.

The first principle of rational choice is that a rise in price reduces quantity demanded. If stuff costs more, people tend to want less of it. This in turn implies the second principle: a rise in price increases the quantity supplied. If people buy widgets and shortages appear, the price of widgets goes up, and this serves as an incentive for suppliers to enter the market and provide more widgets. Note that these laws do not just work in cases of explicit prices; they also work with "shadow prices," such as the relative costs and benefits of crime to a criminal, or relative grades between two sections of the same college course. More precisely, "Even without a market sector . . . each commodity has a relevant marginal 'shadow' price, namely, the time required to produce a unit change in that commodity" (Becker 1976: 6).

It is easy to observe relationships—such as the one between supply and demand—using two variables. You can not only manipulate changes in the variables easily but also derive from them more complex ideas, such as "consumer surplus" (the area under the demand curve and above the price), "indifference curves" (bundles of goods to which the consumer is equally indifferent), and so on. Most important, you can derive policy conclusions about the "real world" elegantly and efficiently. Want to know what a government-mandated increase in the minimum wage will do? Simply raise the price of labor and see what happens: *Voila!* The demand drops, putting people out of work. (This assumes that the demand for labor is "elastic," that is, it responds to changes in price. In some businesses, perhaps most notably the restaurant business, demand for labor is relatively inelastic.)

Rational choice principles have been used to justify capital punishment on the grounds that the existence of capital punishment increases the shadow price of murder (Ehrlich 1975). The usual objection to this argument is that murder is not committed by the "rational actor" implicit in the theory (see Bedau 1982). The response is that rational action is not the same as conscious calculation; further, even if the deranged murderer is not deterred by the death penalty, another potential murderer might be. More important, Ehrlich did no sociological or psychological research on the communicative impact of the death penalty. He created a "toy economy," based on the applied theory of price, and crunched the numbers. The resulting "seven lives saved for every execution" argument was widely used in the rush to reinstitute death penalties during the late 1970s.

A third principle of rational choice is that resources tend to gravitate toward their most valuable uses if voluntary exchange is permitted. The opportunity for profit is a magnet that draws resources into an activity. If the "magnet doesn't work, the economist takes this as a sign not that people are dumb or have weird tastes or have ceased to be rational maximizers but that there are barriers to the free flow of resources. The barrier could be high information costs, externalities, inherent scarcities" (Posner 1992a: 11).

But, if the magnet is working—resources are being used where they are valued most highly—resources are being used efficiently. "Efficiency" is a great devil term among opponents of law-and-economics, immediately conjuring up the worst of Dickensian nightmares. The "perverse realism" of the applied theory of price is unlikely to be persuasive for the general public, which explains the tendency for other systems of norms—anticommunism, conservative Christianity—to develop alongside it. Posner notes that efficiency is not the only "worthwhile criterion" of social choice, but he is certainly accurate in his assessment that most people would agree that it is an important one.

Fourth, although economists would not put the matter quite this way, human communication enters the theory as a process of providing information. Communication generally can be reframed as "transaction," and the exchange of information can be one part of that transaction. Other parts might be the institutional framework of the transaction or the role of another party—say, an attorney who draws up a contract for the transaction. Communication costs, and the notion of transaction and information costs, are extraordinarily important in widening the scope of the economic framework.

To summarize, the messages inherent in economic analysis of human behavior are the following: (1) people respond to incentives; (2) there is an inverse relationship between price and quantity demanded; (3) efficiency defined in terms of wealth maximization is a useful standard for evaluating public policy; and (4) information and transaction costs must be considered when analyzing human behavior and policy outcomes.

PROBLEMS WITH RATIONAL CHOICE

The student usually encounters rational choice theory in Economics 101, and if the teacher is skillful, the student quickly learns that the "rat choice" is surprisingly applicable to all sorts of human behavior. It has an inherent formal, rhetorical appeal for two reasons: (1) it has that characteristic that Kenneth Burke (1968) referred to as the "syllogistic form," in which a text appeals to a reader simply because it ties up all the loose ends, much as the classic mystery story does (124); and (2) it taps into the student's capacity for irony.

There are literally hundreds of interesting rational choice explanations (from why popcorn costs so much at the movie theater to why the custom of giving engagement rings developed), but economists typically do not test them empirically. The economist's equivalent of the magician's "abracadabra" is the Latin phrase *ceteris paribus*—"everything else being equal." You can always escape empirical exceptions to a rational choice prediction simply by claiming that the exceptions reflect some slight (but critical) variation in the nature of the producer, commodity, or consumer, thus not invalidating the general applicability of the prediction. Political scientists Donald P. Green and Ian Shapiro (1994) have documented the startlingly small amount of empirical success that rational choice theory has had in political science. To select the most obvious example, if rational choice theory were universally true, no one would vote, since the possibility of altering an election outcome with a single vote is infinitesimally small. The attempt to "solve" the election outcome problem with rational choice explanation has generated an enormous literature, probably the largest of any aspect of rational choice scholarship (Green and Shapiro 1994: 47–71).

Another problem with rational choice theory, perhaps related to the commonsense public view that it misses some essential aspects of the human person, is that it cannot account for the emergence of social norms or for various kinds of path dependency. If rational choice theory is correct, then in the absence of evil things such as government intervention there should always be efficient, wealth-maximizing outcomes. Yet, there are several counterexamples of certain products or practices being "locked in" (as de facto monopolies) simply because they were the first to come along or because they were able to grab a large market share very quickly, owing to some unique circumstance. Among the most widely cited examples is the "qwerty" layout for typewriters and computer keyboards. It appears that the layout, which is difficult for some to learn, was originally created to lessen the frequency of jamming under a strictly alphabetical arrangement. That is, the earliest typewriters, which utilized an a-to-z arrangement, tended to jam frequently, given the underlying mechanics of the machine. By placing the most frequently used letters under and near the strongest fingers (third and index fingers) in the "home" position, and encouraging the use of *all* the fingers in typing, the most effective speed and least jamming could be effected (Krugman 1994: 221–224; for criticism of the example, see Liebowitz and Margolis 1990). Other examples are the settled victory of VHS videotape technology over Beta, and the ongoing dominance of Microsoft Windows technology over Apple's more "user-friendly" approach. In both cases, an essentially inferior product has driven out a superior one simply because it captured a large market share early on in the competition (in these cases, as a result of quirky corporate decisions—that is, Sony's initial decision not to license Beta technology and IBM's decision to license its PC operating systems from Microsoft).

The primary problem is that rational choice cannot account for the development of social norms. Some social norms may emerge for purely utilitarian cost–benefit reasons; for example, Pentecostal Christianity may be growing more rapidly than Roman Catholicism in Latin

America because of the positive externalities it creates for women (a male Pentecostalist perhaps being more likely to hold a job or be faithful in marriage). And yet rational choice theory cannot explain why a particular form of religion develops in the first place. Why Pentecostalism and not Calvinism? Why not Islam? How do we account for the dramatic decrease in cigarette smoking by African Americans in recent years? Cass Sunstein (1997) maintains that it is largely attributable to a highly successful advertising campaign that included the message: "They used to make us pick it; now they want us to smoke it." The strategic aspect of that campaign, as well as the heightened norm of nonsmoking in the Black community, simply cannot be explained in rational choice terms alone (32–69).

When the question of social norms emerges, the significance of rhetoric and communication emerges as well, for the role of things like epideictic oratory in shaping and reinforcing community norms, as well as the role of strategic persuasion in public life, now have a place even in the analysis of economic behavior. Simply reducing communication to the exchange of information fails to account for attitude and behavior change, and also fails to account for the persuasiveness of the theory itself. In addition to those loci identified by previous scholars, I would argue that a largely unexamined locus in policy argument consists of a representation of an ideal set of communicative practices that govern information gathering and argument about values and outcomes. This locus of good communication serves as a resource for condemning opponents and for valorizing particular cultural constructions of argument, evidence, emotion, and authority. The strains in a given rhetorical idiom often appear more clearly when the locus of good communication is examined.

However useful the economic analysis of human behavior may be in some settings, we have good reason to believe that it may be misleading in guiding public policy. The following case studies examine the application of economic methods to three essentially political issues, and in all three cases, I argue, the use of economic terminology involves more a *deflection* than a reflection of reality.

CASE STUDY 1: THE MINIMUM WAGE

A. O. Hirschman (1991) identifies certain characteristic patterns in the arguments of conservatives against change, from Edmund Burke down to Milton Friedman: conservatives habitually argue that good intentions lead to perverse consequences, that efforts at solving social problems through public policy are inevitably futile, and that large-scale efforts at reform jeopardize existing liberties.

First, the *perversity thesis*: "The attempt to push society in a certain direction will result in its moving all right, but in the opposite direction" (Hirschman 1991: 11). Charles Murray (1994), for instance, "proves" that spending money to eliminate poverty in the 1960s actually *increased* poverty. Hirschman demonstrates that: (1) this thesis is not universally true—change sometimes *does* occur in the direction intended, and there are even unintended *positive* consequences of social change; (2) it serves a psychological function for its adherents ("Could they be embracing the perverse effect for the express purpose of feeling good about themselves? Are they not being unduly arrogant when they are portraying ordinary humans as groping in the dark, while in contrast they themselves are made to look so remarkably perspicacious?"); and (3) it has its appeal because it is grounded in the mythic notion of divine punishment for sin and in the Greek hubris–nemesis pattern (35–42).

The *futility thesis*—the notion that social change simply does not work as expected—is a popular conservative argument (even if it contradicts the perversity thesis that usually accompanies it). Hirschman points out that conservatives usually make this point "with a certain worldly-wise wit as opposed to the alleged earnestness and humorlessness of the believers in progress" (45).

The futility thesis turns on metaphors about masks and veils, holding out the promise of a final recognition scene in which all is revealed (Hirschman 1991: 80). The problem, of course, is that such a promise again relies on the omnipotent wisdom of a class of experts against the alleged stupidity of the masses. Not only is such an assumption arrogant, but it violates its own norms. In other words, it proclaims that people and social systems cannot *learn* which policies work—presumably even from learning the futility thesis. Although Hirschman does not discuss the mythological or theological roots of the futility thesis, I would argue that it is strongly rooted in the Christian concept of original sin, a thesis that was put to effective ideological use by U.S. Protestant theologian Reinhold Niebuhr in defense of the Cold War (see Aune 1996).

There is, finally, the *jeopardy thesis*, the idea that continuing to move forward will jeopardize previous accomplishments. For instance, it is commonly asserted that the federal government's initiatives for greater equality among states' residents nationwide will jeopardize hard-won civil liberties. The world, of course, is more complex than that. Hirschman makes the interesting point that the welfare state came earlier to Germany precisely because it had no strong liberal tradition, thus preventing the marshaling of liberal jeopardy arguments, as in the United States and Britain (1991: 132).

During 1995 and 1996, a debate arose over minimum-wage legislation in the United States in which the perversity argument was deemed not sufficiently persuasive to overturn popular support for a minimum wage increase. I examined a sample of academic and popular arguments about the proposed increase that I found in the ABI/Inform index of business periodicals, and attempted to locate recurring patterns on both sides.

Hirschman (1991) writes: "In economics, more than in the other social and political sciences, the perverse-effect doctrine is closely tied to a central tenet of the discipline: the idea of a self-regulating market. To the extent that this idea is dominant, any public policy aiming to change market outcomes, such as prices or wages, automatically becomes noxious interference with beneficent equilibrating processes" (27). According to Milton Friedman (1982), the standard libertarian argument states that "Minimum wage laws are about as clear a case as one can find of a measure the effects of which are precisely the opposite of those intended by the men of good will who support it" (180). This argument assumes the existence of only two variables at any given time in the labor market, and also assumes a short-term window of analysis. There is virtually never any effort by minimum-wage opponents to argue against the analysis of proponents, other than to question the design of some of the empirical studies.

The standard economic arguments in favor of a higher minimum wage are that (1) increasing it may cause underlying supply and demand curves to shift and (2) a higher minimum wage may also increase productivity, thus boosting profits and employment (see Hirschman 1991: 28). I would add, using the law-and-economics concept of "signaling," that (3) the minimum-wage gauge provides useful "information" to employers as a group about the relative strength of labor and of popular discontent about business practices, thereby forestalling more radical redistributionist threats, and that (4) there is empirical evidence from the 1990 and 1991 wage hikes that appears to refute the perversity thesis (see Card and Krueger 1995; also Spriggs and Klein 1994).

The relative weakness of the case against a higher minimum wage is revealed in the lack of responsiveness to the key arguments in favor of it. The following are all the arguments against the minimum wage that I found in my survey:

1. The minimum wage reduces work opportunities for those who need them most (Verdisco and Cain 1996).
2. Organized labor is being demagogic by going directly to the voters to appeal for a minimum-wage increase (Coryman 1996).
3. It is an insult to U.S. business and industry to say that managers are not honest or caring enough to pay workers a fair salary without a government mandate (Nozar 1996).
4. The restaurant industry is especially hard-hit whenever the minimum wage is increased (Van Warner 1996). (Perhaps that is why Congress also passed $7 billion in tax relief for the food services industry at the same time that it passed the 1996 minimum-wage law.)
5. Most minimum-wage work is simply not worth even the minimum wage (Norton 1996).
6. Minimum-wage laws encourage the sending of jobs overseas (Riley 1996).
7. Any minimum-wage increase creates a slippery slope that hastens the day when the government sets prices as well (Kenney 1995).
8. More serious arguments, such as whether minimum-wage increases are the most efficient means of income redistribution as compared to the earned-income tax credit, appeared in a few places but were not addressed to popular audiences, perhaps because the credit had fallen under the congressional budget ax and because any defense of income redistribution is not "economically correct" (see Niskanen 1995).

The locus of perversity, then, dominates on the libertarian side of the debate. Opponents wisely recognized that, if they could at least create some doubt about the iron-clad certainty of the economic arguments, the sheer appeal of the proposal to audiences concerned about stagnating incomes made the Republican position vulnerable.

Another feature of libertarian economic argument is its tendency to avoid any but the most sweeping sorts of historical arguments. Hirschman demonstrates persuasively that the perversity arguments were first used to criticize the Poor Laws in England in the early nineteenth century. The Poor Laws helped ensure social peace and sustained food production during the Napoleonic Wars, but afterward the new political economy of Bentham, Malthus, and Ricardo argued for deterring the poor from public assistance by "imprisoning [them] in workhouses, compelling them to wear special garb, separating them from their families, cutting them off from communication from the poor outside and, when they died, permitting their bodies to be disposed of for medical experimentation" (Hirschman 1991: 30).

The argument from perversity proposes an implicit view of human action as a sort of hyperactive information-seeking in an extremely volatile environment. Every move may generate a perverse (but *never* beneficial) countermove—hence, the tendency toward unintended (but always *negative*) consequences. Taken to its ultimate extreme, the perversity argument would entail a rejection of all planning, even by private industry, leading either to paralysis or a series of equally perverse leaps of faith, which a few defenders of the Schumpeterian view of capitalism as "creative destruction" have actually advocated.

CASE STUDY 2: THE FARM CRISIS

For those of us who live in small towns or rural areas, the 1980s were a time of devastation, as thousands of "marginal" producers across the United States were forced off the land. Just as Stalin reminded the Russian people that you can't make an omelet without breaking eggs, or the Communist Party generally exhorted its flock to take the "long view," the free market agricultural economists magically wave away human suffering by appealing to the logic of economic history.

Lee J. Alston teaches in the department of economics at the University of Illinois, a public institution. His brief essay "American Farming: If It's Broke, Why Can't We Fix It?" (1993) appears in a book titled *Second Thoughts: Myths and Morals of U.S. Economic His-*

tory. The book, edited by Donald N. McCloskey, designed for undergraduate courses in economics and economic history, is published by Oxford University Press; however, the writing was financed and the book's publication was "arranged" by the Manhattan Institute, a conservative think tank based in New York City.

The introduction to the volume frames the essays by saying: (1) in this book, leading historians "show that commonly accepted wisdom about our economic past is often wrong, and therefore misleading" (3); (2) both big government and big science need to learn from history that social engineering never works—at least in accomplishing its intended ends; and (3) economics is above all a way of thinking, one that enables us to tell coherent and useful stories about the world.

Alston's essay makes the case that government action to solve the farm crisis of the 1980s was doomed to failure. This cautionary tale begins during World War I, when farm prices had increased dramatically during what some have referred to as the "golden age" of U.S. agriculture. Prices were high both because of increased demand and because the European countries' agricultural production had been curtailed by the war. The high prices created an incentive for farmers to bring less-productive land into cultivation. In July 1920 the "agricultural party" ended. By 1921, prices had fallen 30 percent; by 1932, they had fallen another 50 percent. Drought and insects (most notably the boll weevil in the South) also created problems for farmers.

Starting in 1928, farmers sought help from the government. Although President Calvin Coolidge vetoed a price-support measure passed by Congress in 1928, successor Herbert Hoover expanded the role of the federal government in the agricultural economy. The Farm Board was empowered to support prices by offering loans to farmers and permitting them to use future crops as collateral. Farmers would repay the loans if prices were high; if prices fell below the loan price, the farmers would give their crops to the government. Although the Farm Board's policies probably moderated the price slide, the agency had exhausted its funds by 1931.

After his election as president in 1932, Franklin D. Roosevelt adopted two policies to relieve farm distress: price supports and the renegotiation of credit terms. During the New Deal years, "rental and price-support payments made up as much as one-third of the income of some participating farmers" (Alston 1993: 53). States also built on federal effort by passing moratoria on farm foreclosures (twenty-five states did so between 1932 and 1934). Annual farm failures fell by half (from 4 percent to 2 percent), but bankers soon compensated for the inability to foreclose by raising interest rates. Consumers also paid higher prices for clothes and food.

Alston quickly cuts to the 1980s, when farms failed at the highest rates since the end of the Great Depression. During the inflationary 1970s farmers had entered "a bidding frenzy for land." The secretary of agriculture encouraged farmers to plant "fence row to fence row," anticipating continued high prices into the 1980s. But when "crop prices began to fall in 1980, troubles began." (Later, Alston blames the decrease in crop prices on the inflationary monetary and fiscal policy of the 1970s.) Farmers were able to obtain a moratorium on foreclosures in Iowa. In 1986, subsidies still represented one-third of farm income. The Farm Credit System still gave loans to farmers on unusually generous terms, compared with private banks. According to Alston, all this largesse goes to 2 million farmers, roughly 1 percent of the population, and the rest of the country pays for it: some $5 billion extra per year for agricultural goods (as of the early 1990s).

Alston then asks, what would happen if agricultural prices actually were allowed to be guided by the market? Farmers or their offspring would have to move to, say, Chicago and learn a new career, the way "steelworkers in Pittsburgh managed to do over the past decade." There would be trauma, to be sure, but it would reduce (albeit only by a small amount) the food costs of "being a poor parent . . . feeding a family in the Chicago slums." The cheapest and best thing to do would be to allow small family farmers to go out of business, just as we do other small businesses in this country, when they "cannot make it in the marketplace" (54–55).

Alston presents a number of positive benefits to introducing a free market in agriculture. He asserts (without evidence) that: (1) Capital requirements for entry into agriculture would fall, thus benefiting the small farmer; (2) even if corporate farming were to increase, the result would be greater productivity; (3) in the past, farming was efficient in small units because it made monitoring shirkers more practicable—but this is no longer necessary, given increased mechanization and standardization of agricultural production; and (4) comparatively inefficient farmers would have an incentive to diversify their holdings, and we would finally view farms simply as business ventures.

Simple, huh? The rhetorical appeal of Alston's cautionary tale is that of "economic" analysis generally. It reduces social complexity to a few simple principles: the inexorable law of supply and demand, the perfidiousness of government intervention, the glorious and open future promised by the elimination of government intervention. It also is appealing to intellectuals because it relies on irony as a mode of explanation: human actions may have perverse effects, especially in cases of social engineering. Using the *topos* (theme) of perverse effects enables the shrewd economist to wave away with a world-weary look any effort at interfering with the market. This makes the economist appear to have both worldly wisdom *and* a sense of humor, two characteristics often lacking in political radicals, who seem to be angry all the time.

A secondary use of irony is present in the economist's attack on the U.S. myth of the sturdy yeoman farmer and his virtues. Just as Richard Hofstadter attacked agrarian populism in the 1950s as a form of the "paranoid style," Alston appeals to the more cosmopolitan academic's sense that everybody living more than a stone's throw from the coasts is some sort of hick. Actually, the story may be more analogous to that depicted on the television show *Green Acres*, in which the rural hick, Mr. Haney, consistently fools the more cosmopolitan Mr. Douglas, who has made the mistake of romanticizing rural life and has ditched his successful job in Manhattan.

It is not clear, however, that even conventional economic analysis necessarily tells the same story that Alston does. The most disturbing thing about Alston's argument, from an ethical standpoint, is that there is simply no acknowledgment that competing economic explanations exist or that a reasonable person might differ with his policy prescriptions. It is tempting to ask whether the Manhattan Institute would have paid him to write the essay if he had dealt with competing arguments. One also wonders why the academic world is unable to deliver these arguments to readers without a subsidy from a think tank funded by the very rich.

From a strictly economic standpoint, there are several responses to Alston's arguments:

1. The price elasticity of demand for agricultural products is lower than for other commodities. In other words, consumer demand is not affected by price as much as with other commodities. People need to eat, both in good times and bad.

2. When productivity increases, farm income falls. One does poorly by doing well, as David Colander (1995) puts it. The supply curve shifts outward in the inelastic range of the demand curve (746).

3. Consumers—especially the poor woman in the Chicago slums who tugs at our heartstrings in Alston's narrative—are hardly worse off today than they were when farm subsidies began. When Herbert Hoover ran for reelection in 1932, he promised "two chickens in every pot." In today's money, chicken back then would have cost $8 a pound (Colander 1995: 746)—a huge testament to farming productivity over the years.

4. Although producers in other industries can coordinate production, even without cartels, there are still too many farmers to coordinate production easily. Weather and other natural forces also make farming more unpredictable than other industries.

5. Given the realities of the agricultural markets, it is unclear that a purely competitive solution is practical. Without government programs there would be considerable incentive to form (de facto) cartels. As Colander notes, today agriculture in the United States might be controlled by four or five major firms. Agricultural prices might be higher. Agricultural production might be lower.

I have to add here that Colander is no wild-eyed radical; his textbook covers in considerable detail the same points Alston does in his essay, noting additionally that the extraordinary productivity of U.S. agriculture may stem in part from its immunity from occupational safety and health legislation. The accidental death rate for farmers is much higher than the national average for other workers. Farmers work hard and skimp on safety measures. If agriculture became solely a big-business operation, there would be additional clamor for regulation—although not, of course, in Alston's and McCloskey's perfect world.

In short, if you analyze Alston's essay as a piece of rhetoric, a set of strategic choices conveyed via a variety of means of persuasion, and intended for a particular audience, you can make a case for the following conclusions: (1) The essay invites the reader to look at the world in a particular way, as a particular kind of person: one who sees through appearance to the enduring wellsprings of human conduct. One becomes an older, wiser person by taking on the role prescribed by the rhetor. No longer surprised by anything except perhaps the bounty of the unrestrained market, the reader is presented with a sort of cheery reassurance that the world does, after all, make sense. (2) This implied contract between the rhetor and the reader is largely fulfilled through the skillful selection of narrative detail and the omniscient attitude of the narrator. Alternative explanations of the 1980s farm crisis are simply ignored. The characters in the narrative—the farmer, the government, the hapless consumer, the godlike narrator— are fairly rounded and interesting. Since the reader of the narrative is likely to be a consumer, the clear identification of the narrator's interests with the consumer's is a wise choice.[12]

Strangely enough, if taken seriously as a prescription for policy, the essay contradicts its own premises. A sudden end of government price supports and credit control would be the most dramatic form of social engineering since the early days of the New Deal (or the Federal Reserve-engineered recession of 1980). Radical free-market thought here, as in so many other ways, is like a perverse mirror image of communism: the problem of the "transition" is undertheorized. Not only is it not clear how we might get from our current "statism" to the totally unregulated economy, but it is extremely likely that the immediate social consequences would be devastating, perhaps even more so than in the 1980s. Only a leader with the political will of a Stalin would be able to keep the social fabric together during years of radical dislocation that would ensue. As I argue later, in Chapter 6, there is a deep sense in which radical libertarianism requires antidemocratic measures—a dictatorship of the bourgeoisie—to implement its proposals in the teeth of popular resistance.

I am not saying that the economic analysis is inseparable from the rhetorical analysis, a charge made by more radical rhetoricians as well as critics of the rhetorical turn such as Richard Posner. What I am arguing is that Alston does not fulfill the minimum standards required for open and honest inquiry into an important social issue, that his essay is tainted by its funding source, and that the putatively scientific analysis rests on specific strategic choices to suppress certain arguments (through sheer inattention) and bring selected others into clearer focus for the reader.

Case Study 3: The Uses of Labor Unions

As with the minimum wage or agricultural price supports, it is an article of faith among free-market economists that unions are a bad thing.
The standard positive economic analysis of trade unions includes the
following arguments:

1. There is a "market" for labor, just as there is a market for hogs
   or steel.
2. Unions are a monopolistic interference with the labor market,
   raising the price of labor higher than the free-market price.
3. Unions thus prevent the efficient use of resources, decreasing
   productivity and the overall health of their industry and the
   economy as a whole.
4. They cause unemployment because of their wage effects.
5. From a normative standpoint, especially when supported by
   the coercive power of the state, unions undermine the value of
   individual responsibility, because wages are bargained for col-
   lectively rather than determined by merit.
6. Unions interfere with the individual liberty of both employer
   and worker.

This case study examines the analysis of unions by Milton and
Rose Friedman in *Free to Choose* (1980) and by Richard Posner in *The
Economic Analysis of Law* (1992a). The essential form of the arguments
by the Friedmans and Posner against labor unions is "quasi-logical," to
use Perelman's term:

> *Major premise:* The higher the price of anything, the less of it peo-
> ple will be willing to buy.
> *Minor premise:* Labor unions raise the price of labor.
> *Conclusion:* Employers will hire fewer workers.

A corollary argument is that labor unions directly influence the
supply of labor in other job markets. Unions increase the cost of labor
in the union sector of the economy. Since fewer workers are now em-
ployed in the union sector, there is a labor surplus in the nonunion
sector of the economy, a surplus that translates into lower wages for
nonunion workers. Unions are simply a form of licensing: they restrict

entry into the field. The rhetorical appeal of licensing is that it is supposedly designed to protect customers, but the customers are not the ones who lobby legislators for licensing standards. The restriction of entry created by union licensing creates high wages (Friedman and Friedman 1980: 229).

A further strategy is what Perelman calls the argument by contradiction and irony: "to assert a proposition and its negation within one and the same system, bringing out a contradiction which the system contains," making "the system inconsistent and thereby unusable" (Perelman and Olbrechts-Tyteca 1969: 125). The Friedmans point to abuse by union leaders, particularly misuse and misappropriation of union funds; they warn against the automatic equating of the interests of labor union members with the interests of labor as a whole; they point out that unions claim to protect the low-paid worker but actually they serve highly skilled laborers who would be highly paid anyway; finally, they cite the example of airline pilots, who received an annual salary (for a three-day week) of $50,000 in 1976 "even though the skills and responsibilities they have do not warrant their level of pay" (Friedman and Friedman 1980: 222).[13]

Unions also favor a higher minimum wage to protect union members from competition; the higher wage effectively discriminates against people with low skills, especially teenagers. The Friedmans compare the rate of unemployment of teenagers in the 1950s with the rate in 1979; they compare the minimum wage then and now and conclude that there must be a causal relationship. In the article survey described earlier, on minimum-wage legislation in 1995–1996, it was a common strategy for opponents of the minimum wage to play their version of the "race card," claiming that minority youth were the chief victims of such legislation.

More serious from an ethical standpoint is that the Friedmans (and this is true of accounts by free market labor economists generally) fail to anticipate any objections from the other side. Even Friedrich Hayek (1960), certainly no friend of unions, contended that they are useful in arriving at a satisfactory wage structure in a hierarchical organization, in designing effective work rules, and in providing support to workers' families in times of distress (276–277).

There are a number of possible defenses of labor unions from a strictly economic standpoint. Freeman and Medoff (1984), for example, argue that they promote efficiency in the long run by giving workers a voice in the workplace and in politics as well. They also promote the retention of skills (the sort of "tacit knowledge" Hayek was fond of describing) and help disseminate information in the workplace. They reduce transaction costs for employers, thereby reducing turnover.

The Friedmans' critique of unions relies on very little empirical observation or analysis of the impact of unionization in particular industries. A recent study reports that, in the United States, bosses in union-free firms earn 20 percent more than those in similar firms that are fully unionized. Companies with strong unions employ fewer managers. Outside of the United States, the effect is even greater: evidence from twelve industrialized countries indicates that bosses in nonunion firms earn up to five times more than those in union firms. Thus, it may well be that the impact of unions is not only on consumers and employees but also on managers ("Who Pays for Unions?" 1998).

From a non-Chicago-school standpoint, as with minimum-wage legislation, it may be argued that union wages increase aggregate demand, thus creating growth in the economy as a whole. From an ethical standpoint, the lessons of solidarity and craftsmanship promoted in unions make the unions useful sources of "human capital." Finally, it is not clear that "labor" is best treated as a commodity undifferentiated from any other. One of the most radical libertarian theorists, Richard Epstein (1995), contends that academic tenure is necessary because it equalizes relationships between relatively powerless faculty and powerful boards of regents, thus promoting knowledge (169). It is a pity that Epstein and his ilk refuse to understand the need to "equalize" relations in workplaces other than the university.

CONCLUSION

Our three case studies reveal several rhetorical strategies of economic analysis that draw upon the basic principles I described in the first part of the chapter.

> *Strategy 1:* Define any object, person, or relationship as a commodity that can be bought or sold.
>
> *Strategy 2:* Rely heavily on quasi-logical and quasi-statistical argument to enhance credibility and a sense of disinterested objectivity.

Strategy 3: Appeal to the reader's sense of irony by pointing out the inevitable perversity of well-intentioned social programs.

Strategy 4: Appeal to the reader's sense of moral indignation, equating failure to promote economic growth with condemning the poor to starve.

Strategy 5: Avoid responding to opposing arguments, because to do so would call into question the scientific character of your own argument; in *real* science, when fundamental questions are settled, only cranks dispute them.

Strategy 6: Leave empirical investigation to the sociologists or historians.

But, as James K. Galbraith (1998a) describes it, the hub of the problem lies in Strategy 1:

> We need a rebellion against the metaphor of the labor market—an entity that no one has ever seen, where no one has ever been. . . . Economics needs a rebellion that is almost less against the system under which we live, as against the sources of our complacency about that system. We need a rebellion, not so much against existing market institutions, as against the analytical tyranny of the idea of the market, as it applies to pay. (265–266)

CHAPTER TWO

Economic Rhetoric and the Realist Style

(or, There Ain't No Such Thing as a Free Lunch)

Every beginning student of economics is taught the TANSTAAFL principle: "There ain't no such thing as a free lunch."[1] This principle is a good example of the economic "realist style." The preceding chapter identified the economist's invention of arguments through a set of familiar *topoi*, or rhetorical templates. But economic rhetoric also speaks and gestures in a recognizable *style*, as you can see from the distinctive examples given here.

First, in the words of Adam Smith (1776/1976):

> It is not from the benevolence of the butcher, the brewer, or the baker, that we expect our dinner, but from their regard to their own interest. We address ourselves, not to their humanity but to their self-love, and never talk to them of our own necessities but of their advantages. Nobody but a beggar chuses to depend chiefly upon the benevolence of his fellow citizens. (18)

David Ricardo's (1817/1996) theory states:

By gradually contracting the sphere of the poor laws; by impressing on the poor the value of independence, by teaching them that they must look not to systematic or casual charity, but to their own exertions for support, that prudence and forethought are neither unnecessary nor unprofitable virtues, we shall by degrees approach a sounder and more healthful state. (74–75)

Richard Whately's (1832) "style" is evident in this passage:

I wish for my own part there were no such thing as Political Economy. I mean not now the mere name of the study: but I wish there had never been any necessity for directing our attention to the study itself. If men had always been secured in person and property, and left at full liberty to employ both as they saw fit; and had merely been precluded from unjust interference with each other—had the most perfect freedom of intercourse between all mankind been always allowed—had there never been any wars—nor (which in that case would have easily been avoided) any taxation—then, though every exchange that took place would have been one of the phenomena of which Political Economy takes cognizance, all would have proceeded so smoothly, that probably no attention would ever have been called to the subject. (84–85)

From Alfred Marshall (1920/1997):

[I]n a world in which all men were perfectly virtuous, competition would be out of place; but so also would be private property and every form of private right. Men would think only of their duties; and no one would desire to have a larger share of the comforts and luxuries of life than his neighbours. Strong producers could easily bear a touch of hardship; so they would wish that their weaker neighbours, while producing less should consume more. Happy in this thought, they would work for the general good with all the energy, the inventiveness, and the eager initiative that belonged to them; and mankind would be victorious in contests with nature at every turn. Such is the Golden Age to which poets and dreamers may look forward. But in the responsible conduct of affairs, it is worse than folly to ignore the imperfections which still cling to human nature. (9)

And, Judge Richard Posner (1988) and the "no free lunch" principle:

> [T]he economic approach to human behavior insists on just the sort of gritty realism that the New Criticism taxed some Romantic poetry with trying to evade. In its insistence on the centrality of self-interest (and hence of incentives) in motivating human action, in its insistence that everything has a cost—that there is no such thing as a free lunch—and in its consequent skepticism about Utopian projects, economics is revealed as a bastion of Enlightenment values. The absence of Romantic uplift is precisely what makes economics—the rejection of Romanticism in the sphere of government—so repugnant to the heirs of Romanticism. (312)

These arguments are *styled* in a "realistic" way. They reflect a worldview that is pleased with itself for "seeing through" the pretensions of poets, dreamers, and romantics. It is not difficult to imagine the right set of gestures for *performing* these utterances: the controlled, even vocal tone; the ironic shrug; the relaxed physical posture (perhaps accompanied by a few puffs on a pipe).

This chapter examines the political style of economic rhetoric, applying the insights of Francis Beer and Robert Hariman (1996a) on the discourse of realism. I will argue that realism is the default rhetoric for defenders of the free market. The realist economic style works by radically separating power and textuality, constructing the political realm as a state of nature, and by depicting its opponents as prisoners of verbal illusions. Realism is recognizable as a style, and that style in turn reinforces the realist ideology, which is convinced it can do without rhetoric. A serious acceptance of the economic realist view of politics (especially as manifested in the theory of public choice) promotes a widespread cynicism that is fundamentally destructive of democratic politics.

The chapter goes on to examine the realist rhetorical theory of Judge Richard Posner, currently one of the most prominent free-market advocates, and concludes with my own argument that an economic realist theory of persuasion fails to account for many important aspects of human action, notably the development and communication of social norms.

THE NO-NONSENSE NATURE OF THE REALIST STYLE

Although style and delivery were treated as separate from and secondary to invention by most theorists of rhetoric, historically the actual teaching of public speaking typically has emphasized either the careful learning and application of dozens of tropes and schemes or the repeated analysis and labeling of patterns of vocal and physical performance. Students who begin a public speaking class often are surprised to learn that they will be taught audience analysis or modes of proof. They are not surprised to learn that their language use and their delivery skills will be critiqued.

The prominent contemporary rhetorical theorist Robert Hariman (1995, 1996) has developed (in his words) a "cautious, postmodernist" approach to the study of style and rhetorical performance. He writes that successful politicians know intuitively that political success involves "conventions of persuasive composition that depend on aesthetic reactions. . . . In a word, our political experience is *styled*" (Hariman 1995: 2–3). We come to recognize a distinctive *political style* as "*a coherent repertoire of rhetorical conventions depending on aesthetic reactions for political effect*" (4). Hariman identifies four types of political style: realist, republican, courtly, and bureaucratic. He analyzes the rhetoric of Machiavelli and Henry Kissinger as masters of realism who created "a characteristically modern political style that crafts an aesthetically unified world of sheer power and constant calculation" (13). The discursive practice of realism asserts simultaneously an epistemology, a political theory, and a rhetoric. Realists profess to see the world clearly. They assume that international politics is a competition among states and that domestic politics is a competition among interest groups. Participants in this competition pursue power through rational calculation; they presume that attending to issues other than power (such as "values" or "morality") is a distraction (Beer and Hariman 1996b: 6). Finally, realists use an antirhetorical rhetoric that favors the plain style and avoids verbal ornament. They denigrate opponents as "rhetorical," too caught up in their own textuality to focus on rational calculation (Hariman 1995: 17). Realist rhetoric thus is configured within the master trope of *metonymy*: the reduction of political life to a calculus of power.

Machiavelli, like all realists, crafts the illusion that his rhetoric is merely a neutral instrument for transmitting to the reader the hard facts about the world. Politics is reduced to a calculus of power. Rhetoric is reduced to the transparent exchange of information. The political actor suffers a reduction as well:

> Only a person of a certain type will survive in a world of hard realities and sovereign powers. When reality is defined against textuality, one is sublimating the sociality of politics. If a discourse is a true representation of its subject because it is devoid of ornament (that is, because it is not directed to please others), then it must stand independently of a social situation, free of social motives such as the quest for higher status. Once one discovers the vectors of power in a field of material forces, there is no need to understand social practices, regulations, or entertainment except as they are manipulated. (Hariman 1995: 30)

The problem with the realist style is twofold: (1) It is disingenuous in denying its own "rhetoricity." As Aristotle wrote in the *Rhetoric*, "a writer must disguise his art and give the impression of speaking naturally and not artificially" (cited in Hariman 1995: 203n16). Realism is a form of artifice, as members of rhetorical cultures understand, but repetitive emphasis on the "merely" rhetorical arguments of one's opponents tends to undermine the possibility of metacommunicating about argument itself. (2) By disparaging political discourse, the realist undermines the persuasive norms that govern a healthy democratic culture. Deliberation never occurs on the basis of the common good, but within "a vernacular of sovereign powers, calculations of interest, and the like." Conceiving of democratic deliberation in this way leaves a "brittle sense of social order and a pessimistic view of history" (Hariman 1995: 44). The realist style thus not only disempowers democratic publics if widely practiced among opinion leaders, but it also fails as a basis for persuading publics in times of crisis.

If we apply Beer and Hariman's (1996a) insights, we see that the economic realist style works in the following ways:

1. *It defines human nature down.* It is safest to concentrate on self-interest as the fundamental human motivation. Those who do not are hopelessly "romantic" or "utopian."

2. *It defines the political in terms of the social.* As Sheldon Wolin (1960, 1989) has argued, the classical economists eroded the concept

of the distinctively political. Politics became associated with "govern-ment." Society was a spontaneous, self-adjusting order with no need for a principle of authority other than the pressure of social confor-mity, guaranteed by the presence of Adam Smith's "impartial specta-tor" within each human breast.

3. *It defines efficiency as a default norm, including efficiency of infor-mation exchange.* The economic realist reduces all questions of value to individual taste: "*de gustibus non est disputandum*" (there's no disputing about taste), as Gary Becker and George Stigler (1996) emphasized in a famous article. "Tastes are the unchallengeable axioms of a man's behavior: he may properly (usefully) be criticized for inefficiency in satisfying his desires, but the desires themselves are *data*" (24). The only common ground for communication between people is agreement on individual tastes or else the good of "efficiency." Consider, for ex-ample, such an ad in the personals column: "Single White Female economist, in search of Single White Male economist, into French wines, Vizsla puppies, and the Dead Kennedys, for conjoint utility maximization." Do not, the economic realist says, attempt to play the Hitler card here and contend that Nazism must just be a matter of taste, too. It is not the value-free economist who is responsible for Na-zism. Nazism was the product of a collective effort to force agreement on the nature of virtue or distributive justice. Virtue talk always ends up being coercive (see Posner 1999).

The clearest illustration of the economic realist style in action is public choice theory, which reduces political activity to "rent-seek-ing," that is, the attempt of special interest groups to extract favors from government.

PUBLIC CHOICE THEORY VERSUS DEMOCRACY

Public choice theory is the application of microeconomics to political science. The four core texts that best illuminate the theory are Ken-neth Arrow, *Social Choice and Individual Values* (1951); Anthony Downs, *An Economic Theory of Democracy* (1957); James Buchanan and Gordon Tullock, *The Calculus of Consent* (1962); and Mancur Olson, *The Logic of Collective Action* (1971).[2] The core principle of public choice is that "the representative or the average individual acts on the basis of the same over-all value scale when he participates in market activity and in political activity" (Buchanan and Tullock 1962: 20).

Perhaps the most complex and widely studied concept in public choice theory is the Arrow Impossibility Theorem, which "proves" that it is impossible to arrive at a social welfare function that is not imposed in a coercive manner. The standard argument goes as follows. Three voters (I, II, III) vote on three outcomes (A, B, C), agreeing to abide by majority rule. Voter I prefers A to B and B to C; voter II prefers B to C and C to A; and voter III prefers C to A and A to B. The result is twofold: a voting cycle emerges, with A defeated by C, in turn defeated by B, and in turn defeated by A; also, majority rule is undermined because, while B represents a compromise choice between voters I and II, the outcome is C, which is lower on both their scales of preference. There is thus a built-in problem with democracy and majority rule whenever more than two possible outcomes are popular. This insight, for which Arrow won the Nobel Prize, has often been used to justify the realist claim that any common notion of "virtue" or "the good" is impossible to legislate into existence without undue coercion.

While Arrow's theorem is useful in reflecting on "voting behavior," the design of elections, the analysis of parliamentary strategy, and more technical aspects of political science, it is distinctly counter to commonsense assumptions about how politics works. There are times when a "general will" of the people *does* get expressed; three relatively noncontroversial examples might be the American Revolution, the ratification debates over the Constitution, and the dramatic end of laissez-faire in constitutional law after 1937 (see Ackerman 1991). The decision to rebel against Britain was the product of considerable discussion and debate; those who opposed the decision eventually came to support it or else exercised their "exit" option by moving to Canada or elsewhere. The debate over the Constitution perhaps led to less consensus, but the adoption of a Bill of Rights and the emergence of a two-party system gave opponents a "voice" in the new regime. The U.S. public in 1937 rejected President Roosevelt's efforts to pack the Supreme Court but also were strongly supportive of a change in the court's approach to economic legislation. Half a century later, even President Reagan did not wish to overturn the New Deal.

There is a Manichaean quality to the rhetoric of Arrow's theorem, one that is common in libertarian political theory, suggesting that, without firm constitutional guarantees of liberty, people are always trumping someone else's rights. More specifically, note that in this model *the voters do not talk with one another*. Communication and rhetoric are mere epiphenomena: only interests count.

A related notion is Anthony Downs's Rational Voter Paradox. Downs argued that voter apathy and ignorance are not bad things; the rational voter, in fact, spends little energy gathering information about politics, because he realizes that his vote has only a negligible impact on the actual outcome of an election. Although the Paradox has generated one of the largest bodies of scholarly literature in U.S. politics, it seems largely not to have been verified. Green and Shapiro write that it has "contributed fewer insights than examples of defective social science research," including "post hoc theorizing, slippery predictions, and an inability to formulate a cogent null hypothesis" (Green and Shapiro 1994: 48). Once again, the Rational Voter Paradox assumes that the only role for communication and persuasion in public life is in gaining "information" that is weighed by the rational actor.

What came to be called the "free-rider problem" was implicit in the Rational Voter Paradox. Before Mancur Olson came along, the dominant perspective in political science was that organized groups are the basic unit of politics. Olson offered a different account of the logic of collective action: only specific incentives will inspire rational individuals in latent groups "to act in a group-oriented way" (Olson 1971: 51). The "free rider" is one who recognizes that an economic or political good will be provided by a group independently of his action and who consumes that good without contributing to the group. Olson actually used the free-rider problem to justify the closed union shop on the grounds that unions cannot obtain any goods from collective bargaining if free riders are permitted by labor law (66–97). But the typical application of the free-rider concept by right-wing economists has been to reinforce the idea that politics is simply an effort by special interests to gain special favors from government. Only small, well-organized groups have much political impact, since they reduce the number of free riders.

The concept of rent-seeking behavior also relates to the free-rider concept. Buchanan and Tullock argued that much governmental activity is the product of rent-seeking behavior by special interests—a "rent" here being defined as an income earned when supply is restricted. Pressure by farmers to obtain prices for their crops higher than supply–demand equilibrium prices is a classic example of "rent-seeking" behavior. In fact, virtually all political activity is an attempt to extract rents by government guarantee (see the studies in Buchanan et al. 1980). The only solution, recently proposed by James Buchanan and R. D. Congleton (1998), is to propose a constitutional amendment prohibiting any group from receiving any government benefit not available to any other group.

The theory of rent-seeking has contributed to the widespread perception that government is incapable of solving social problems. Any oppressed group can now be labeled as rent-seeking rather than as seeking "justice." In fact, justice exists within public choice theory simply at the "constitutional level," that is, absolute equality before the law. The most interesting development of public choice theory has been in constitutional law. Justice Antonin Scalia has expressed sympathy with the public choice literature and has proposed an activist role for the judiciary in preventing legislative decision making about issues related to property. An expansive interpretation of the "takings" clause of the Constitution would prevent democratic majorities from tampering with private property rights, whether in environmental legislation or in legislation that "interferes" with the "labor market" (e.g., a mandatory minimum wage or provisions for occupational safety and health) (see Farber and Frickey 1991: 89–102).

These principles of rational choice—the impossibility of deriving an unforced consensus about the public good, the pervasiveness of rent-seeking in politics, and the free-rider problem—have become all-purpose templates, or rhetorical *topoi*, for making complex cases of political and economic behavior understandable and explainable. When limited to the status of tools for social-scientific inquiry, these principles can be very useful. When elevated to a metaphysics, they become dangerous. When they are *subsidized* by right-wing foundations, they become the greatest threat to equality and democracy since the pre-1937 Supreme Court. In terms of the focus of this book, the principles of rational choice represent the triumph of the realist style, a style that is fundamentally corrosive to public order. And, perhaps most important, their realism stems from their steadfast refusal to consider communication and rhetorical action as important features of politics.

The economic realist style rests on a set of antirhetorical assumptions. Judge Richard Posner of the Seventh Circuit Court of Appeals attempted to develop an account of rhetoric in economic terms, limiting rhetoric to the "tricks" that help an advocate undermine an audience's reasoning process. If Posner's account is inadequate, as I argue that it is, the claim of economic realism to have developed *the* comprehensive explanation of public life can be shown to be false.

A POSNERIAN THEORY OF RHETORIC

Law-and-economics is of particular interest to the student of free-market rhetoric because it represents the most audacious (and heavily funded) attempt by economics to colonize an entire academic discipline and social institution, and because Richard Posner, the most important theorist and practitioner of econo-legal analysis, has written some interesting things about the art of rhetoric. Most of the time when we analyze the relationships among political, legal, economic, and rhetorical theory, we are left with a few odd marginal comments, such as Kant's abrupt dismissal of rhetoric in his *Critique of Judgment* (Kant 1951: 165–166, 171–172) or Marx's confession to his father about "cooling his fevered brain" by translating parts of Aristotle's *Rhetoric* (see Aune 1994: 15–16). It is rare for the student of argument to find an explicit statement of an influential jurist's method of rhetorical criticism as well as a provocative statement about the nature of rhetoric itself. Posner frames the art of rhetoric in terms of information costs, which is potentially a useful insight. But Posner is unable to account for two important aspects of classical rhetorical theory: the theory of *topoi* (stock issues, or rhetorical templates) as a tool for inventing arguments and the theory of *epideictic* (ceremonial) *oratory* as a means of reinforcing community norms. Furthermore, close attention to the role of rhetoric in public affairs reveals the limitations of the efficiency argument, which governs much academic defense of an unfettered free market.

Posner's comments on rhetoric appear in several different places, notably in the 1981 book *Economics of Justice*, in the 1988 *Law and Literature: A Misunderstood Relation*, and most systematically in an essay, "Rhetoric, Legal Advocacy, and Legal Reasoning," in his 1995 book *Overcoming Law*. The tone of the essay is unusually shrill for Posner; his references to "rhetoric prigs" no doubt reflect the many negative reactions to his earlier remarks on rhetoric, especially by Donald

McCloskey (1991), who accused Posner of having a "roto-rooter" theory of communication (209; see also McCloskey 1988b).

Posner's first discussion of rhetoric appears in a chapter on primitive law in *The Economics of Justice* (1983). He makes three arguments:

1. Speech and manners in less developed societies are more formal and decorous. The reason? Such societies lack conversational privacy, thus increasing the costs of misunderstanding. "People who lack conversational privacy must learn to express themselves precisely and circumspectly, since many of their conversations are bound to be overheard" (172).

2. The art of rhetoric is more highly valued in primitive cultures than in modern ones. The primary explanation is that information is more costly in primitive cultures, and the art of rhetoric economizes on the search for information.

3. Rhetoric economizes on information primarily through "the ethical appeal." Posner writes that "Character is a proxy for credibility that becomes important only where the costs of information are high" (173). Another implication of viewing "ethos" in terms of information costs is that it helps us recognize the extent to which a fully "rhetorical culture" in the traditional sense is also of necessity a culture of *deference* (see Weaver 1964, 1953).

In *Law and Literature: A Misunderstood Relation* (1988), Posner discusses rhetoric somewhat more extensively. He had written in *The Economics of Justice* that there are few modern textbooks on the subject of rhetoric; by 1988 he had discovered "the long American tradition of rhetorical analysis in the Aristotelian manner" (271n6). In this work Posner makes several arguments.

He first rejects the equation of rhetoric with practical reasoning or "right reason." He criticizes twentieth-century writers (Kenneth Burke is an exception) for neglecting the "amoral" character of rhetoric. He further criticizes recent analysts of judicial opinions for expanding the scope of rhetoric by making praise or criticism of the rhetoric of the opinion "synonymous with praising or criticizing the opinion, period."[3]

Posner then performs a fascinating analysis of the rhetoric of Oliver Wendell Holmes, Jr.'s dissenting opinion in *Lochner v. New York*. He claims that the opinion fails by legal craft standards but is successful by rhetorical standards (the evidence being that we are still reading the opinion today). He analyzes both Holmes's use of the ethical appeal (reinforcing the theme that it works because of high audience information costs), his use of "Mr. Herbert Spencer's Social Statics" as a metonymy for laissez-faire, and his somewhat sloppy use of evidence and precedent. He then compares the *Lochner* dissent to the odious *Buck v. Bell* opinion, and notes that they share the same "rhetorical" brilliance. Posner writes, "Scholarly analysis of the 'rhetoric' of judicial decisions would be more fruitful, and certainly clearer, if scholars stopped trying to equate rhetoric with goodness" (289).

Finally, Posner defends the use of "economic rhetoric" in law (which seems like a shift in definition) against critics such as Terry Teachout, James Boyd White, and Robin West. He argues that simply because economic analysis "does not wear its emotions on its sleeve" it is not therefore callous: "Would Teachout think a medical paper insensitive or 'disintegrative' if its author did not express sympathy for the people whose disease he was writing about?" (311). To use a different example, the writings of Bruno Bettelheim on child psychology were compassionate, well-written, and broadly cultured. They were also horribly wrong, largely about the genesis and treatment of autism (see Pollak 1997).

Posner also argues that he is simply providing an additional perspective on human interaction. New perspectives often require overstatement or a kind of tunnel vision. But a set of political and cultural values underlies Posner's project, which he describes in a rare flight of emotion:

> In its insistence on the centrality of self-interest (and hence of incentives) in motivating human action, in its insistence that everything has a cost—that there is no such thing as a free lunch—and in its consequent skepticism about Utopian projects, economics is revealed as a bastion of Enlightenment values. The absence of Romantic uplift is precisely what makes economics—the rejection of Romanticism in the sphere of government—so repugnant to the heirs of Romanticism. (312)

Posner makes a more complete statement about the economic analysis of rhetoric in *Overcoming Law* (1995), wherein he identifies two methods a speaker uses to influence an audience. The first is to supply information. The second is to use "signals of one sort or another to enhance the credibility of the speaker's arguments," notably the "ethical appeal."

Persuaders will have a range of goals, "ranked from the most to the least desired, and he may not aim at the most desired because the cost of persuading the audience to accept it may be prohibitive" (500–501). Although Posner does not say so, this is a good restatement of Aristotle's notion of the "available means of persuasion." Posner identifies "distance" and "tenacity" as two variables that determine the cost of persuasion. "The cost of persuading an audience to believe X will be lower, other things being equal, the shorter the distance between X and Y, where Y is the audience's prior belief concerning the subject of the speech." Tenacity is the relative strength with which a belief is held. Skillful rhetoricians build bridges between their arguments and the audience's existing beliefs—"hence the importance of analogy as a rhetorical device" (501).

Posner then introduces the concept of information costs and criticizes McCloskey for neglecting it. He distinguishes between a scientific paper and a speech to a jury in terms of the fact that the cost of information is much lower to a scientific audience. In fact, the concept of information costs helps explain the decline of rhetoric since the Renaissance:

> Outside of specialized areas of discourse and inquiry, information costs have declined with the spread of literacy, universal education, better communications, increased knowledge, the emergence of information specialists, the growing prestige of scientific and other rational methods of inquiry, and the development of institutions ranging from schools and universities to product warranties, department stores, and representative (as distinct from direct) democracy, for economizing on information costs. All these are alternatives to rhetoric and have contracted its domain. (Posner 1995: 504)

Posner goes on to analyze the debate between Plato and Aristotle, and draws some conclusions about their differing views of law. Plato would probably have favored the professional judiciary of the Continent whereas Aristotle would have been more comfortable with the jury system. Posner points out, quite sensibly, that the Athenian legal system simply gave too much scope to inflammatory rhetoric. There needs to be a balance between the analytic role of the legal counselor and the rhetorical role of the advocate (506–517).

Posner anticipates the objection that he ignores the idea of rhetoric as a kind of thinking, including analogical reasoning, metaphor, and casuistry. He argues that rhetoric is best defined as "the nonlogical, nonscientific, nonempirical methods of persuasion." Without such a definition, it becomes impossible to "admire the rhetorical prowess of a Hitler," who illustrated the two primary ways in which rhetoric can be pernicious. Hitler first conveyed information about how to oppress another group. He also discovered ways of subverting the audience's cognitive apparatus (528). Posner appears to be saying that a logical division of labor in the academy is to give rhetoricians control of delivery, organization, ornamental figures of speech, and emotional appeal.

A consistent but somewhat more positive view of rhetoric appears in Posner's book on Justice Benjamin Cardozo (1990a). There he identifies "rhetorical prowess" as one reason for Cardozo's influence as a judge. The component parts of Cardozo's rhetorical prowess are: (1) "A vivid, even dramatic, bodying forth of the judge's concerns," (2) "Lucid presentation of arresting particulars," (3) the ability to relate the particulars to larger themes, (4) a point of view that transcends the particulars of the case, (5) "A power of clear and forceful statement," and 6) "A high degree of sensitivity to the expectations of one's audience" (133–134). One might add to these Posner's argument earlier in the book that Cardozo's jurisprudence was "rhetorical" in the sense that he was concerned to reduce the gap between lay and legal conceptions of justices by taking his cues from the moral standards of the community (28–30). His pragmatic jurisprudence was audience-centered and economized on information costs to the lay audience.

To summarize, Posner's view of rhetoric consists of the following arguments:

1. Rhetoric and science are distinct practices.
2. The study and practice of rhetoric are most influential when information costs are high.
3. Rhetoric is best thought of as appealing to the irrational side of the self.
4. The primary rhetorical devices are the ethical appeal, provi-

sion of true and false information, and stylistic choices used to circumvent cognition.

5. Rhetorical analysis of judicial opinions must be distinguished from the legal craft aspects of those opinions. Still, the study of judicial opinion writing is extremely important, as a means of understanding judicial influence; it may be especially necessary in view of the decline of U.S. humanities education. (Posner argues that the poor quality of judicial opinions in recent years stems from the tendency to turn opinion-writing over to law clerks [1990: 48].)

INFORMATION COSTS VERSUS SOCIAL AND POLITICAL NORMS

Posner's theory of rhetoric follows the same conceptual path as his introduction of economics into legal analysis. First, Posner narrows the scope of the rhetorical enterprise to cost–benefit analysis. The persuader's choice of the available means of persuasion can be described in this way: "The persuader whose goal is fixed will choose that mixture of rhetorical devices—including true information, lies, signals, and emotional appeals—that, at least cost to himself, will maximize the likelihood of achieving that goal. . . . The cost of persuading the audience depends on the distance between X and Y, where Y is the audience's prior belief concerning the subject matter of the speech." It also depends on the tenacity with which those beliefs are held (1995: 500–501).

Second, he defines actual communication between speaker and audience primarily in terms of information exchange. A speaker influences the beliefs of audiences by supplying information, which for Posner includes false as well as true information, deductions, and inductions; and by "using signals of some sort to enhance the credibility of the speaker's arguments—such signals as speaking with great self-assurance or furnishing particulars about oneself that make one seem a credible person." Posner notes that this strategy usually appears first to make the audience receptive, and says, "The creation of this receptive mood was called in classical rhetoric the 'ethical appeal' " (1995: 500).

Posner's characterization of *ethos* as simply the creation of a receptive mood is simply wrong. Aristotle's *Rhetoric* defines *ethos* as a mode of proof provided "in the character of the speaker," or, more precisely, the character of the speaker as it is manifested in the speech. Posner apparently confuses *ethos* with *pathos*; ignoring the significance of *ethos* means leaving out the historical and cultural dimension of rhetoric. Posner cannot account for the role of the orator as an embodiment of cultural ideals; nor can he account for the way in which exceptionally eloquent rhetorical texts such as Lincoln's "Second Inaugural" enter into the public consciousness of a nation.

Third, Posner rigidly separates rhetoric from ethics. After a rather breathless analysis of Plato's *Gorgias* as well as Aristotle's *Rhetoric*, he concludes that one simply should avoid any kind of normative evaluation of advocacy. He also notes in parenthesis that "the efforts of the defenders of rhetoric to do so may be one reason for the low esteem in which the discipline is held. Poor rhetoricians they, they overargue their case" (Posner 1995: 516). In these passages, the voice of Holmes begins to come out very clearly. Just as in his famous address "The Path of the Law" Holmes had rigorously attempted to separate law and morality, Posner wishes to do the same with rhetoric and morality (see Posner's useful 1992 anthology of Holmes's writings). It is unfair to characterize rhetoricians as playing the old lawyer's game; Posner constructs a straw version of "morality" as a simplistic answer to questions of right and wrong. Aristotle understood, as did generations of rhetoricians, philosophers, and lawyers after him, that politics, law, and ethics are inextricably linked by the human capacity for reasoning. Posner is right that a lot of bad rhetorical criticism exists that simply attacks the rhetor for not adhering to the critic's prejudices, but surely he knows that it is possible to examine respectfully the ethical reasoning of a rhetor without agreeing with it. Posner's objection applies equally to his own rhetoric in *Overcoming Law*, which is full of dismissive epithets ("rhetoric prigs") cloaked in the guise of scientific judgments.

Fourth, Posner rigidly separates rhetoric and science. The rhetorician discovers nothing: "The rhetorician doesn't stick his neck out. No Socrates, he is respectful of public opinion, or less politely the prejudices of his audience. That is one reason why the literature of rhetoric is duller than that of science or philosophy." Science, Posner says, works by falsifying propositions, thus promoting truth, while rhetoric has no such tendency (1995: 528–529). Posner, who ostensibly is an admirer of Protagoras, here reinscribes an essentially Platonic view of rhetoric in which clear lines are drawn between rhetoric and science.

Not only does such line-drawing ignore the enduring role of rhetorical masterpieces in sustaining a nation's public consciousness, but it also prevents insight into the rhetorical tools used by scientists with audiences with low information costs. McCloskey's (1994) comparative historical analysis of changes in the "implied author" of economic articles from the historian-philosopher of 1929 to the mathematician of 1989 is but one example of the uses of rhetorical analysis of economic "science" (see chs. 9–13).

Fifth, Posner gives us an incomplete history of rhetorical theory. Posner's is a history of rhetoric from which Isocrates, Cicero, and Quintilian, among others, are absent. He constructs a history of rhetoric in which the "extremes" of Plato and Aristotle are seen as unrealistic, leaving the sophistic rhetoric of Protagoras as winner by default. Legal rhetoric in the West, much as with law itself, is largely a creature of the Roman rhetoricians, who combined a sophistic attention to effectiveness with a philosophical view of ethics and politics. Posner neglects the Ciceronian rhetorical tradition, which, in the long run, was more influential on education and law than the Aristotelian tradition. Some of the more interesting recent studies in legal rhetoric, notably William Wiethoff's (1996) analysis of antebellum southern judges and John W. Cairns (1991) on Scottish legal education, point to the essential role of cultural differences in rhetorical education that have influenced legal communities. We also know that the study of rhetoric (especially Roman rhetoric) was a particular interest of Justice Hugo Black and that he urged Earl Warren to read Aristotle's *Rhetoric* as a way of preparing himself to write judicial opinions (see Newman 1994: 427).

Sixth, and most important, Posner never mentions the role of epideictic oratory in Aristotle or in the rhetorical tradition. Cass Sunstein has developed an important analysis of the role of norms rather than "preferences" as the foundation of individual rationality. Sunstein (1997) discusses the concepts of "norm entrepreneurship" to describe the way in which social norms get changed (becoming "norm bandwagons" or "norm cascades") (32–69). The classical rhetoricians knew that epideictic oratory had a central role to play in the communal definition and reinforcement of social norms. As Perelman (1982) writes, "The epideictic genre is central to discourse because its role is to intensify adherence to values, adherence without which discourses that aim at providing action cannot find the lever to move or to inspire their audiences" (19). It is also impossible to understand judicial or deliberative rhetoric without noting the role of norms as major premises for enthymemes. The reduction of argument to communication of information, the elimination of cultural tradition as a factor in ethical appeal, the ignoring of the role of the audience (as well as the presence of multiple audiences) in negotiating rhetorical meaning, the simplistic and "literary" focus on the single speech text, as well as the unrealistic character of Posner's depiction of an essentially unidirectional flow of information from speaker to audience, are other criticisms of Posner's view of rhetoric.

Finally, Posner neglects the particular strength of the rhetorical tradition as a pedagogical program. Training in public speaking, debate, and argumentative writing deserve at least equal representation with literary criticism in high schools and colleges. Posner's account of the decline of rhetoric neglects to provide an explanation both for rhetoric's survival in the United States, outside of the Ivy League, as well as its tentative revival since the 1970s.[4] Even on Posner's own terms, it would make sense that the rhetorical revival would occur precisely at the point where academic specialization as well as increasing cultural diversity have actually *increased* the costs of general information about public issues. The specific cognitive role that rhetorical education has to play in undergraduate education seems to lie in its ability to develop habits of mind such as audience-centeredness. Hans-Georg Gadamer (1995) identified the chief benefits of humanist rhetorical education as the cultivation of *Bildung, sensus communis,* judgment, and taste (10–39). These need not be viewed as habits that conflict with science but as distinctive intellectual capacities that cut across all disciplines and are particularly necessary for democratic discussion and debate. An information-exchange theory of persuasion fails to account for the richness of human symbolic action, including Posner's own rhetorical prowess.

What does critique of Posner have to do w/ realist style??

CONCLUSION

The economic realist style and its reductive sense of rhetoric fails, finally, as an adequate account of human action because of its inability to engage in democratic discussion and debate. Even in economic terms, the emphasis on "exit" by free-market theorists ignores the market action / adequate protection?

equally important role of "voice." In Albert O. Hirschman's classic 1970 work *Exit, Voice, and Loyalty*, he defined "exit" as the choice to leave because a better good or service can be provided by another firm or organization. "Voice," on the other hand, refers to the act of communicating grievances to a firm or organization. Where competition exists, exit can improve the performance of an organization. But the problem with exit, writes Hirschman, is that it can "atrophy the development of the art of voice" (5). Further, when applied to political organizations, exit may only create a "race to the bottom." A recent conservative book on federalism contends that we should return virtually all political power to the states, even including the choice of establishing a state religion. After all, the writer contends, citizens can "vote with their feet" (Greve 1999: 3). But the case for conservative principles is a product of the art of "voice," and even if everyone has the equal opportunity to "exit," the long-term consequence is the devaluation of public discussion and debate.

Markets are useful things, but they should not have been turned into a religion. Politics is, ultimately, the search for the optimum balance of exit and voice in a polity. It is no accident that the quality of public argument has declined so dramatically in the years since the ascendancy of the market. The free-marketeers can only dismiss democratic participation as "rent-seeking behavior."

The good news is that realism appears to be less persuasive with the general public than it is with academics in law and economics. The market faith needs a sense of passion if it is to persuade democratic majorities.

PART II

What Libertarians Want

CHAPTER THREE

Checking
Ayn Rand's Premises

(or, The Revenge of the Nerds)

In 1991 a joint survey by the Library of Congress and the Book of the Month Club found that Ayn Rand's *Atlas Shrugged* was second only to the Bible in the overall list of books that had made a major impact on the lives of the respondents (cited in Sciabarra 1995: 1–2). In the survey, the following people, among others, named Ayn Rand[1] as a significant influence on their lives: British Prime Minister Margaret Thatcher; Simon LeBon of the rock group Duran Duran; financial commentator Louis Rukeyser; Martin Anderson, President Ronald Reagan's chief domestic and economic adviser; Hillary Rodham Clinton; Steve Ditko, the creator of Spider Man; Alan Greenspan, once a member of Rand's inner circle and now the chairman of the Federal Reserve System; Robert Heinlein; Kathryn Eickhoff, associate director of the Office of Management and Budget under President Reagan; the late Rock Hudson; philosophers Robert Nozick and John Hospers; actress Jill St. John; Charles Murray, author of *Losing Ground* and *The Bell Curve*; the rock group Rush; and Supreme Court Justice Clarence Thomas.[2]

The "self-esteem" movement in psychotherapy that was the emphasis of a controversial California State program in the 1970s is a creation of Nathaniel Branden, Rand's former lover and later a "non-person" in the eyes of orthodox Objectivists. (Objectivism is the preferred name for Rand's philosophy, based on her core philosophic insight: A is A, or, there's an objective world out there.)[3]

An article in the libertarian magazine *Reason* cites a 1979 survey of the sixties generation in which one in six mention Rand as a person whom they admired. Among authors, Rand was tied for sixth place with Germaine Greer, behind Kurt Vonnegut, Kahlil Gibran, Tom Wolfe, Jean-Paul Sartre, Albert Camus, and Allen Ginsberg, respectively, but ahead of Rod McKuen, Hermann Hesse, Paul Goodman, Simone de Beauvoir, Norman Mailer, and James Jones, in that order (Riggenbach 1982).

The interest in Rand's work has not abated. Publishers normally sell some 300,000 copies of her works annually (*Investor's Business Daily* 1998). The U.S. Postal Service issued an Ayn Rand 33-cent postage stamp on April 22, 1999. A made-for-cable movie of Barbara Branden's *The Passion of Ayn Rand* appeared on the Showtime network on May 30, 1999 (Rust 1999). *The Chronicle of Higher Education* (Sharlet 1999) recently noted increasing scholarly interest in Rand's works. Rand is a pervasive presence on the World Wide Web, from the orthodox Ayn Rand Institute, run by her heir, Leonard Peikoff, to the "revisionist" Institute of Objectivist Studies run by David L. Kelley.[4]

The words "orthodox," "purge," and "revisionist" conjure up images of Stalinism, although, as any Randian would quickly retort, Rand never sent anyone to a gulag nor had anyone shot. Still, the intense psychological hold Rand had over her disciples is, to say the least, a bit unusual. Both Barbara Branden's and Nathaniel Branden's books evidence the authors' seemingly undiminished awe for Rand, nearly twenty years after their expulsion from Rand's circle. John Hospers, the noted U.S. philosopher, was one of Rand's first "respectable" academic followers. Rand broke with him when he gave a critical, academic response to a paper she delivered at the annual meeting of the American Society for Aesthetics at Harvard, in October 1962. Years later, when Barbara Branden interviewed Hospers for her book, he said, "I found myself weeping. Isn't that remarkable?" (Branden 1989: 308).

Despite Rand's influence, there has been remarkably little academic study of her work and her influence—and most of that has been done by writers sympathetic to her project, notably Mimi Gladstein (1984), who has pursued Rand's implications for feminism, and Robert Nozick (1982), the noted political theorist, who wrote a widely cited essay, "On the Randian Argument." So, in this chapter I analyze perhaps the most influential texts written by Rand, two lengthy speeches in *Atlas Shrugged*: first, Francisco's "money" speech and, second, the sixty-page radio speech of John Galt, the shadowy leader of the creative people who go on strike against the world.

Much traditional rhetoric and literature have relied on the strategy of "presence," the ability of the rhetor to single out certain things for the audience's attention. The rhetor connects things remote in time or space to the audience's sentimental commitments using vivid depictions, such as Mark Antony brandishing Caesar's bloody tunic or a prosecutor showing the children of the victim of the accused (Perelman 1982: 35–38). Rand, to the contrary, often works her rhetorical magic by systematically *removing* presence from her characters' rhetoric—John Galt's disembodied radio voice is just one example. But there is one exception: the role of what today might be called "rough sex" in her novels (which is most likely part of her continuing appeal to awkward, adolescent readers curious about sex). By eliminating all transindividual claims of affection, sentiment, or authority, Rand is able to amplify the impact of her central theme, "the virtue of selfishness."

A further conclusion from a careful examination of Rand's stylistic choices and her implicit theory of rhetoric is that, despite her overall emphasis on liberty and the individual, *the form of her writing is remarkably totalitarian in that every potential response by the reader is completely controlled.*[5] It comes as no surprise that Rand hated Shakespeare and loved Mickey Spillane (Barbara Branden 1986: 278). Every sentence, every page hammers into the reader's mind the same theme and appeals to the same longings for recognition and for sexual release, unrelieved by irony, whimsy, or the slightest ambiguity.

IF YOU ALWAYS READ FOR THE PLOT, PLEASE SKIP THIS SECTION

Kenneth Burke (1968) noted in *Counter-Statement* that many works appeal to audiences solely on the basis of form. His analysis of different types of formal appeals—ranging from the "conventional form" of the ritual or the familiar genre to the "syllogistic form" of the classic detective novel—is now an accepted part of the critical vocabulary.[6] One type of appeal he neglects to mention, however, is well exemplified by Rand's work. I am tempted to call it the *Herculean form*, based on the idea that some works appeal to us chiefly for the Herculean effort required to navigate their sheer length. There is a certain appeal (perhaps greatest among adolescent readers) of actually making it to the *end* of a 1,085-page book. U.S. best-sellers by James Michener, for example, seem to exhibit this appeal.

Atlas Shrugged (1957) combines aspects of several genres (the detective story, science fiction, and the "bodice-ripper") into what Mimi Gladstein (1984) calls a "theodicy of capitalism" (38). Like all of Rand's literary works, it follows a distinctive melodramatic plot pattern in which a heroic male individualist battles the forces of collectivism (Gladstein 1984: 22). The heroic male is always tall and strong, with grey eyes. The woman who falls for the hero is always slender and intelligent. An exaggerated sexuality—something like an intellectual 1950s adolescent's version of heavy-metal videos—suffuses the work. As Gladstein notes:

> Instant recognition of the like-minded is an ability shared by Rand's heroes and villains alike. . . . In two of Rand's stories, the first meeting of hero and heroine is accompanied by a rape-like encounter, which, rather than distancing the couple, cements the relationship. . . . John Galt's first sexual experience with Dagny is a ritualized rape in the tunnels of Taggart Transcontinental. For Rand these romanticized rapes are symbolic of the head-on clash of two strong personalities. The rapist is conquered just as his victim is.

Gladstein, obviously a fan, goes on to say, "When Rand's characters love, they love without reservation" (23).

The novel is set in a future United States, not totally dissimilar from the 1950s although there are some differences: the head of the nation is not called the president; much of Europe and Latin America have become "peoples' states"; and the economy is in crisis. Dagny Taggart, whom Gladstein calls "the most heroic female protagonist in American fiction," runs Taggart Transcontinental Railroad. Her brother James is its titular president. Her leadership tasks are constantly frustrated by government agencies. In the process of rebuilding one of Taggart's old railroad lines, she meets Hank Reardan, an industrialist who has invented a new metal stronger than steel. They fall in love and together attempt to defeat the forces of collectivism. She finds an abandoned motor in the ruins of an old factory in Wisconsin and goes on a search for its inventor, a search that intensifies as she realizes that many talented thinkers, industrialists, and artists keep dropping out of sight.

Her search leads her to a utopian community in Colorado where the dropouts have set up their own free enterprise system; called Mulligan's Valley or Galt's Gulch, this community is a refuge from the "looters," "scabs," and "moochers" who live off the productivity of others. Exemplifying a typical Rand reversal of a traditional maxim, the community lives not by the socialist principle "from each according to his ability, to each according to his need," but rather by this oath: "I swear by my life and my love of it that I will never live for the sake of another man nor ask another man to live for mine" (Gladstein 1984: 39). Dagny meets, and immediately falls in love with, John Galt, the leader of the dropouts and the inventor of the motor.

[handwritten margin note: So patriotic sacrifice is impossible — unimaginable]

Dagny does not stay, because she is not yet ready to give up on her struggle. Instead, she returns to a world beset by crisis. A national broadcast by Mr. Thompson, the "head of state," is announced, but John Galt takes over the airwaves and gives a lengthy speech about the *real* causes of the world crisis: mysticism, the concept of original sin, altruism, and what he calls the cult of "zero-worship." Agents of the government eventually capture Galt and torture him in an attempt to make him speak to the people and help legitimate the collectivist regime. But he is ultimately rescued by the other dropouts, as civilization finally collapses completely, symbolized by the blackout of New York City. The novel ends as Dagny and Galt make plans to rebuild civilization.

An interesting and contradictory moment in the novel lies in the public's reaction to Galt's speech. The "looters" recognize that the public responds to Galt's charismatic rhetoric, which is why they try to torture him into helping the regime. But it is unclear whether the masses are entirely capable of responding "mind to mind." Their response to Galt is more like the submissive response to the Alpha male in the pack—mirroring in a larger scale Dagny's sexual response to him. Rand's larger philosophical project requires the dissolution of the traditional dichotomy between body and mind, thus removing the objection that Dagny's response is somehow irrational. Nonetheless, there is more than a whiff of fascism in the depiction of the passive ("feminine") masses giving in to the strong leader (see Burke 1969).

Gladstein is particularly good at identifying the ways in which Rand's various characters embody a set of virtues and vices. Her protagonists are all "romantic rebels against restrictive and mundane societies. In their rebellion, they act alone and on principle" (41). Although Dagny, Galt, and Rearden are the main characters, they are assisted by other romantic rebels, most notably Francisco D'Anconia. D'Anconia, the heir to a copper fortune (the verbal parallel with Anaconda Copper is presumably no coincidence), helps bring about the economic collapse of the "looter" states. He also is assigned the task of educating Hank Rearden, most notably through his famous encomium to money. Another major helper, Ragnar Danneskjold, had attended college with Galt and D'Anconia, intending to become a philosopher, but instead he becomes a pirate, sinking ships bearing raw materials to the looters' factories and thus hastening the collapse of collectivism. He is a kind of reverse (that is, income-blind) Robin Hood, stealing from the undeserving and giving to the deserving.

Other characters represent individualists' virtues in their respective fields: Hugh Akston, a philosophy professor at Patrick Henry University and mentor to Galt, Francisco, and Ragnar—he was the last academic to affirm the possibility of truth; Richard Halley, a composer; Michael "Midas" Mulligan, the richest man in the country and proprietor of the community where the dropouts hide (he also runs a bank using only gold for exchange—a return to the gold standard being an article of faith among Rand's followers and other libertarians); and Judge Narragansett, who once presided over the Superior Court of Illinois but resigned when an appeals court reversed his ruling that those who earn are more entitled to the product of their labor than those whose only claim is need.

The novel's archvillains are mostly intellectuals who have given up on truth. Dr. Floyd Ferris uses the resources of the Science Institute to flummox logic in his book *Why Do You Think You Think?* Dr. Robert Stadler, once a great physicist and teacher of Galt, Francisco, and Ragnar at the university, trades his integrity willingly for wealth. James Taggart, Dagny's brother and president of Taggart Transcontinental, is so deathly afraid of personal responsibility that, when he marries, he deliberately chooses someone who is so inferior, in his view, that she will be bound to adore him. Minor villains include: Orren Boyle, a businessman who makes a fortune with government money; Emma "Ma" Chambers, a mystic and Buddhist who tries to convert the country to a soybean diet, a scheme that ends up ruining the wheat harvest; Fred Kinnan, a racketeer who heads the Amalgamated Laborers of America and is the most honest of the looters because he does not pretend that he is doing anything other than running a racket; Cuffy Meigs, a drunken thug who takes over an important weapons project and pulls the wrong lever, blowing everything up; Chick Morrison, the "morale conditioner," or the public relations flak; Dr. Simon Pritchett, author of *The Metaphysical Contradictions of the Universe*, in which he maintains that human beings are just chemistry and biology and metaphysics is just a matter of opinion; and, finally, Mr. Thompson, the "head of state," who is convinced that everyone is open to a deal.

Rand's characters in *Atlas Shrugged* thus play out a sort of allegory of 1950s politics. But how are we to make sense of the larger narrative in which the characters interact? A useful critical question is, What kind of social and political problem solving does the narrative accomplish? Fredric Jameson (1981) has developed the important insight that "ideology is not something which informs or invests symbolic production; rather the aesthetic act is itself ideological, and the production of aesthetic or narrative form is to be seen as an ideological act in its own right, with the function of inventing imaginary or formal 'solutions' to unresolvable social contradictions" (79).

Jameson goes on to describe the narrative category of romance as possessing a sense of good and evil as magical forces, a salvational sense of history, and a transitional moment in which two distinct modes of production or moments of socioeconomic development coexist, with its resolution projected "in the form of a nostalgic (or less often, a Utopian) harmony" (148). Like many defenses of the free market, *Atlas Shrugged* is a *romance* (see Haworth 1994: 5). Despite its surface claims to rationality, the novel exhibits the characteristics described by Jameson: a magical sense of vice and virtue, a depiction of historical crisis and salvation. I also would contend that the novel works as a problem-solving device for the anxiety generated both by the insecure status of the intelligentsia under capitalism and by the transition of capitalism from its "pure" laissez-faire form to "late" capitalism. Specifically, the characters in the novel illustrate a sense of disconnection between mind and body.

Only Galt is a fully integrated man, able to transcend the false dichotomy between mind and body. Hank Rearden, whose mind is capable of great things (for example, creating a new metal), is so out of touch with his body that he stays with his wife out of a vague sense of obligation, and in an odd speech to Dagny after their first coupling he tries to deny the spiritual component of his sexual desire. The novel dramatizes the movement of the world as defined by this narrow character system into the orbit of Galt's synthesis of the fundamental contradiction.

One person's false dichotomy is another's contradiction, and it seems reasonable to look for other accounts of the mind–body dichotomy. In an interesting passage, Nathaniel Branden describes his initial sexual encounter with his future wife Barbara: "Through the act of sex I discovered my own body, as if only now had it fully come into existence" (Nathaniel Branden 1989: 32) After Ayn Rand discovers that Branden has dumped her (and Barbara) for a younger Objectivist, Rand wails, "If you have an ounce of morality left in you, an ounce of psychological health—you'll be impotent for the next twenty years! And if you achieve any potency sooner, you'll know it's a sign of still worse moral degradation! ... The man to whom I dedicated *Atlas Shrugged* would never want anything less than me! I don't care if I'm ninety years old and in a wheelchair!" (Nathaniel Branden 1989: 371; compare Barbara Branden 1986: 346).

This fierce effort to unite mind and body is a distinctive theme in Rand's work. But Rand fails to recognize that the mind–body split is not an inevitable feature of human nature, but is created by the process of commodity exchange and by the alienation of labor. An interesting feature of Rand fans is that they seldom are artisans or industrialists. If you go back to the list at the beginning of the chapter, you will note that her appeal is chiefly to entertainers, psychologists, economists, and businesspeople involved with finance capital rather than with the actual production of *things*. This appeal also is relevant at a time when the transition from laissez-faire capitalism to its more complex "late" form is occurring. It is thus appropriate that one of Rand's most important fictional speeches is an encomium to money.

FRANCISCO'S MONEY SPEECH

The setting is a wedding reception for James Taggart. Bertram Scudder, one of the "looters," tells a young woman next to him not to be disturbed by Francisco, since he is a typical product of money, the root of all evil. Francisco turns to them, smiling politely, and begins his speech.

The first part is organized as a set of antithetical comparisons, ending with variations of the rhetorical question "Is this why you say money is the root of all evil?" Francisco, like Ayn Rand, asks the *radical* question, the root question, namely, What is the root of money? Money is:

1. A tool of exchange.
2. The material sign of the principle of fairness.
3. Taken away by moochers and looters.
4. Made possible by men who produce things, men with the capacity of rational thought.
5. A statement of hope that there are people who will not default on moral principle.
6. Based on the axiom that every person is the owner of his mind and effort.
7. Permission for you to obtain what your goods and labor are worth, but no more.
8. Permission for no deals other than of mutual benefit.
9. A demand for the recognition that human beings must work for their own benefit.
10. A demand for the recognition that the common bond human beings share is not suffering, but the exchange of goods.
11. Something that will die without its root in the rational mind.

In a transitional paragraph, responding to the objection of St. Paul that the love of money is the root of all evil, Francisco contends that the rational person does not love money in and of itself, but as the sign of the creative power of the individual. Rand appears to allude here to the Christian doctrine of the sacraments as "outward and visible signs of inward and spiritual grace" (*Book of Common Prayer* 1948: 581). Just as the water of baptism signifies the spiritual rebirth of a person into the Christian community, money signifies a better kind of spiritual rebirth into the community of creative, rational people. Money in fact demands the highest virtues of its owner. Men without courage, pride, or self-esteem will not remain rich for long. Then, in an echo of Abraham Lincoln's "house divided" speech, Francisco says, "When you see that trading is done, not by consent, but by compulsion—when you see that in order to produce, you need to obtain permission from men who produce nothing—when you see that money is flowing to those who deal, not in goods, but in favors—when you see that men get richer by graft and pull than by work, and your laws don't protect you against them, but protect them against you—when you see corruption being rewarded and honesty becoming a self-sacrifice—you may know that your society is doomed. Money . . . will not permit a country to survive as half-property, half-loot" (390). The destroyers will start by destroying money: They will end the gold standard, thus making an objective measure of value impossible.

Furthermore, Francisco contends, the argument that money is the root of all evil came from a time when wealth was produced by slaves. That time is no longer, thanks to the United States, the first and only "country of money," meaning: "a country of reason, justice, freedom, production, achievement" (391). The United States created the highest form of human being, the industrialist. The proudest distinction of Americans is that they created the phrase "to make money" (391). It had always been treated as something to be seized or begged; Americans understand that wealth has to be created. Making money is the essence of human morality. But now the looters' credo is that making money is immoral. The result of this belief will be destruction, since, if you do not use money as the basis for dealing with other human beings, the only other alternative is violence.

In response to his audience's exclamations of horror, Francisco challenges his hearers to refute a single sentence he uttered. They cannot. One woman says she can feel he's wrong, even if he's good at logic. Francisco retorts that when everyone is starving to death, her feelings will not help them (392).

The speech works in Rand's characteristic way of de-presencing human experience. There are no concrete historical examples, only generalized references to past slavery or to the founding of the United States. The constant use of anaphora foregrounds the abstract noun *money*. The speech is essentially barren of metaphor. It relies entirely on schematic devices for its hold on the reader: a relatively mechanical use of anaphora (the figure of repetition, such as King's use of "I Have a Dream" in his famous speech) and antithesis that creates a predictable pattern in the hearer's mind, what Burke (1968) called "minor, or incidental, form," carrying the audience along independently of the content of the message (127–128). The insistent rhythm reinforces the sense of the orator hammering against misconceptions, with the occasional release after a long series of repetitive clauses.

The style of the speech raises some conceptual difficulties for Rand's argument. If it is best that minds simply speak to other minds, why rely so heavily on the brute, mechanical force of the stylistic devices? If money, productivity, and exchange are interconnected, where does symbolic action, the literary and rhetorical motive, fit into Francisco's equation? If money is often held by those who commit fraud or do work they hate, where is the highest form of man? When did he (or she) actually dwell on this earth? Only Francisco, Dagny, and Rearden, of the characters we have met thus far in the novel, actually approach this quality. What are the rest? If they are moochers and looters, then why make the effort to communicate with them at all? Most importantly, where do *children* fit into this scheme?[7] The most glaring absence in Rand's writings is any extended reflection on the moral duty toward children. Addressed to an "inner adolescent" who has triumphantly silenced its "inner child," Rand, through Francisco, and especially through John Galt, crafts an oddly childless world.

"THIS IS JOHN GALT SPEAKING"

Nathaniel Branden has described the context in which Ayn Rand wrote the Galt speech. First, Nathaniel and Ayn announced to Barbara and Frank (Ayn's husband) that they were in love: "It's a rational universe," Ayn said, "*this had to happen*" (Branden 1989: 156). Eventually they had sex: "She made love with the same single-track concentration that she did everything else; nothing existed but the moment, our bodies, this sensation, then the next. What was electrifying was that in her gentlest, most sensual touch I could feel the full force of her personality, as if the voltage of her mind and the voltage of her flesh were one" (162). He goes on to describe their making love in her living room, Ayn still in her fur coat. "In this relationship I was making love not only to a woman but to a world—as if through the act of penetration, I was making contact anew with all of my most precious values. Sex was a bridge to another level of consciousness, to another kind of reality" (217). Lying in bed, she quoted from Hugo's *L'Homme qui rit:* "Woman is clay, longing to become mire" (222). The John Galt speech took Rand two years to write: "the two most painfully difficult years of her career. But it was not merely the difficulty of the project that made the writing take that long; it was the fact that her mind and time were divided between the novel and our relationship" (163). Branden came to realize that the underlying problem in all psychological complaints is lack of self-esteem: "A flawed self-concept, intellectual self-doubt, a sense of unworthiness or guilt, an experience of inadequacy, a feeling that 'Something is wrong with me' or 'I am not enough' " (172). He told Ayn about this insight and found out she was just then writing about self-esteem in Galt's speech: " 'In Galt's speech, you'll see that I describe self-esteem as one of the three cardinal values of my moral code. I define it as the conviction that you are competent to live and worthy of living' " (175). Galt says: "To live, man must hold three things as the supreme and ruling values of his life: Reason—Purpose—Self-esteem. Reason, as his only tool of knowledge—Purpose, as his choice of the happiness that tool must proceed to achieve—Self-esteem, as his inviolate certainty that his mind is competent to think and that his person is worthy of happiness, which means: is worthy of living" (cited in Branden 1989: 183).

Some interesting features of the Galt speech are: (1) it is delivered over the radio; (2) we really know nothing about Galt except that he was brilliant in college, tried to make it as an engineer, and now is leading the strike—we do not know him as a child, nor do we really know anything about his inner life in the same way that we know about Dagny Taggart's or Hank Rearden's; (3) the speech illustrates Rand's implicit theory of rhetoric: the importance of the mind speaking to another mind as the best form of persuasion; (4) there is an absence of figurative language, other than in his use of anaphora (repetition); (5) the fact that "the masses" respond to him so positively is surprising, since they are by definition not one of the higher classes whom Galt is primarily addressing; and (6) the speech is remarkably long. When Bennett Cerf tried to get Rand to shorten Galt's speech, she said: "Would you cut the Bible?" Branden says that it fit the scale of the book: "To me, it was a marvel of economy" (1989: 226).

At 8:00 P.M., November 22, the "head of state," Mr. Thompson, is scheduled to address the nation. At 8:00 on the dot, a voice comes over the radio receiver: "Ladies and gentlemen, Mr. Thompson will not speak to you tonight. His time is up. I have taken it over. You were to hear a report on the world crisis. That is what you are going to hear" (Rand 1957: 936). The voice is "clear, calm, implacable," sounding as if it were directed "not to a group but to one man; not the tone of addressing a meeting, but the tone of addressing a mind" (936). It quickly establishes its ethos, in the form of an "I am" anaphora. I am: the man who loves his life, does not sacrifice his love or his values, has deprived you of victims and thus destroyed your world, and will now tell you why you are perishing.

The combination of anaphora and antithesis continues relentlessly. Galt accuses his audience of having sacrificed justice to mercy, independence to unity, reason to faith, self-esteem to denial, and happiness to duty. These choices have produced the current disasters. Galt's strike has simply given them what their choices have ordained. Galt orders his audience: Do not try to find us, because we do not choose to be found. Do not cry that it is our duty to serve you, because we do not recognize such duty. We are on strike against self-immolation, the creed of unearned rewards and unrewarded duties, the dogma that the pursuit of one's happiness is evil, that life is guilt. *And we do not need you.* The rest of the speech defies analysis based on any rational structure, consisting of a string of aphorisms about morality, punctuated as always by the schemes of anaphora and antithesis, culminating in a peroration about the new world that is possible when the strike ends. Key points include:

1. A morality of reason is the morality proper to man; man's life is its standard of value. What enhances the life of a rational being is good, but what destroys it is evil.

2. A single axiom is at the root of this code: existence exists. A is A. A thing is itself. True and false, right and wrong, are one and the same. It is "depraved" to look for any reason other than one's own.

3. Human beings require three fundamental values in order to live: Reason—Purpose—Self-esteem.

4. These values require the virtues of "rationality, independence, integrity, honesty, justice, productiveness, pride." Rationality means

that existence exists. Independence means you cannot escape the responsibility of judgment. Integrity means you cannot fake your consciousness. Honesty means you cannot fake existence. Justice means you cannot fake the character of men. Productiveness means that all work is creative work if done by a thinking mind. Pride is recognition of the fact that you are your own highest value, and it has to be earned.

5. The symbol of the moral person is the trader.

6. There is one act of evil we must all agree on refraining from, namely, the initiation of physical force against others.

7. The ideologies of "mysticism" (apparently Christianity and religion in general) and "materialism" (communism), though seemingly opposed, have in common the hatred of the individual. The "mystics" have split man in two (body and soul), thus exalting self-sacrifice. The "materialists" (later, "mystics of muscle") have subordinated man to society. Both are wrong in requiring any sacrifice of self at all. They treat altruism as a "magic formula" that can justify anything, including the slaughter of millions. All that mystics want is death and destruction.

Galt then reveals a bit more about himself: twelve years ago, he worked as an inventor, developing a new source of energy as important as steam or oil, but he was attacked at a meeting of his factory and was then able to see clearly the incompetence and evil of the world. And that is when he went on strike against the cult of "zero-worship" (Rand 1957: 974).

Like all prophetic rhetoric, Galt's jeremiad then proceeds to identify and address a prophetic "remnant": those with "the dignity and will to love one's life" but who are confused, wondering why they "live without dignity, love without fire and die without resistance" (976, 978). This part of the audience is still capable of choosing to be like John Galt: "That choice is yours to make. That choice—the dedication to one's highest potential—is made by accepting the fact that the noblest act you have ever performed is the act of your mind in the process of grasping that two and two make four" (982).

The jeremiad then turns into a high school commencement speech, with specific advice for living one's life: accept the fact that your life depends on your mind; accept the task of becoming a man;

accept the fact that you are not omniscient; accept nothing less than perfection in the realm of morality; accept happiness as the only moral purpose of your life; and learn to treat as the mark of the cannibal any man's demand for your help.

An apostrophe (figure of direct address to an absent audience) to Francisco D'Anconia and Ragnar the pirate reemphasizes the theme of the blindness of the world to the reality of mind and personal achievement. Galt, Francisco, and Ragnar together have resolved to rally to U.S. ideals against those of a decaying Europe. This country was not built on handouts, on the mind–body split. It was the product of *reason*, the notion of *rights*. "*Rights* are conditions of existence required by man's nature for his proper survival. If man is to live on earth, it is *right* for him to use his mind, it is *right* to act on his own free judgment, it is *right* to work for his values and to keep the product of his work" (985–986).

The theme continues. Government exists to protect man's rights, to protect him from physical violence. A proper government is *only* a policeman. You need not worry that the men of strong intelligence are a threat to your livelihood; when you work in a modern factory you are paid not only for your labor but also for that of the inventor, the industrialist, and the investor who made that factory possible. Galt does not use the term "surplus value," but the next passage is a direct response to that Marxist concept: "Would you dare claim that the size of your pay check was created solely by your physical labor and that those rails were the product of your muscles? The standard of living of that blacksmith is all that your muscles are worth; the rest is a gift from Hank Rearden" (Rand 1957: 988). The worker, then, lives off the surplus value created by the inventor and the capitalist, not the other way around. In return for this surplus all that the capitalist sought was freedom, but that was too much for the world to grant.

Galt then reidentifies the saving remnant: "those among you who have retained some sovereign shred of their soul, unsold and unstamped: 'to the order of others.' If, in the chaos of the motives that have made you listen to the radio tonight, there was an honest, rational desire to learn what is wrong with the world, you are the man whom I wished to address. By the rules and terms of my code, one owes a rational statement to those whom it does concern and who're making an effort to know. Those who're making an effort to fail to understand me, are not a concern of mine" (990). Galt's message to the remnant is "stop supporting your own destroyers." Wait until the looters' state collapses into impotent chaos, with starving robber gangs fighting against one another. Wait until the advocates of sacrifice are dead. Then we will return.

The peroration paints a picture of the new world coming when the men of mind return: it will be a productive city of factories and orchards and markets and "inviolate" homes. Everyone will happily labor under the sign of the dollar—the symbol of free trade and free minds (Rand 1957: 991). The political system will be contained in the single premise that one shall obtain values from others through physical force. It will restore to citizens the spirit of childhood, "that spirit of eagerness, adventure and certainty which comes from dealing with a rational universe." Citizens will receive from others not alms, pity, money, or forgiveness of sins, but a single value: *justice*.

Those men of mind still struggling or held prisoner in the world must leave the destroyers. Galt turns his attention to Dagny: "Do you hear me . . . my love?" The commencement address tone returns: "In the name of the best within you . . . don't let your fire go out. . . . Do not let the hero in your soul perish. . . . The world you desired can be won, it exists, it is real, it is possible, it's yours" (993). You will win when you are ready to pronounce the oath Galt took at the beginning of his battle: "I swear—by my life and my love of it— that I will never live for the sake of another man, nor ask another man to live for mine" (993). And so the speech ends: part jeremiad, part commencement address. The realization that Galt (like his creator) cheerfully wishes the destruction of the vast majority of human life on the planet only sinks in on the second or third reading. Despite the claims about liberty, the reality is that Rand's world is to be run by an intellectual meritocracy, with the remainder grateful for the crumbs of surplus value extracted from the intellectuals' labor. Millions of people around the world will have to die in order for the reign of the "looters" to end. Only the intelligent and self-reliant will be fit to rule. Rand's voice, at the end, with its repetitions and antitheses relentlessly hammering away at the reader's mind, is the voice of one who, as Whittaker Chambers (1990) wrote, can easily be imagined shrieking "To a gas chamber, go!" (122).

CONCLUSION

Ayn Rand's rhetoric is a distinctive defense of the free market, because
it rests on strictly moral grounds, often thought to be the weakest link
in capitalism. While other thinkers might concentrate on justifying
the market on grounds of "realism" or "efficiency," Rand wants to defend the market as an "unknown ideal" not fully realized. It does not
matter whether the market is "efficient" or not, since it is the contribution to the individual's achievement that is of value, not some utilitarian calculus. At the end of *Atlas Shrugged*, all of civilization is in ruins, but the fundamental morality of the heroes is affirmed, and that is
all that really matters. Capitalism has had a rhetorical problem from
its inception. The "bourgeois virtues," as McCloskey termed them, are
not quite as inspiring as aristocratic virtues. Capitalism looked inspiring compared to the "drab grey world of socialism" depicted by Mrs.
Thatcher, but, in the absence of a communist menace, how is a capitalist social order to legitimate itself? What Rand provided was an inspiring moral justification for capitalism, addressed to that audience
most vulnerable to utopian appeals, namely, young intellectuals.

There are times when human beings need to hear inspirational
messages about self-reliance and the struggle to "be all you can be."
The primary developmental task of adolescence, psychologists tell us,
is for adolescents to carve out a sense of individual identity by beginning the difficult task of separating from their parents. A sense of self-
worth comes in part from setting boundaries between the self and the
other. Independence, self-reliance, and the setting of strong boundaries have been coded as masculine qualities for a long time. It is not
surprising that Ayn Rand's novels seem to speak powerfully to women,
who often have not been allowed such qualities. In the conformist cli-
mate of the U.S. high school—particularly in the 1950s—the message
of John Galt was especially attractive to those who did not fit in.

So there are some forms of rhetoric that are particularly apposite
to a particular audience at a particular time, and Ayn Rand's rhetoric
may qualify for that distinction. But it is one thing to read Ayn Rand
when you are a lonely, zit-ridden, horny adolescent and quite another
thing to spend your whole life searching for a Dagny or a John Galt.
Every powerful rhetoric eventually finds its most appropriate audience.
To recognize yourself in the last pages of *Atlas Shrugged*, gloating over

the ruins of civilization, may be fine if you are fantasizing about schoolyard bullies and snobbish cheerleaders receiving their comeuppance. But to turn such anger into a politics and a religion is not a fit preoccupation for adults. To be an adult is to recognize a sense of obligation: to a partner, a child, a community. Ayn Rand came to America because her relatives in Chicago helped her. They were an ordinary, hard-working, religious Russian Jewish family. I wonder if she ever thanked them.

CHAPTER FOUR

Anarchy, State, and Utopia

A Rhetorical Reading

CAPTAIN'S LOG: STARDATE 13256.8

The Enterprise is on its way to Planet Libertas in the Hobbesian system. We have received a distress call from a Robert Nozick, who claims to be a professor at a Harvard University, and he is demanding that we rescue him.

Lieutenant Commander Data has confirmed that Nozick was a professor of philosophy at a prominent U.S. university in the latter half of the twentieth century. He was most famous for his book *Anarchy, State, and Utopia*, which won a National Book Award in 1974, in which he argued that only a minimal state is justified and that a utopia based on libertarian principles is possible. Just before the socialist revolution that created the United Federation of Planets, he volunteered for a cryogenics experiment funded by Richard Scaife. Convinced that civilization was about to end, Scaife sought to preserve a saving remnant of libertarian thinkers who would wait for the revolution eventually to self-destruct and would then reassert their dominion. Starship Cato took off from Earth in Old Earth Date March 2007, and has not been heard from until now.

In this imaginary episode of *Star Trek: The Next Generation*, Nozick and his fellow libertarians have landed on a planet where, partially as an experiment, they have forbidden the creation of a state, allowing only for competing protective associations. The four protective associations (formed by the paleoconservative followers of Murray Rothbard, the more moderate followers of Friedrich Hayek, some Chicagoans, and the disciples of Ayn Rand) have warred against one another for years, constantly improving their warfare and surveillance technology. The Rothbardians, concluding that they would rather be dead than Randian, started a final battle that ended in "mutually assured destruction." The Hayekians and the Chicago school then merged forces, leading to a monopoly protective agency, but the negative externalities (radiation) from the earlier Rothbardian–Randian exchange killed off all of them except for Nozick, who had begun a sideline selling fallout shelters. (Only Nozick had one, since the rest viewed buying a shelter as an effort at "planning" and decided to trust to the outcome of the market in protective agencies.) Nozick recounts the foregoing tale to a scouting team from the Enterprise and is momentarily convinced that he has an ally in Data. Captain Picard and the rest of his crew, however, conclude that Nozick is best left on Planet Libertas. In a humane gesture, they transport him to a Holodeck hastily built near his fallout shelter and program it to replay a graduate seminar in political philosophy for eternity.

Although this imagined scenario is a bit of whimsy, as John Nelson (1989) has written, most of the best contemporary political philosophy takes the form of science fiction (I would add that much current political philosophy reads more like *bad* science fiction). The most influential philosopher of libertarianism at present is Harvard-based philosopher Robert Nozick, whose *Anarchy, State, and Utopia* reached a wide audience after its publication in 1974. It has continued to influence discussions of rights and the legitimacy of the state, even in Marxist circles. Its use of "counterfactual" arguments and radical depresencing of history and politics makes it read a bit like a science fiction novel.

Anarchy, State, and Utopia is an effort to demonstrate three propositions: (1) a minimal state—limited to protection against force, theft, fraud, and to the protection of contracts—is justified; (2) any more extensive state would violate persons' rights and therefore not be justified; and (3) the minimal state is not only right—it is *inspiring* (ix). Nozick, like Rand, has recognized capitalism's rhetorical problem; namely, that the realist rhetoric of *Homo economicus* is not very

appealing to young or idealistic audiences. Nozick's book addresses
Rand's audience after they have grown older, studied a little philosophy and economics, and perhaps flirted with communal living (remember, it was the seventies).

The following rhetorical analysis of Nozick's masterwork reveals
both the unexamined assumptions of his defense of the "nightwatch-
man state" and the underlying basis of the persuasiveness of radical libertarianism to certain audiences. *Anarchy, State, and Utopia* is of particular interest to me in the context of this book, because, like Rand's
Atlas Shrugged, it is an attempt to conceptualize a free-market utopia.
Some classical liberal thinkers have occasionally likened nineteenth-
century England to the idyllic setting of an Old Milwaukee beer commercial: "It doesn't get any better than this." For Nozick, however, the
best is yet to come. He hopes to persuade anarcho-capitalists that a
minimal state can still manage to preserve rights, and he hopes to persuade the children of the sixties that a minimal state is not some
dreary fantasy of economists but rather the only possible world in
which everyone "can do their own thing." Other free-market advocates have rejected utopia outright in the name of a "realistic" assessment of human nature and the limits of government. Radicals like
Rand and Rothbard have written angry indictments of the existing political order. Nozick injects a much-needed dose of humor and a positive program into the libertarian project.

Nozick first adduces a "potential explanation" of the origin of the
state out of a state of nature, carefully avoiding historical or empirical
arguments. He then develops a theory of rights that unfortunately ignores human relationships altogether. For example, he attacks even
voluntary redistribution of property as immoral. He concludes by creating a blueprint for a libertarian utopia. This utopia is carefully
crafted to appeal both to radical capitalists and to sixties-style rebels,
but its rejection of public deliberation limits its applicability as a potential real-world political program.

THE RHETORIC OF PHILOSOPHY

Before examining Nozick's arguments, let us briefly consider *Anarchy,
State, and Utopia* as a text. Is Nozick's "philosophical" justification of

the free market markedly different from Rand's "literary" justification? Are both different from, say, a speech by Margaret Thatcher or a libertarian manifesto by Charles Murray? If so, in what ways?

Edward Schiappa (1991) has demonstrated that the word "rhetoric" does not appear in Greek writings until Plato's *Gorgias*. In that dialogue Plato dissociates (dissunites) the art of the *logos* (knowledge) into the binary opposition between "rhetoric" and "philosophy." *Rhetoric*, akin to cosmetics or cookery, merely appeals to the uninformed or to the baser instincts of the populace. *Philosophy*, on the other hand, is a way of life, accessible only to those who participate in the give-and-take of dialectic. In the *Phaedrus*, however, Plato appears to find a role for the art of rhetoric in his philosophical system. It requires thorough knowledge of the subject at hand, as well as the ability to craft messages adapted to the souls of one's audience. The good rhetorician, like the philosopher, is able to show audiences "better versions of themselves" (Weaver 1953: 25).

Aristotle refined Plato's philosophic rhetoric into a practical art for the statesman: "the faculty of discovering in the given case the available means of persuasion." Chaim Perelman and Lucie Olbrechts-Tyteca (1969) developed Aristotle's insight into a rhetoric of philosophy, contending that philosophers address a "universal audience," that ensemble of ideally rational hearers who will yield to the force of the better argument. Extending Perelman's insight, David Zarefsky (1995) defined argument, as distinct from rhetoric, as the practice of justifying decisions made under conditions of uncertainty (54–59). To engage in "argument," in the philosophical sense, requires a willingness to suspend judgment, to acknowledge the presence of opposing views, and to represent those opposing views fairly (see Ehninger 1970; Johnstone 1966). Jürgen Habermas (1979) introduced the idea of the "ideal speech situation" as a regulative ideal for argument, in which: (1) no truth claims are exempt from questioning; (2) no one-sided (that is, authoritarian) social norms will be present in the discussion; and (3) everyone has an equal opportunity to speak (see also Aune 1994).

The real world of politics, however, often requires that advocates address arguments to specific audiences, simplify complex issues, and appeal to partisan interests. The art of rhetoric is a useful tool of survival in politics and law, where an opponent cannot be trusted to adhere to the canons of good argument.

Political philosophy is an interesting borderline genre between speculative philosophy and practical rhetoric. While they do not necessarily address specific political conjunctures in the way that, say, someone campaigning for office does, political philosophers inevitably react to political events and seek to give advice to politicians and future politicians about the nature of the ideal regime. After Locke (who called rhetoric "a perfect cheat") and Kant (who accused rhetoric of merely "playing" with serious topics), the art of rhetoric gradually disappeared as a topic in political philosophy, only to reappear in a limited form in the late twentieth century. Robert Nozick writes firmly within the Lockean tradition—indeed, he writes as if there were no political philosophy before Locke. In fact, the very nature of libertarianism requires a fundamental suspicion of the art of persuasion, since the effort to persuade another appears to violate the value of personal autonomy.

Yet, if there is any single message that comes through from the rhetorical revival, it lies in the insight that rhetoric cannot be escaped. You can try to approach the ideal of discourse addressed to a universal audience, but you cannot escape the fact that political philosophy is addressed to audiences, selects facts from the real world, invents rhetorical examples, and strives for advantage over opponents.

NOZICK'S PREMISES: STATE OF NATURE, RIGHTS, AUTONOMY

Nozick begins his book by contending that the fundamental question of political philosophy is "Why should there be a state at all?" (4), but he provides no evidence for this claim. He has framed his argument in terms that reflect the cultural presumption that state-of-nature theory is the logical starting point for serious political philosophy. As Chaim Perelman (1982) writes, "Presumptions are based on the idea that that which happens is normal." They impose the burden of proof upon the person who departs from normal expectations. Nozick assumes that his audience—whether anarchists or Rawlsian liberals—views his starting point as uncontroversial. But Aristotle or Plato or Aquinas would not have started a discussion of politics this way. It is as if one were to examine a group of bees and ask, "Should there be a hive at all?"[1]

The unspoken assumptions underlying Nozick's starting point are: (1) serious discussion of political philosophy begins with Hobbes;

(2) serious discussion therefore begins with the admittedly artificial construct of the state of nature; and (3) a view of human beings as individual rights-bearers is the only one worth taking seriously. Nozick's "universal audience," his ideal of a competent and reasonable audience, is committed to these abstract values. Concrete values attached to "a specific being, object, group, or institution, in its uniqueness," are not shared by this universal audience, which treats abstract "rights" as being of fundamental value (Perelman 1982: 27). Perelman writes that reasoning based on "concrete values seems characteristic of conservative societies. Abstract values, in contrast, serve more easily as a basis for critiques of society, and can be tied to a justification for change, to a revolutionary spirit" (28). This commitment to abstract rights distinguishes Nozick from true conservatives who, as Edmund Burke noted at the time of the French Revolution, are more likely to talk about the "rights of Englishmen" than the "rights of Man." As we shall see, Nozick anticipated not only the Reagan and Thatcher revolutions but also the revolutionary end of the nation-state itself.

The presumption of the state-of-nature argument and the insistence on abstract rather than concrete values are in turn linked to a particular locus of the "preferable." A locus, Perelman writes, is an affirmation of what is presumed to be of higher value in any circumstance whatsoever. A utilitarian, for instance, may frame an argument in terms of the locus of *quantity*: "the greatest good for the greatest number." As Mark P. Moore (1993) has pointed out in his analysis of the spotted owl controversy in the Pacific Northwest, the timber industry argued in terms of a locus of *quantity* (the preservation of jobs for thousands of people) while environmentalists argued in terms of a locus of *quality* (the irreplaceable value of a particular species). In this case, Nozick frames political philosophy in terms of the locus of *autonomy*: the value of the individual as rights-bearer.

Another concept from Perelman that is useful in analyzing Nozick's rhetorical strategy is the argument by dissociation: "When, faced with the incompatibilities that ordinary thought encounters, a person does not limit himself to conjuring away the difficulty by pretending not to see it, but instead tries to resolve it in a theoretically satisfying manner by reestablishing a coherent vision of reality, he will most often attain such a resolution by a dissociation of most of the ideas accepted from the start" (Perelman 1982: 126). For example, Kant had resolved the problem of moral freedom by dissociating (that is, separating) the ideal of reality into phenomenal reality, ruled by universal laws of cause and effect, and noumenal reality, where causality rules through freedom. The study of persuasion in Western culture has been driven by Plato's original dissociation of the art of the *logos* ("speech," "reason") into "philosophy" and "rhetoric," a dissociation that Perelman and other new rhetoricians have attempted to dissolve. The two terms in a dissociative pair are structured in such a way that term 1 corresponds to appearance and term 2 corresponds to a normative "reality" underlying the appearance. Perelman did not discuss the "reassociation" of previously dissociated ideas, although the concept is implicit in his work. Nozick's strategy is to reassociate under the abstract term "individual rights" terms that had been dissociated by Rawls, Dworkin, and other defenders of New Deal liberalism. Dworkin (1977), like the post-1937 Supreme Court, had contended that "civil liberties" (freedom of speech, press, religion, and association) are more fundamental rights than property rights, which may be curtailed to promote the equality of all persons to attain a position of equal concern and respect in the community. Nozick, like all the classical liberals and libertarians discussed in this book, not only rejects this dissociation but creates a hierarchy of valued rights in which the right to property stands at the top (somewhat like a neo-Platonic god) and from which all other rights emanate.

In keeping with the values of his intended audience, Nozick also invokes the methods of science to describe his approach to the problem of the state. Real science, it seems, is not mere empirical description. Nozick borrows from the philosopher of science Carl Hempel the notion of *a potential explanation* (1965). A potential explanation creates an account of a realm of experience or nature, and we can learn a lot from it even if the explanation has no relation to reality whatsoever.

Nozick's invocation of the method of potential explanation has three rhetorical benefits: (1) it borrows the prestige of the natural sciences for the notoriously more imprecise practice of political philosophy (using what Perelman calls "quasi-logical" arguments, arguments that mimic formal logic, but with probable rather than certain premises and with questionable formal validity); (2) it removes the ability of an opponent to appeal to historical arguments or evidence in refuting his position; and (3) it removes the nagging doubt about the appropriateness of his own initial framing of the problems of politics in

Lockean terms: in an odd combination of *a fortiori* argument and argument from authority, he contends that he cannot be expected to do something Locke also was unable to do.

In constructing his potential explanation of the origin of the state, Nozick proposes to start with a nonstate situation in which people generally satisfy moral constraints and act as they ought. The state can be justified under one or more of the following conditions: if the state is better than the nonstate situation where people act morally, if the state is the best we can realistically attain, if the state arises from anarchy without violating moral principles, or if the state is an improvement over anarchy (Nozick 1974: 5).

Nozick identifies problems that would arise in Locke's state of nature. Personal and private enforcement of the individual's rights might lead to feuds, with no firm way to settle them. If there's a stronger adversary, an individual may lack the power to enforce those rights (11–12). The individual might solve this with mutual-protection associations, but they would be inconvenient when problems arise within the association, such as a "paranoid or cantankerous" member. Members also would always have to be "on call" (12–13). (Note that even a rotating form of service to the community as a whole is viewed inherently as a burden by a Nozickian proponent.) Such problems could be solved by the division of labor: some entrepreneur would form protective services and hire people to perform protective functions (13).

Another alternative would be to hire a neutral arbitrator, as in a religious court. Nozick quickly cuts back to present-day reality from his "potential explanation," thus enhancing its credibility. We tend, he says, to forget possibilities of acting outside the state. Would you really pick Congress first if you were looking for a group of wise and sensitive persons to regulate you for your own good? (14). To Nozick, it was unclear what a wise and sensitive person would look like.

Other problems raised by protective agencies include the following. Would a protective agency enforce rights against a client of the agency? What happens when there are conflicts between clients of different protective agencies? What happens if you have an outlaw agency? (Nozick 1974: 17) One outcome might be that two agencies would do battle, with one always winning. Another would be separate turf: one agency would be powerful in one geographic area, the other in a different area. This would lead to border battles, but if they fought evenly and often, they might eventually set up a system of appeals courts (16).

One purpose of this extended potential explanation is to provide a striking metaphoric reframing of the notion of the state itself. Nozick asks, innocently: "How, if at all, does a dominant protective association differ from the state?" (18). He has by a strategy of synecdoche (the rhetorical figure equivalent to zooming in for a close-up) identified the state (itself already implicitly dissociated from "community" or "people") with one of its parts.

The more overt justification for this story of conflicting protective associations is to use a form of explanation dear to Nozick's intended audience: the invisible-hand explanation, which is appealing because of its elegance and simplicity. The state, like dinner in *The Wealth of Nations*, results from the guidance of an invisible hand. It occurs as a by-product of selfish human action, not by human design. Nozick provides an aria-like list of sixteen intriguing invisible hand explanations. For example, Jews have higher IQs than Catholics because their learned men, rabbis, were encouraged to have large families, whereas learned Catholics, priests, and monks were required to be celibate.

The invisible-hand explanation has other appeals beyond those identified by Nozick: (1) it reinforces the libertarian objection to planning of any sort (except for the rational planning done by entrepreneurs); (2) it appeals to the intellectual's craving for explanation, especially any explanation that lies below the surface or confounds everyday common sense; and (3) it uses the vestiges of the argument from design in theology not to prove the existence of God, but of a rational, ordered universe discoverable by the scientific mind. Interestingly, as Albert O. Hirschman has noted in his discussion of the "Futility Thesis," conservatives and libertarians usually emphasize negative unintended consequences when discussing governmental action. In this case, Nozick is more interested in positive unintended consequences (perhaps in keeping with his relentlessly upbeat version of libertarianism).

So, Nozick asks, have we provided an invisible hand explanation of the state? A necessary condition for the existence of a state is the announcement that, to the best of its ability, it will punish everyone whom it discovers to have used force without its express permission (24). But the protective associations don't seem to have this monopoly character. And they fail to provide protection for all in their territory. This difference between the state and the protective association leads to Nozick's discussion of rights.

NOZICK ON RIGHTS

Nozick's discussion of rights relies on a form of argument known as the
"slippery slope": if you do *x* (give the student an extension on this paper, allow an assault weapons ban, have an impure thought), you will
inevitably do *y* (have no academic standards, take away firearms from
law-abiding citizens, commit adultery). Douglas Walton (1992), the
foremost contemporary analyst of informal logic, has devoted an entire
book to the slippery slope argument, suggesting some boundaries between fallacious and potentially valid forms. In legal systems that rely
on the concept of precedent, there is a clearly identifiable link between identifying a general right (say, "right to privacy in the marital
relationship," as in *Griswold v. Connecticut*) to a related, but more controversial right ("right to privacy" in reproductive choice, as in *Roe v.
Wade*). Walton says that fallacious slippery slope arguments are ones
that cannot specify the links between an initial state and undesirable
consequences. Walton does not draw a connection with Kant's Cate-
gorical Imperative ("Act only on that principle that you can will to be
universal law"), but it seems plausible to suggest that much moral theory (of the variety known as deontological—duty-based) after Kant relies heavily on the slippery slope argument that if you break a universal
rule of any kind, you will develop the bad habit of rationalizing away
morality entirely. Kant's emphasis on moral autonomy and individual
rights is one important precursor of libertarianism, which borrows
from Kant (in largely unacknowledged ways) the idea that once you
let the nose of the camel (the state) into the tent, pretty soon the
whole camel follows. Nozick's aim is to show his anarchist reader the
possibility that the slippery slope of rights-invasion might be stoppable
at a defensible point.

The night-watchman state of classical liberal theory appears to be
redistributive—it compels some people to pay for the protection of
others—hence, a "slippery slope" that justifies other attractive pur-
poses requiring redistribution; the ultraminimal state, in contrast, provides protection only to those who pay for it (Nozick 1974: 26).
Nozick seems not to recognize the existence of positive externalities in
the relationship between the night-watchman state and the individual. A childless person who is taxed to support, say, public education
obtains certain benefits from living among educated people. Nozick's
strategy here (like Howard Jarvis and other leaders of the tax revolt of

the 1970s) is to depict the citizen as engaged in a transaction with the state. The citizen should receive an itemized list of the goods and services purchased with her tax money, and if she is not satisfied, then the tax is redistributive. (Some cities, notably Milwaukee, have actually begun such a process of itemization for local tax bills.) But there is redistribution and there is *redistribution*. If my taxes subsidize city parks, but I never go to them, has my wealth been redistributed? The framing of the citizen–state transaction shifts the burden of proof onto the "state" to justify expenses in individual terms, which makes the notion of *res publica* (public things) inherently suspect.

Nozick then considers utilitarian objections to his position. He ignores pre-Lockean ethical positions—notably, virtue ethics—but the notion that a community might have a common understanding of virtues is utterly foreign to Nozick's world. He criticizes utilitarianism for not taking rights and their violation sufficiently into account. Rights could be thought of as side constraints in a utilitarian theory, but, Nozick writes, "Political philosophy is concerned only with *certain* ways that persons may not use others; primarily, physically aggressing against them." There is no justified sacrifice of some of us for others (1974: 32–33).

The central value of individual autonomy is reinforced by Nozick's clever discussion of what he calls the "experience machine," which sounds a bit like the Holodeck on *Star Trek: The Next Generation*. Even if we could simulate any experience on demand, or even develop a transformation machine to make us whatever sort of person we want to be, it is inherently disturbing to think of some thing or someone else living our lives for us.

The experience and transformation machines raise the question: What if beings from other galaxies treated us the way we treat animals? (Nozick 1974: 45). What characteristics of persons create moral constraints for those interacting with persons? Traditional lists of favorable traits include: sentience and self-consciousness, rationality, free will, and having a soul. Of special moral importance, Nozick contends, is the capacity "to form a picture of one's whole life" and "to act in terms of some overall conception of the life one wishes to lead" (50). Having a "soul" may mean simply this sort of striving to give meaning to one's life.

The case of a person with Down's syndrome or autism is a useful counterexample to Nozick's position. Is a severely autistic person without living parents or relatives capable of acting in terms of some overall conception of his life? Probably not. Who should take care of him? Not the state, because that would involve redistribution. The person with severe autism or any sort of debilitating handicap is dependent on the largesse of those whose "overall conception of life" might involve enjoying changing a fifty-year-old's diapers. The idea that a parent or the "state" might have an "obligation" to the handicapped person could only be the first step down the slippery slope to the confiscatory welfare state that Nozick is trying to deconstruct. What would a political philosophy that began with the needs of the autistic child look like?[2]

Nozick concludes this section by noting that he has fulfilled his goal of demonstrating how a minimal state could emerge out of anarchy (1974: 52) and has raised the problem of redistribution by noting how the general provision of protective services would arise as well (52).

AGAINST THE REDISTRIBUTIVE STATE

The implied audience of Part I of Nozick's book is an anarcho-capitalist, such as David Friedman or Murray Rothbard. The implied audience of Part II is ostensibly the person of good will who may have leanings toward some form of welfare state, however modest. But the actual audience is more likely the reader who is already persuaded of Nozick's position and is searching for arguments to defend it. The audience is most emphatically not the socialist or social democrat, since Nozick basically refuses to engage the socialist position other than in caricature.[3]

Nozick begins this section by defining the notion of "justice in holdings." The just holding of property consists in: (a) original acquisition of holdings—principle of justice in acquisition; (b) transfer of holdings—principle of justice in transfer; and (c) if (a) and (b) are true, there is just distribution (150–153).

Nozick frames the socialist objection entirely in terms of the labor theory of value and contends that the mistake of the socialist lies in basing her analysis on a faulty time-slice of the distribution process (155). The welfare or redistributive state believes in "patterning," that is, finding a principle for justifying redistribution. Examples might be moral merit or neediness. Following Friedrich Hayek, Nozick rejects the very idea of patterning: we cannot know enough about each person's situation to distribute to each according to his moral merit (158). However, one strand in a free capitalist society would permit distribution according to benefits to others.

Capitalism does not reward independents like Thoreau—it rewards people who are occupied with serving others and winning them as customers (159n). Nozick then proposes a little motto (somewhat reminiscent of the slogan in Galt's Gulch): "From each as they choose, to each as they are chosen" (160).

The refutation of socialism moves along briskly. Nozick first creates a straw person notion of socialism, avoiding the issues of workplace democracy and the problem of de-skilling that have occupied socialist thought in recent years. Second, like Deirdre McCloskey's, Nozick's picture of capitalism suggests the model of a small-town main street or, more aptly, an upscale mall in a university town. The straw socialist here is depicted as hating the honest merchant who just wants to serve his or her customer well. But surely it strains one's credulity a bit to picture Donald Trump, Bill Gates, or even George Soros as *primarily* in the business of pleasing customers! Just as with McCloskey, Posner, and other free-marketeers, the model of human interaction is *dyadic*, not communal. There is a buyer and a seller. Sometimes they trade laces, but there is no network of institutions or intermediaries, much less workers, who are stakeholders in this interaction. To admit the presence of additional intermediaries and stakeholders would involve asking some rather difficult questions that cannot easily be answered by Nozick's simplistic view of property rights, namely, what happens when market exchanges affect the larger community?

Perhaps the most widely cited part of *Anarchy, State, and Utopia* is the Wilt Chamberlain exemplum.[4] Wilt Chamberlain signs with a ball club. He plays under the following agreement: he gets 25 cents for every ticket sold. So, if management sells a million tickets at a dollar apiece, freely bought by people who want to see him, Chamberlain gets $250,000. How is this even remotely unjust? (160–162). Not only that, but a truly socialist society would have to prohibit "capitalist acts between consenting adults," because there will always be an incentive to put in work on your own time after hours (Nozick 1974: 163). You cannot attain any end-state principle or patterned principle of justice without continuous interference with people's lives (163). Nozick then raises a particularly revealing rhetorical question: Should a family use its scarce resources to help its most talented child or its least talented? The most talented, of course. And what is true of a family is even more true of society as a whole: there is no reason to expend scarce resources to enhance the lot of the less fortunate (167n). This is the standard argument used against mainstreaming handicapped children in public schools. If resources are devoted to them, then the gifted will be held back. The notion that the gifted might obtain certain benefits (developing the tolerance and sensitivity that may pay off later on) or that including the handicapped might have additional moral implications is harder to measure by a simple cost–benefit analysis.

The next move by Nozick is predictable: any set of holdings realizing a particular pattern may be transformed by voluntary exchanges or gifts into another set of holdings that does not fit that pattern (219). In other words, private charity can solve the problems of the less advantaged. But this argument assumes there are always sufficient incentives for voluntary exchanges or gifts. The historical evidence for the claim that private philanthropy might pick up the slack from the welfare state is very thin. But, even granting the case for private philanthropy, the astounding aspect of Nozick's ethics is that he views it as far more moral to let a retarded child starve than for a Bill Gates to be forced to pay a dollar in taxes. The open-minded philosopher in my audience may be thinking "surely this is why rhetoric and philosophy are not the same thing. Mr. Aune is shamelessly pulling out the retarded child card again. Real philosophers don't appeal to the emotions that way or frame arguments in the most extreme way possible." Would that were true, dear reader, for Nozick goes on to make the incredible claim that taxation of earnings from labor is tantamount to forced labor (1974: 169). Any effort to create an end-state of equality involves a shift from the classical liberal notion of self-ownership to the idea that the state may at least partially own persons (172). To be taxed is to be enslaved. Note that there is no implication that I may vote to be taxed or that most people, unless brainwashed by libertarians, would do so as well. Nozick appears to be suggesting, like some Marxist caricature, that all of us are deeply in false consciousness if we are not willing to man the barricades to prevent ourselves from being enslaved every April 15th.

It is a comparatively short step, alas, from Nozick's argument to the rantings of the National Rifle Association about the confiscation of guns, or the right-wing militias' contention that any form of government extending beyond the role of a county sheriff is illegitimate. Libertarians spent much of the 1980s and 1990s decrying a culture of "victimhood" promoted by the left. But the right has come to power largely by creating and exploiting a sense of victimhood on the part of "the ordinary, hard-working taxpayer"—and Nozick has provided the philosophical ammunition for that argument.

Next Nozick takes on John Rawls, his liberal competitor, directly. In Rawls's *A Theory of Justice* (1971), he asks the reader to imagine that a "veil of ignorance" has descended upon people who have to make a decision about the political ordering of their society. They must decide how goods and rights will be distributed, but they know nothing about their own endowments (intellectual or property) beforehand. Rawls contends that a reasonable person would arrange a society in such a way as to ensure that the least-well-off person is benefited, so long as everyone else is not made worse off. In other words, Rawls provides an elegant justification, in the arcane quasi-economic language of analytic philosophy, for the social-democratic state. Nozick provides a counteranalogy to the original position: a group of students has studied during the year, and received grades from 0 to 100 that the students haven't learned of yet. They are asked to allocate grades among themselves so that the grades add up to a given sum, determined by the sum of the grades they have actually received from the teacher. Would these people agree to a non-end-state historical principle of distribution? That is, would they give people grades according to how their exams were evaluated by a qualified, impartial observer? Of course not, Nozick says. Therefore, Rawls's justification of redistribution fails, even under the veil of ignorance (202). The three principles of justice—acquisition, transfer, and rectification—are process principles, not end-state principles of distributive justice. Rawls says the original position will generate principles of justice, but these have to be end-state principles, not process ones. Nozick identifies a dilemma in Rawls's argument: if processes are so great, the theory is defective because it cannot produce them; if processes are not so great, then insufficient support has been provided for the principles agreed to in the original position (1974: 208). The only psychological reason why the Rawlsian conception of justice is appealing is that it is based on envy (229). Once again, Nozick's insistence on the dyadic structure of human interaction is clear: I cannot assume that my community should require a living wage or care for the handicapped, because that involves the sin of envy. Nozick accuses defenders of an egalitarian end-state of failing to argue for their position. It just does not matter to say that the wealthiest n percentage of the population holds more than that percentage of the wealth and that the poorest n percentage holds less, etc. There must be a historical account of how that alleged maldistribution came about. Nozick contends that there is a dearth of adequate arguments against maldistribution. One wonders, though, what gets to count as an argument. The great conservative statesman Disraeli argued for greater equality, not out of envy but out of concern that the continued existence of "two nations" would eventually destroy the social order. Nozick does not even admit the possibility of different degrees of maldistribution. Nozick does discuss the rationale for equal access to medical care. He cites the ethicist Bernard Williams, who says that the only proper criterion for the distribution of medical care is medical need. Nozick develops three analogies in response to Williams. He discusses equal rights to barbering, gardening, and the choice of a spouse. If Williams is right, then the only basis for allocating haircuts is "barbering need," the gardener must mow only those lawns that need it the most, and a woman must reject an intelligent and good-looking suitor lest he complain of unfairness. One might even, under Williams's logic, be forced to pay for the plastic surgery of unattractive people in order equalize the marriage market (233–235).

By constructing the nonlibertarian opponent as an envious utopian, Nozick is able to evade questions about *fundamental* needs (to health care, education, food, shelter, meaningful work) that may actually *enhance* the exercise of the rights he values (see Walzer 1983: 88n).

Nozick then preempts the Marxist critique of alienation with an analysis of the concept of self-esteem. (The search for meaningful work is hardly reducible to "self-esteem," but again we have to remember the audience for whom Nozick is writing.) Envy is a vice because it allows self-esteem to be affected by other people's activities or characteristics. Legitimate self-esteem can only derive from a person's own activities or characteristics (Nozick 1974: 240). The Marxian insistence on meaningful work thus is reduced to the idea that being ordered about lowers your self-esteem, and you need more democratic input in order to feel better (246). But suppose a more meaningful job isn't worth that much to a worker. He won't take lower wages to get it (249). So, why don't unions start new businesses, then? Where did the means of production come from? Whose entrepreneurial alertness operated throughout, foregoing current consumption? (254n). And now large portions of the working force have cash reserves in personal property as well as union pension funds. Why don't they use this money to establish worker-controlled factories? Nozick spends considerable time in this section of the book accusing Marxists of exploiting people's ignorance of economics. You have to wonder whether Nozick has studied the nature of capital markets at all, given his argument about pension funds. When the great wave of deindustrialization occurred in the late 1970s, several community groups attempted precisely what Nozick suggested, but they simply were not able to develop the level of access to investment capital that was required (see Lynd 1982).

Next, Nozick relies on a recurring tactic of his, namely, the strained analogy: "Does Thidwick, the Big-Hearted Moose, have to abide by the vote of all the animals living in his antlers that he not go across the lake to an area in which food is more plentiful?" If you lend a group of people your bus for a period of time, and the people come to depend on the bus, surely they do not then acquire a right to say what you do with the bus in the future (269). But note that in both analogies the animals and the bus users have contributed nothing to the value of the antlers or the bus. Even allowing that the owner of a firm should be compensated for her risk-taking, surely workers or employees have contributed something to the welfare of the firm. Nozick returns to the question of caring for the poor. He contends that philanthropy and forms of insurance could provide for the needs of the poor without the state becoming involved. As Jonathan Wolff (1991) points out, however, those born poor or sick will hardly be acceptable risks to an insurance company. Further, those in financial difficulties often make insurance the first nonessential expenditure sacrificed (13). There is nothing in Nozick's theory that would even encourage philanthropy. In fact, people's respect for other's rights should positively encourage everyone to bear the consequences of any lack of entrepreneurial foresight on their part. Otherwise, given the principles of rational choice, some future family might trust to philanthropy for a bailout and thus fail to exercise sufficient caution in expenditures or in procreation.

To sum up Nozick's argument thus far: (1) a minimal state emerges from the competition among private protective associations, thereby improving on anarchism; (2) only a minimal state that provides for common security can be justified morally, given a strong sense of private property rights; and (3) the impulse to ensure equality of outcomes is not only impractical but also morally unattractive as well, because it is based on envy.

NOZICK'S UTOPIA (OR, A RHETORIC FOR LIBERTARIANS)

Part III of Nozick's book, "A Framework for Utopia," recognizes an inherent problem with libertarianism, namely, that it just isn't very inspiring. He asks, would anyone "man the barricades" under the banner of the minimal state? While other libertarians have used the fear of "serfdom" (regimentation, as in the former Soviet Union) or paranoid fantasies about the "new world order" to motivate their audiences, Nozick seems to recognize that neither strategy will work for his baby-boomer audience. This audience has three significant characteristics: (1) its extraordinary economic success was largely built on trade union struggles and highly redistributive government programs (the G.I. Bill, in particular) that had become largely invisible by the time the boomers had reached college age; (2) its experience with government largely involved evading the draft; and (3) its economic anxiety was manifested, as Barbara Ehrenreich (1989) puts it, in a "fear of falling." That is, the highly educated boomers in the professional-managerial class increasingly felt squeezed during the 1970s (especially by the inflation in housing prices), blocked from full ascendancy into the ruling class, and fearful of descending into the working-class world of their grandparents.

An especially appealing notion to this audience was the idea of a meritocracy. After all, the college-educated in this generation had learned to make the grade through standardized tests, and were likely to be resentful of those who had attained their status through some sort of exclusive group membership. The baby boomers were also the most mobile and experimental generation since their immigrant grandparents or great-grandparents had come over from the Old Country.

They often attended college far from home. They frequently married outside their traditional ethnic or cultural background. They knew what it was like to reinvent themselves, striking out fearlessly "on the road." For this audience, the promised utopia of libertarianism seemed like a restatement of the best aspects of their college years: legal dope, free love, no draft, and you get to keep that 25–50 percent of your salary that the welfare–warfare state was eating up in taxes.

Nozick begins the description of *his* utopia as a "realist," contending that it is impossible to realize simultaneously all social and political goods, given the nature of the human condition. Utopia must be "the best for all of us; the best world imaginable, for each of us" (1974: 298). Nozick takes his "market romance" one remarkable step further, not only defending the positive role of the market but also contending that the full realization of the free market *is* utopia. So, you end up with an economist's model of a competitive market, which is great because it gives us "immediate access to a powerful, elaborate, and sophisticated body of theory and analysis" (302).

Since people are different, there will be no way to satisfy all the values of more than one person. If only one set of values can be satisfied, you need a diverse range of communities (309). "No one should attempt to describe a utopia unless he's recently reread, for example, the works of Shakespeare, Tolstoy, Jane Austen, Rabelais, and Dostoevski to remind himself of how different people are" (311). Utopia will consist of utopias; it is a framework for utopias, a metautopia or utopian smorgasbord in which utopian experiments may be tried out; people are free to do their own thing (312). Previous utopian schemes have relied on design devices. Filter devices are better, Nozick contends, because they allow you to try out different communities and then leave if you find a better one (316). In other words, we need a market in utopian communities in order to attain utopia. Only the market provides the necessary feedback that enables products to be improved.

Whenever the virtues of the market are raised, an evolutionary argument cannot be far behind. Evolutionists point out the advantages of genetic heterogeneity whenever conditions change greatly. The same would be true of different utopian communities; by valuing different kinds of skills and abilities, they improve the overall chance of survival. This process, Nozick writes, will be appealing to "existential" and "missionary" utopians, if not to imperialistic ones.

market/evolution —

Now comes Nozick's appeal to the countercultural desire for lifestyle experimentation: "Though the framework is libertarian and laissez-faire, *individual communities within it need not be*, and perhaps no community within it will choose to be so" (320). Nozick finds it strange that young people who want to be "natural" and "go with the flow" are so hostile to market mechanisms (321n). He rejects planning a utopian community inclusive of all in advance, but he sympathizes with voluntary utopian experimentation. The market in utopias and the filtering process of "free and open discussion" will reveal the advantages of both the utopian and antiutopian positions (333).

Interestingly enough, this brief reference to free and open discussion is the only mention of *communication* in Nozick's book. As Robert Paul Wolff (1981) points out:

> Nozick's models, methods, and arguments all treat social relationships as transparent rather than as opaque. He portrays social interactions as marginal to the existence, integrity, and coherent identity of the individuals who participate in them, rather than as central and constitutive. (95)

Despite Nozick's claim to having accommodated both utopianism and commitment to diversity, there is no recognition of an independent sphere of political discussion and debate in Nozick's "political" philosophy. Like the classical economists, he displaces the political with the social. By bracketing out communication and persuasion as a problem, Nozick is able to evade the central difficulty attending free-market rhetoric, namely, how to account for differing levels of access to political forums or, in this case, to the different utopia providers. Surely a working-class mother of five children has less incentive and time to go utopia shopping than a 1974 Harvard graduate who leaves home to "find himself."

CONCLUSION

In summing up his book, Nozick reveals that each of its three parts is an independent justification of the minimal state. The minimal state arises naturally out of the human need for self-protection. The minimal state is *more moral* than a redistributive state. The minimal state ensures cultural diversity. Based on these appeals, there are, then, three implied audiences of the book: the Rothbardian anarchist, the wavering social democrat, and the 1960s utopian. Nozick warms up to his peroration, providing a seemingly universal defense of his utopia:

> The minimal state treats us as inviolate individuals, who may not be used in certain ways by others as means or tools or instruments or resources; it treats us as persons having individual rights with the dignity this constitutes. Treating us with respect by respecting our rights, it allows us, individually or with whom we choose, to choose our life and to realize our ends and our conception of ourselves, insofar as we can, aided by the voluntary cooperation of other individuals possessing the same dignity. How dare any state or group of individuals do more. Or less. (Nozick 1974: 334)

No matter how appealing this final argument may be to a person who values his or her autonomy and self-reliance, it fails to accomplish the task of prescribing a logical transition to this utopia. What kind of political organizations will be needed to implement the utopia? Will those who resist be forced to be free? Will the "withering away of the state" occur through some painless evolutionary process? Not only is there no place for politics in Nozick's actual design for utopia, but also there is no rhetorical strategy to persuade a democratic public to accept it. The typical libertarian distrust of public discussion and debate suggests that utopia either is impossible or paradoxically can develop only under an initially authoritarian regime. My purpose in this chapter has been to identify Nozick's libertarian arguments as strategies. Nozick borrows the prestige of the natural sciences to frame his political arguments. He attempts to close off appeals to history or experience with a convoluted set of thought experiments. He rests a revolutionary rejection of redistributive policies on nothing more than a slippery slope argument. Finally, he smuggles in the 1960's dreams of equality and community as realizable only under hypercapitalism while at the same time identifying the successful as the true victims of the modern welfare state.

Nozick's elaborate fictions of "potential explanation," elegant invocations of the invisible hand, strained analogies, and appeal to a sense of victimhood all end up, not with a realizable utopia, but with the recognition that life under a Thatcher or Reagan regime *is* utopia, the best of "all possible worlds"—at least if you are white, young, male, and wealthy. And how *dare* anyone take away a dime of your money!

CHAPTER FIVE

What Libertarians Want, According to Murray Rothbard and Charles Murray

There is a widespread perception that libertarians are the only political group with "new ideas." The Cato Institute, the Adam Smith Institute, and the 150 or so other free-market think tanks positively bristle with proposals for privatizing every public good, from education to welfare to military defense. Libertarian policies have a special appeal to baby boomers in the professional-managerial class and to people in the high technology industries. Were a libertarian candidate to come along with the leadership and rhetorical skills to reach out to a broader constituency, a fundamental realignment in U.S. politics might well result. The practical problem, however, is that libertarianism is founded on a deep antipathy to democratic discussion and debate.

Every ideology, when considered as rhetorical action, addresses what critic Edwin Black (1970) calls "the second persona," a model of what the rhetor would have his or her real audience become.[1] At a very basic level, who would not want to be the sort of audience addressed by libertarian rhetoric? The job listing or personals ad seeking out a libertarian might run something like this:

Wanted: a person who is intelligent and a self-starter. You are dis-
gusted by the rent-seeking of both big business and big labor. You
would never think of taking a handout. Your private life is your
own—you don't want the government in your bedroom or in your
medicine chest. You work hard, and you play hard. You are free to re-
locate anywhere that values talent. You are not held back by family,
religious, or ethnic ties. You would rather make love than war, but
you have a closet full of guns. You care enough for the poor, the handicapped, and the aged to want to free them from paternalism and
dependency. Above all, you know that history is on your side. Government is obsolete, and the dialectic of history has led to this culminating moment: the triumph of you, the Sovereign Individual.

There is a certain sunniness, a basic optimism, in libertarian rhetoric that makes it rather attractive, especially at a time when the dominant political emotion on the U.S. left seems to be smoldering rage.
But below the surface of the cheerful rhetoric of the folks at the Cato
Institute is another side, tapping into deep class and racial resentments
and coded as "antigovernment" resistance.

In this chapter I examine the rhetorical genre of the libertarian
manifesto, focusing closely on the first and most important one, by
Murray Rothbard, titled *For a New Liberty* (1978), and the most recent
one, by Charles Murray, *What It Means to Be a Libertarian* (1997). As
with Nozick and Rand, I study the arrangement of the arguments in
the text fairly closely, identifying recurring images and strategies.
Rothbard is distinctive in offering a historical argument for libertarianism—Nozick and Rand generally avoid appeals to historical example. Murray's manifesto is in the spirit of "classical liberalism" rather
than Rothbard's "anarcho-capitalism." Rothbard and Murray share the
devaluation of politics characteristic of libertarians, although Murray
proposes a massive expansion of common-law adjudication to solve social problems. Both are distinctively "American" in that they never
draw on the experience of other nations in their indictment of the
U.S. welfare state. Rothbard cannot tell the story of liberty in the
United States without inventing powerful conspiracy theories to account for liberty's decline—theories that lead his version of libertarianism into the darker currents of U.S. nativism and racism. Murray's
defense of racism under the rubric of "freedom of association" is more
subtle, but it meshes well with his arguments about race and intelligence in *The Bell Curve*.

ROTHBARD ON THE NATURE OF INDIVIDUAL LIBERTY

Although libertarianism may be most aptly characterized as the obsessive search for market solutions to all public problems, there are two distinct schools of economics that have significantly influenced the movement.

The Chicago school of economics has produced the mainstream form of libertarianism, which is traditionally closely identified with the Republican Party. Mainstream libertarianism adheres to the methodology of positive economics, acknowledges that government has a role to play in cases of "market failure," and is generally the most flexible and "reasonable" of the libertarian positions. The law-and-economics movement, developed by Richard Posner, is Chicago-school economics applied to legal issues.

A "purer" approach to libertarianism is embodied in Austrian economics, founded by Carl Menger in the 1880s and is most associated with Friedrich Hayek, Ludwig von Mises, and Murray Rothbard. Hayek's book *The Road to Serfdom* (1944) was widely read in conservative circles, although his economic theory was not well received in the United States until he won the Nobel Prize in 1974. Hayek was unable to secure a teaching appointment at the University of Chicago in the economics department and had to settle for a position in the Committee on Political and Social Thought. Hayek's teacher, Ludwig von Mises, was more radical than Hayek (at the University of Chicago Mises stalked out of a meeting of the Mount Pelerin Society, an influential group of free-market economists that included Hayek and Milton Friedman among others, claiming that they were a "bunch of socialists" [Rockwell 1998]). Mises developed a close identification with the National Association of Manufacturers during the 1940s and subsequently taught for many years at New York University (although his chair in economics was actually paid for by the Volcker Fund, a now defunct precursor of today's conservative foundations). Mises's most important book, *Human Action* (1949), is representative of the Austrian school. Mises rejected the use of mathematics in economic analysis, was fairly nonempirical in his methodology, viewed "value" as entirely subjective, and was much more hostile to government intervention than proponents of the Chicago school. "True" Austrians are distinguished from the Chicago school not only by their distaste for mathematics but also by their opposition to the Federal Reserve

System and their support for "free banking" (that is, the absence of a Federal Reserve) and a return to the gold standard.

Murray Rothbard, who wrote his doctoral dissertation on economics under Mises at NYU, became the standard-bearer for Austrian-style libertarianism during the 1960s. Unable to obtain a teaching post at a research university, he taught for many years at Brooklyn Polytechnic Institute, where his opposition to the Vietnam War made him acceptable to the left-leaning faculty. Rothbard was a founder of the Libertarian Party, the Cato Institute, and other important libertarian groups; during the 1980s he left the Libertarian Party, thereafter preferring to align himself with old-line Taft Republicans in the John Randolph Society, the Mises Institute at Auburn University, and the League of the South (of which he was a charter member). Rothbard had supported Strom Thurmond's States' Rights candidacy for president in 1948, so his later attempt to unite libertarianism and paleoconservatism was consistent with his general philosophy (see Francis 1995).

The most concise statement of Rothbard's political views is his 1978 manifesto *For a New Liberty*. The book has three parts: a statement of principles, relying on "natural law" libertarianism and U.S. history; a set of practical proposals for libertarian policy; and, finally, a discussion of "what is to be done"—the political strategy required to bring about a libertarian revolution.

Rothbard begins by affirming the importance of *ideology*. Revolutions are not made by the type of pragmatic accommodation that is characteristic of U.S. politics. To create a new revolution for liberty, we need to go back to the classical liberal ideology that shaped the Revolution and that was, alas, undermined by the ratification of the Federalist Constitution. Classical liberals wanted separation of church and state *and* "separation of the economy from the State" (1978: 3). The earliest liberals were John Locke and the radical libertarian "True Whigs" (3). *Cato's Letters*, by True Whigs John Trenchard and Thomas Gordon, describes human history as a record of irrepressible conflict between power and liberty. In the interests of liberty, power must always be kept small (4). Unfortunately, the True Whigs among the revolutionaries were eventually defeated by conservative and reactionary forces who wanted to retain the mercantilist British system of high taxes, controls, and monopoly privileges conferred by the government (6). Thomas Jefferson himself abandoned the principles of liberty with the imperialist drive toward war with Britain in his second term, his concessions to the Federalists, the "unconstitutional" Louisiana Purchase, high military expenditures, the establishment of a central bank and imposition of protective tariffs, direct federal taxes, and funding of public works (7).

Charles Murray, in his libertarian manifesto, makes a similar appeal to the libertarian writings of the eighteenth century, even choosing his chapter titles as if to reflect pamphlet titles from that time. The remarkable thing about this libertarian appeal to the eighteenth-century experience is how little resemblance the libertarian version of Radical Whig ideology bears to its actual practice.

There are a number of features of Radical Whiggism and civic republicanism that bear no resemblance to the libertarian version.

1. Radical Whigs did not counterpose government and society—that is a later invention of the classical economists. They were distrustful of centralized government power and of the role of wealth in sponsoring imperialist policies; however, their answer to these problems was not to eliminate government but to improve the nature of political representation (see Bailyn 1967 and Wood 1972).

2. Radical Whigs' notion of liberty was inextricably connected with what today would be called "equality of result." They often appealed to a Saxon golden age of liberty and equality that was overthrown by the "Norman Yoke."

3. Based on their heavy reading of Roman history, rhetoric, and politics, Radical Whigs crafted an ideal of "republicanism" in which the "great, manly, and warlike virtues" were celebrated (as John Adams put it) and in which people "were instructed from early infancy to deem themselves the property of the State [and] were ever ready to sacrifice their concerns to her interests" (Adams and Charles Lee, cited in Wood 1972: 53). Cicero's notion of the *republica*, the Commonwealth, in which the people have a communal interest in justice (see the epigraph to this volume), was widely cited. "A Citizen," observed Samuel Adams, "owes everything to the Commonwealth." "Every man in a republic," declared Benjamin Rush, "is public property" (cited in Wood 1972: 61).

4. It was accepted that government and the judiciary had a substantial role to play in fostering economic development, both at the local and national levels. In colonial times courts assessed taxes, ad-

ministered their spending on public works, determined rights-of-way, and issued commercial licenses of all sorts (see Ellis 1971: 5–6). Because these local courts were controlled by juries, there was a strong emphasis on the right to trial by jury as a cornerstone of republican rights (see Rakove 1996: 299). The role of the state in facilitating economic growth was simply taken for granted until the late nineteenth century (see Horwitz 1977). Earlier disagreements on finance, such as the quarrel over instituting a national bank, reflected concerns over concentrations of economic power, not "statism" per se.

Another historical theme emphasized by Rothbard is the role of public education in the destruction of liberty. The attack on schooling was a common theme in 1960s radicalism, including the Summerhill experiment (A. S. Neill's discipline-free private school) and the writings of Paul Goodman and Ivan Illich. By the 1990s this attack on public education had come to enlist an odd coalition of Roman Catholics, fundamentalist homeschoolers, yuppies, and libertarians. Rothbard used a conspiracy theory of public education that could be interpreted either in sixties' radical or fundamentalist terms:

> To insure the dominance of the new statism over public opinion, to insure that the public's consent would be engineered, the governments of the Western world in the late nineteenth and early twentieth centuries moved to seize control over education, over the minds of men: over the universities, and over general education through compulsory school attendance laws and a network of public schools. The public schools were consciously used to inculcate obedience to the State as well as other civic virtues among their young charges. Furthermore, this statizing of education insured that one of the biggest vested interests in expanding statism would be the nation's teachers and professional educationists. (1978: 12)

There is really no difference, in the eyes of Rothbard and other libertarian critics of public education, between the public schools and a totalitarian state, or between public school teachers and Communist Party apparatchiks.

Rothbard's critique of public education rests on a strong concept of individual rights. Although many libertarians argue for a market economy on strictly utilitarian terms, Rothbard reserves some of his harshest language for the British utilitarians and social Darwinists. He condemns them for ending up as apologists for the existing order: "This utilitarian crippling of libertarianism is still with us. Thus, in the early days of economic thought, utilitarianism captured free-market economics with the influence of Bentham and Ricardo, and this influence is today fully as strong as ever." What Rothbard appears to mean here is that the classical economists made the mistake of justifying the market as a means to general happiness. Rothbard is completely uninterested in general happiness. The market is a means unto itself: "Current free-market economics is all too rife with appeals to gradualism; with scorn for ethics, justice, and consistent principle; and with a willingness to abandon free-market principles at the drop of a cost–benefit hat" (16).

Rothbard has been criticized by some traditional conservatives for his "extreme apriorism." William F. Buckley, Jr. (1995), for example, in his obituary for Rothbard, wrote that Rothbard believed in liberty much in the same manner that David Koresh believed in God. When Kruschchev came to the United States in 1959, Rothbard applauded Kruschchev publicly, because, he said, the Soviet leader had killed fewer people than Eisenhower had.

Like his mentor, Ludwig von Mises, Rothbard believed that the understanding of "human action" can be deduced from a few basic principles.[2] "The libertarian creed rests upon one central axiom: that no man or group of men may aggress against the person or property of anyone else. This may be called the 'nonaggression axiom.' 'Aggression' is defined as the initiation of the use or threat of physical violence against the person or property of anyone else. Aggression is therefore synonymous with invasion" (Rothbard 1978: 23). The libertarian insists on applying the general moral law to everyone, with no special exemptions. He considers it one of his main tasks to "spread the demystification and desanctification of the State among its hapless subjects," to show that "all governments subsist by exploitive rule over the public; and that such rule is the reverse of objective necessity" (25).

Unlike Nozick, Rothbard seeks to justify his basic axiom. He examines three potential foundations: emotivism, utilitarianism, and natural law. The problem with emotivism is that it cannot convince anyone else (all values being subjective to the emotivist). Utilitarianism cannot decide if a given act is good or evil, only its consequences. Only natural law provides a sound basis for the nonaggression axiom.

Rothbard considered himself an Aristotelian and a Thomist, although it is unclear that he actually read any of their political writings. He says that we live in a world of many entities, each of which has a distinct nature that can be investigated by man's reason; the species "man" requires the ability "to learn, choose, develop his faculties, and act upon his knowledge and values" (28). So far, the argument is straight Aristotelianism, but instead of taking the step toward including political participation as part of the human *telos* (aim), Rothbard then smuggles in Locke: The natural-rights principles include the right to self-ownership, to "control the body free of coercive interference," and the right to one's own labor, and to whatever property one has created out of the unowned state of nature (28–33).[3]

Rothbard condemns contemporary liberals for separating property rights from other natural rights. The right of a free press, for example, is grounded in the right to own newsprint. The person who falsely shouts fire in a crowded theater should be arrested, not because he overstepped "free speech" rights but because he violated the property rights of the person who owns the theater. By buying a ticket, the person contracted not to disrupt the performance for others (44).

Rothbard then begins his great "Hymn against the State" (using the same simple rhetorical device of anaphora that we saw in Ayn Rand's writing):

> For centuries, the State (or more strictly, individuals acting in their roles as "members of the government") has cloaked its criminal activity in high-sounding rhetoric. For centuries the State has committed mass murder and called it "war," then ennobled the mass slaughter that "war" involves. For centuries the State has enslaved people into its armed battalions and called it "conscription" in the "national service." For centuries the State has robbed people at bayonet point and called it "taxation." In fact, if you wish to know how libertarians regard the State and any of its acts, simply think of the State as a criminal band, and all of the libertarian attitudes will logically fall into place. (46)

There really should be a name for the inability to make moral distinctions. Rothbard, like Nozick, is unable to see any difference between the "Jew tax" that was levied to enter the ghetto in Germany and a tax (for which citizens have voted) to support a local elementary school. Living in the contemporary United States is no different than living in Stalin's Soviet Union. No wonder Rothbard is the favorite economist of the Patriot militias, the Holocaust revisionists, and the Christian Right.[4]

Rothbard is especially critical of the role of intellectuals in promoting the idea of the benevolence of the state, staffing the state bureaucracies, and engaging in social engineering (54–55). Intellectuals also play an important role in condemning "conspiracy theories of history": "For a search for 'conspiracies,' as misguided as the results often are, means a search for motives, and an attribution of individual responsibility for the historical misdeeds of ruling elites" (57). Intellectuals infuse guilt about "materialism" or "greed"; they use pseudoscientific jargon to "weave apologia for State rule which rival the ancient priestcraft in obscurantism":

> For example, a thief who presumed to justify his theft by saying that he was really helping his victims by his spending, thus giving retail trade a needed boost, would be hooted down without delay. But when this same theory is clothed in Keynesian mathematical equations and impressive references to the "multiplier effect," it carries far more conviction with a bamboozled public. (59)

The public is bamboozled, the intellectuals are traitors to liberty, and there is a vast conspiracy against your rights. It is but one short step from Rothbard to Timothy McVeigh.

ROTHBARD'S POLICY PRESCRIPTIONS

Rothbard begins the policy section of his book with a powerful evocation of the U.S. dystopia: high taxes, the urban fiscal crisis, Vietnam and other foreign interventions, crime in the streets, traffic congestion, the military–industrial complex, frequent transportation delays, river pollution, water shortages, air pollution, power shortages and blackouts, poor telephone and postal service, mindless television programs, a corrupt welfare system, inadequate urban housing, union strikes and restrictions, poor educational standards, inflation and stagflation, Watergate (73–78)—*all* caused by government.

Rothbard believes that all of the following are immoral invasions of the right of self-ownership: military conscription, antistrike laws, the income tax, the withholding tax, the power to subpoena(!), and compulsory commitment to mental health institutions (79–93). Forc-

ing a taxpayer to fill out an income tax form violates the Fifth Amendment right against self-incrimination, as well as making one work
without pay (86).

According to Rothbard, there should be no laws of libel and slan-
der. Streets should be privately owned and then easily rented out for
demonstrations, if needed (97). Pornography must be legalized. If pros-
titution is made legal, there will be higher-quality and safer service
(106). Abortion must be legalized: every woman has the right to own-
ership of her own body (108). Laws against gambling are "absurd and
iniquitous" (109). Narcotics must be legalized; otherwise, we will have
to ban cigarettes, tight shoes, improperly fitting false teeth, excessive
exposure to the sun, and excessive intake of dairy products (112). Police corruption occurs most often when entrepreneurs (drug dealers,
bookies, and pimps) attempt to deliver voluntary services to consumers but the government gets in the way (113). Gun laws prevent the
creation of a peaceful, altruistic society: "a society where peaceful citizens are armed is far more likely to be one where Good Samaritans
who voluntarily go to the aid of victims of crime will flourish" (118).

Compulsory education creates a vast prison system, with teachers
and administrators serving as wardens and guards. Child-labor laws
should be abolished so that children can learn to do what they are
most suited for (121). After all, the United States was built by citizens
with little or no formal schooling (121). If we abolish public schools, a
market in education will appear, just as it has in newspapers and maga-
zines and books (128). Suburbia will disappear when zoning restrictions are abolished, thus ending upper-middle-class white privilege
(133). Public higher education forces the poor to subsidize the education of the wealthier (138). Higher education gets skewed to the demands of government and foundations rather than those of the students, since the students don't pay most of the bill (140).

Rothbard goes on to proclaim that welfare must be abolished.
Workhouses would be a better deterrent to poverty (Rothbard 1978:
148). Every organization could set up a welfare system similar to the
Mormons' system (148), in which church members receive support
from the church when unemployed, financed by a 10% "tithe" by all
members. The poor have higher rates of alcoholism, narcotics addiction, venereal disease, and homicide for "cultural," not economic, reasons (152).

Inflation and stagflation can be eliminated only if we adopt the
prescriptions of the Austrian school of economics. The natural state of

the economy is deflation, not inflation (174). The elimination of the Federal Reserve and a return to the gold standard will cushion the shocks of the trade cycle. (Even Milton Friedman admits that laissez-faire policies during the Great Depression would simply have made things worse. Note that Rothbard has no way of accounting for the critical political role played by President Franklin D. Roosevelt in restoring public confidence.)

We must privatize the police, as they would then have a greater incentive to be courteous and avoid brutality (217). Would private police forces be in perpetual conflict? Maybe, but even then there would be no more Dresdens or Hiroshimas (221). Courts should be privatized, too, perhaps financed by fees or a monthly subscription service. The military should be disbanded; if we had a Russian invasion, the worst that could happen would be guerrilla warfare, and we would win (241) in that case. U.S. foreign policy has long been guided by imperialist designs. Keynesian corporate liberalism brought the military–industrial complex to the United States in the first place (280).[5]

Rothbard's libertarianism is so far beyond conventional capitalism that it defies any clear left–right labels. Free markets require some degree of predictability: security of contracts, reduction of transaction costs, a provision of "public goods" such as education or defense or a transportation and energy infrastructure, as even such Chicago school economists as Milton Friedman and Gary Becker recognize. Rothbard provides a more radical assault on the contemporary state and on big business than virtually any contemporary socialist thinker. His policy prescriptions are not so much based on greater efficiency (although he asserts it in all of the examples I just provided) as they are on their greater congruence with his peculiar notion of morality. According to Rothbard, it is more moral to starve a retarded child than to coerce someone into feeding the child. Rothbard's confounded ability to switch back and forth between moral and utilitarian justifications is part of the rhetorical kit of all contemporary libertarians. But would anyone want to live in his utopia?

THE QUESTION OF STRATEGY 1

The last section of Rothbard's book deals with the question of strategy: How can we get from "our current State-ridden and imperfect world to

the great goal of liberty?" (1978: 297). He makes the following sugges-
tions:

1. Develop a movement with a sense of "community and *esprit de corps*."
2. Learn from the Marxists about strategic thinking, since they have been at it longer than any other group. Their concepts of left-wing sectarianism and right-wing opportunism will be particularly useful (299).
3. Make the building of a free society an intellectual adventure, requiring great acts of courage: "Who . . . will go to the barricades for a two percent tax reduction?" (301).
4. Cooperate with any policy that does not work against the long-run purpose, but avoid "contradictions in rhetoric" (307).
5. The primary audiences for the movement will be campus youth, the media ("because the consistency of libertarianism attracts a group of people who are most alert to new social and political trends"), overtaxed middle America, small-business people, big-business people outside the "monopoly establishment" (311–312).
6. Be ready for the crisis situation that will make revolution possible. Writing in 1978, Rothbard contends: "It is Watergate that gives us the single greatest hope for the short-run victory of liberty in the U.S. For Watergate, as politicians have been warning us ever since, destroyed the public's 'faith in government'—and it was high time, too" (318).

Rothbard is not terribly specific about the nature of the crisis that will doom the existing order. He has no theory of unfolding contradictions, as the classical Marxists did. He was instrumental in founding the Libertarian Party and Cato Institute, although he eventually left both, preferring to align himself with what came to be called the "paleoconservatives." This was not an unexpected move. Rothbard had supported Strom Thurmond for president in 1948. He was one of the charter members of the League of the South, which promotes "peaceful" secession from the United States and encourages a return to the "Christian republic" of the Old South.[6] The League of the South and the Mises Institute at Auburn have been instrumental in promoting Christian Right resistance to federal power. Mark Thornton, a close associate of Rothbard's from the Mises Institute, is a top adviser to Governor Fob James of Alabama, who has denied that the Bill of Rights applies to the states and has threatened to call out the Alabama National Guard to protect the right of a local judge to display the Ten Commandments in his courtroom and pray publicly before sessions of his court.

Rothbard's uncompromising libertarianism and his defense of the Old South are not likely to appeal to the genteel yuppie or the computer entrepreneur. The split between Rothbard and the more practical libertarians of the Cato Institute parallels the split between Pat Buchanan and Newt Gingrich over the nature of the Reagan legacy. What I find admirable about Rothbard is his willingness to take the consequences of his ideology "to the end of the line," as Kenneth Burke would say. He illustrates the truth that, once you accept his initial premises about individual rights, you must view all government as immoral. But the slippery slope works just as well in the opposite direction. *Libertarians have no set of principles that might enable them to stop the process of privatization.* Charles Murray attempts to provide a more practical libertarian program, but his work illustrates even more clearly than Rothbard's the sort of social devastation that would ensue after "the Revolution."

CHARLES MURRAY'S MANIFESTO

What It Means to Be a Libertarian (1997) was subsidized by the American Heritage Institute and by the Bradley Foundation, both of which Murray praises in his acknowledgments for their support of "intellectual freedom." Murray had gotten into trouble with the Manhattan Institute for *The Bell Curve* (1994), a rehabilitation of traditional scientific racism that he had coauthored with the late Harvard psychologist Richard Herrnstein. There is no mention of *The Bell Curve* in Murray's manifesto, although reading them jointly provides some useful insights into the hidden assumptions of libertarianism. Libertarianism really is an ideology for Murray's "cognitive elite."

Like Rothbard's book, Murray's manifesto is divided into three parts: principle, policy, and strategy. Unlike Rothbard, Murray explicitly uses the language of economic analysis (public goods, incentives, rent-seeking) to establish his principles. He first criticizes our public culture for having given up on public celebrations of "freedom." "So-cialists," he writes, "made it intellectually fashionable to mock free-dom" (3). Then, like Rothbard, he defines government as possessing a monopoly on the use of physical force, the police power. Force is bad, cooperation is good. People in a free society should not be impeded from engaging in voluntary and informed transactions.

The legitimate reasons for use of the police power of the state are: criminal law; tort law; enforcement of contracts; the provision of "public goods," goods that are nonexclusive, that is, they can be con-sumed by one person without diminishing their availability to others; street lighting; clean air; and public roads. Murray's willingness to ad-mit the existence of public goods, he writes, distinguishes him as a classical liberal from radical libertarians like Rothbard. Unfortunately, "socialists" have vastly expanded what counts as a public good, so we should go back and ask three questions of any program proposed under that heading: Is the good something that cannot be provided by indi-viduals without government help? Am I asking my neighbor to pay for a government service he doesn't want? Am I asking my neighbor to pay for a government service that benefits me, or people whom I favor, more than it benefits him? (Murray 1997: 13). In any case, public goods should be provided at the most local level feasible. Murray here invokes the principle of "subsidiarity," which was much used during the time of the "Contract with America" in 1994. The peculiar thing about the notion of subsidiarity is that it comes out of Roman Catholic political thought, where it was also applied to business, the importance of a family wage, and all the aspects of the "commonwealth" that Catholic thought inherited from Cicero (see Greeley 1976). As with eighteenth-century republicanism, libertarians like to seize doctrines out of historical context and read into them their own preoccupations.

Unlike Rothbard, who seems more interested in morality than happiness, Murray forthrightly frames the justification for libertarian-ism in terms of the "pursuit of happiness." One cannot be happy with-out: freedom and personal responsibility; freedom of association; economic freedom (which encourages equal treatment of everyone re-gardless of race, ethnicity, religion, or social status); property rights; and freedom of personal behavior.

A federal government that respected these values would still re-quire departments of State, Defense, and Justice, although foreign aid would be eliminated. There would still be an Environmental Protection Agency, Yellowstone Park, and Washington Monument. (Murray asserts this. Why couldn't Yellowstone and the Washington Monument be run by private firms?) But he would add $3,000 unrestricted tuition vouchers for every child in the United States attending elementary and secondary school. He would eliminate the regulation of products and services (Food and Drug Administration, Consumer Product Safety Commission), because tort liability would suffice. He would eliminate all labor regulations except laws against force and fraud in employment. He would eliminate safety regulations in the workplace, and employers would be liable for on-the-job injuries. Business and agricultural subsidies would be eliminated. Civil rights regulations would be eliminated. Government would not spend money on general science, technology, or the arts. Government would maintain the interstate highway system. The Postal Service and FCC would be eliminated. Social Security, Medicaid, Medicare, Assistance for Dependent Children, the food stamp program, public housing, SSI (supplemental social security for the disabled and mentally retarded), and unemployment compensation would be eliminated. The federal government would then be two-fifths of its present size. State and local governments would pick up any necessary functions that had been eliminated at the federal level.

Murray discusses all these things at such an abstract level that you hardly realize the two glaring problems with his proposal, even on libertarian terms:

1. How is the transition to state-based welfare systems to occur? Wisconsin, for example, which has pioneered the "welfare-to-work" program touted by many analysts across the political spectrum, has found itself actually expending much more money on its work incentives program in the short term than on actual welfare benefits. It has been unable to implement its new policy without considerable federal assistance ("Crunch Comes for Welfare Reform" 1999). What do folks "dependent" on these programs do until the state or local programs kick in?

2. Murray does not engage the "race-to-the-bottom" argument that is a staple of the federalism debate. Only the national government is in any position to engage in redistributive policies, because when states or local governments raise taxes for health care or other welfare items, they are competing with other states or localities for tax dollars.

Given the easy mobility of plants and capital across state boundaries, a "race to the bottom" ensues.[7] Even the "truly needy" are harmed. Recipients of SSI, which is administered by the states, now receive, on average, 50 percent less money than they did in 1970.[8] Incentives matter, as the free-marketeers keep telling us.

You can read Murray's book without realizing just how chilling its implications are. Libertarians usually are associated with supporters of drug legalization or occasionally gay rights (this, at least, has been my experience with libertarians on college campuses—the drug legalization idea seems to be a primary source of the appeal of libertarianism). What Murray really wants is to restore the Old South, although he is less honest about it than Rothbard was toward the end of his life.

Part II of the book addresses the policy implications of libertarianism in more detail. Murray contends that tort liability could take care of the need for occupational safety and health legislation. He argues that racial integration was going to occur voluntarily anyway—the civil rights movement just speeded up the process (87). Naturally, he provides no proof for this assertion. He contends that poor patients would be able to rely on doctors who would provide service at reduced fees. Perhaps most strangely, he blames poverty itself on government—even though the children of the poor already live in cardboard boxes and the rich live in armed enclaves (13). Given the rate of economic growth we have had in this century, there should not be any poverty by now (126). Eliminating welfare will make the poor more careful about procreation as well.

Insofar as Murray provides any evidence for his sweeping claims about the relationship between government and poverty, he does so entirely with the "trend lines" he also used in *Losing Ground* (1994), the influential assault on "welfare as we know it." He identifies a social problem, notes a point at which government intervenes, and then shows how the social problem has gotten worse. Murray's central strategy is *post hoc ergo propter hoc* ("after this, therefore, because of this") reasoning. He refuses to admit the existence of multiple causes for the problems he examines. He refuses to entertain the possibility that social problems might have worsened had government not been involved. He also is silent on questions of finance capital. Will the Federal Reserve System still operate? Will corporations receive incentives to locate jobs outside the United States? Those are examples of government programs that have had dire consequences for working people.

It is instructive to compare Murray's comments on poverty in his manifesto with the concluding chapter of *The Bell Curve*, "A Place for Everyone." There authors Herrnstein and Murray argue that their "cognitive elites" (those with high IQs) have been able to create political rules that actually disadvantage those who "aren't very smart." Compared to Ayn Rand, Herrnstein and Murray come off as bleeding hearts. They propose to eliminate all business regulations and credentialing (for example, for doctors or for day-care workers). Members of the cognitive elite know how to jump through bureaucratic hoops, but stupid people do not. (The corollary argument seems to be missed, though: with so many stupid people, the flood gates are opened to unlicensed physicians promising miracle cures.) Herrnstein and Murray want to restore marriage as a central value, since that is the only way the lower classes will learn moral responsibility. They want to restore local neighborhoods, where the stupid can find a place to make a contribution to society (I propose Murray's neighborhood). Here again, the superior morality and sense of social "place" of the Old South seem to come through. Murray's great contribution to libertarian rhetoric is to find a set of appeals sufficiently coded that they can appeal simultaneously to white racists, recreational drug users, Silicon Valley entrepreneurs, and—well—the stupid.

THE QUESTION OF STRATEGY 2

Murray, like most libertarians, eschews metaphoric language, but he uses an interesting metaphor in the third section of his manifesto. He contends that "tectonic shifts" in U.S. politics are occurring now (1997: 143). He notes four such shifts:

First, now that government is widely seen as Them rather than Us, large changes become possible.

Second, more and more U.S. citizens are beginning to want to be left alone: small business owners, parents of school-aged kids, people planning for their retirement, social conservatives tired of having gay rights and other non-Christian principles shoved at them.

Third, elites have come to see that they possess privileges denied to others. This has radicalized them. Baby boomers have participated in the "secession of the successful" and are increasingly buying out of the systems of social security and public education. So are the people in the computer and telecommunications revolution. Murray contends that the primary political task of libertarians is "to talk to both generations, the affluent baby boomers and the technologically fluent post-baby boomers, about the connections between losses of different freedoms" (161). Never mind that both the boomers and the technological elites have had their prosperity based on two of the most important federal programs of the century: the GI Bill and the defense spending that led to the Internet.

Finally, as people seek to rediscover and gain control of their everyday lives, they begin to see the importance of family values, community, and "civil society." They see that civic participation can occur independently of politics, and this radicalizes them. Another libertarian writer, Grover Norquist (1996), identifies the natural audience of radical libertarian arguments as the "Leave-Us-Alone Coalition": gun owners, school choice and home schooling groups, the term-limits movement, religious advocacy groups, and small-business owners.

Although Murray proposes to restore democratic control at the local level, he is surprisingly willing to give greater power to the branch of government least responsive to popular pressure—the courts. Social problems formerly dealt with by regulation will be resolved in the courts, usually via the application of tort law (albeit with a substantially reduced set of incentives for plaintiffs). The reason Murray wants the courts involved is the same reason that judges such as Antonin Scalia or Frank Easterbrook do, namely, they represent a convenient way to eliminate the power of democratic majorities in the U.S. system. Even though at present those majorities are broadly against government intervention, hostility to business elites simmers just beneath the surface of public opinion. The only way to protect against further economic legislation, in Murray's utopia, is to take economic questions entirely out of the hands of legislatures. And, once all political questions either become problems solved by local "morality" or become legal questions, the disparity of access to legal help and legal information will ensure that the cognitive elite maintains its control over the stupid. As Mary Ann Glendon (1994) points out, the reason there is so much litigation in the United States as compared with western Europe is that the United States does not provide the kind of social safety net that serves as a disincentive for people to seek large financial rewards in court.

CONCLUSION

Libertarianism is based not only on a fundamental hatred of politics but also on a fundamental hatred of democracy, for democracy provides a potential threat not only to wealth but also to the reign of the cognitive elite. Unlike Rothbard, Murray has shown how a libertarian rhetoric can appeal to multiple constituencies—old-fashioned racists, the digitally literate, business people, militia members, intellectuals. Yet, taken as a whole, libertarian rhetoric remains too "pure" to capture a mass constituency. Large corporations, for example, tend to prefer a strong national government (if only to reduce the transaction costs created by conflicting local regulations). Christian conservatives are adamantly opposed to extending personal liberties, especially over matters of sexuality and reproduction. Advocates of a strong national defense and an international role for the United States are likely to balk at the libertarian assault on the nation-state. Further, no national leader with strong libertarian credentials has emerged. Conventional party politics in the United States requires too much compromise for the devoted libertarian. Even the political figure closest to the libertarians, Ronald Reagan, was only partially successful in mediating the conflicting claims of the market and traditional U.S. values.

PART III

The Struggle over Reagan's Free-Market Legacy

CHAPTER SIX

From Reagan to Buchanan

National Glory and Globalization

Despite the development of powerful discourses and institutional sites for radical critique during the 1980s, there has been surprisingly little analysis from the Left of the rhetoric of Ronald Reagan and Margaret Thatcher.[1] Their very rhetorical skill seemed to confirm the left's general Platonic bias against eloquence. Despite the rapid growth of discursive analysis—at the expense of traditional class analysis—in radical circles since the 1980s, the actual practical effect of political discourse on audiences has remained less significant for cultural studies scholars than, say, the latest thing Madonna is up to.

This chapter examines Ronald Reagan's rhetoric in defense of the great u-turn away from the Keynesian and liberal-democratic revolution. A careful analysis of Reagan's rhetoric, using both the tools of traditional rhetorical analysis as practiced in the U.S. tradition of public address study and the tools of recent literary theory, reveals the ability of a skilled rhetor to transcend both ideological and material contradictions. In fact, the art of rhetoric is itself the art of contradiction management. The material and ideological contradictions of the U.S. political order, however, have become increasingly apparent with the advent of "globalization." In my view, the purpose of rhetorical criticism is to identify the contradictions in an ideology and thus show opponents of that ideology effective ways to target arguments. In a more conventional scholarly sense, rhetorical criticism of ideology develops an account of how ideologies grow and decay in the presence of internal and external problems.

My argument unfolds in this way:

1. Ronald Reagan helped build a larger audience for conservative rhetoric. He used the apocalyptic religious imagery that appealed to the hard-core right and yet effectively made it seem less radical and negative.
2. Reagan's pastoral or priestly rhetorical style and his skillful use of romantic narrative helped to build support for him personally yet failed to gather wide support for his social agenda.
3. Specifically, over time President Reagan became less and less able to hold together the warring factions of the conservative movement: the libertarians, the traditionalists, and the Cold Warriors. This instability in conservatism's fortunes can be seen most clearly in President Reagan's response to the congressional debate in 1988 over the prenotification of plant closings (discussed later in this chapter).
4. The major source of instability in conservatism lies in the irreconcilability of an unfettered free market's pressures toward globalization and the continuing value of patriotism.
5. Globalization has created a resurgence of conspiracy rhetoric on the right, with the Federal Reserve System emerging as the primary alleged villain.
6. Patrick Buchanan's assault on free trade represents a creative attempt to dissociate the values of the free market from globalization, although it has thus far failed to bring the Reagan coalition back together.

REAGAN'S RHETORIC: THE VIEW
FROM PUBLIC ADDRESS STUDIES

In contrast to the near silence about Reagan in radical circles, traditional U.S. public address scholars have produced a considerable body of work about Reagan's speech making, and there has emerged something of a consensus about the nature of his rhetorical artistry. The typical liberal- and left-wing critique of Reagan was that he was simply a "talking head" programmed by unacknowledged corporate–capitalist handlers. This caricature expresses both those groups' disdain for Reagan's public speaking ability and a lack of understanding of his intellectual development. Although, like all public figures today, Reagan retained a large speech-writing staff as governor and as president, he did write his own speeches during his early career and remained very involved in the composition and revision of his major public pronouncements until late into his second term.

The best analysis of Reagan's rhetoric over the course of his public life may be found in Kurt Ritter and David Henry's book, titled *Ronald Reagan: The Great Communicator* (1992). I want to highlight a few of their arguments.

First, Ritter and Henry identify the most salient features of Reagan's rhetoric:

- Frequent un-self-conscious references to God
- An emphasis on heroes
- Appeals to the value of freedom and of progress
- An appropriate presentational manner
- Frequent attempts to link the sacred and the secular

In general, "Reagan's oratorical success owes as much to his capacity to imbue secular political events and issues with the trappings of religious ritual as it does to his undeniably appealing delivery skills" (Ritter and Henry 1992: 5). Ritter and Henry identify three rhetorical-religious forms used by Reagan during his career.

During the first period, when he was a spokesman for General Electric and emerged as a conservative activist, Reagan used a "secular apocalyptic rhetoric" emphasizing the following themes:

- Lamentation: the expression of deep concern about the condition of the United States.
- Warnings of Armageddon: alerting one and all to a final, cosmic struggle between good and evil in which, typically, political figures and movements represent larger spiritual forces.

These apocalyptic themes are part of the biblical heritage of Christianity and (to a lesser extent) the heritage of Judaism. When such stark metaphysical dichotomies appear in public discourse, there is a convention in Western democracies of labeling the discourse as "extremist."

Reagan's first contribution to the practical management of conservative rhetoric came with his unique twist on apocalyptic themes. As with most rhetorical strategies, there was a trade-off in the use of apocalyptic rhetoric; that is, while images of Armageddon might resonate with churchgoers—especially Protestant fundamentalists and evangelicals—they frighten secular audiences or members of religious groups who have rejected apocalyptic theology. As Ritter and Henry note, it was during this period that Reagan crafted his ability to speak to several different audiences simultaneously. His secular apocalyptic rhetoric was different from religious apocalyptic in two ways. First, secular apocalyptic in general (and it was no different for Reagan) treats historical events as contingent on human action, whereas religious apocalyptic sees individuals as overwhelmed by supernatural forces. Second, Reagan was able to shift subtly from "the desperate prospect of a secular Armageddon to the reform motive of restoration rhetoric. He did this without betraying a hint of internal inconsistency or a scintilla of contradiction" (Ritter and Henry 1992: 28).

During the second designated period, from the late 1960s to the late 1970s, Reagan spoke in a new rhetorical-religious form, the secular jeremiad. The jeremiad form, which dates back to the Hebrew prophets and Puritan preaching practices, has three distinctive features:

- The Promise: a covenant with God, promising blessings on the Promised Land—in this case, the United States.
- The Declension: the United States' failure to live up to its obligations as the chosen people.
- The Prophecy: if the United States will repent and reform, the promise can still be fulfilled.

Reagan was known to have admired the speech by John Winthrop on the ship *Arabella*, en route to found the Massachusetts Bay Colony.

We shall find that the God of Israel is among us, when ten of us shall be able to resist a thousand of our enemies [and] when He shall make us a praise and glory that men shall say of succeeding plantations:

"The Lord make it like that of New England"; for we must consider that we shall be as [Matthew 5:14] a city upon a hill. The eyes of all people are upon us; so that if we shall deal falsely with our God in this work we have undertaken and so cause Him to withdraw His present help from us, we shall be made a story and a by-word through the world. (Winthrop 1995: 34)

Winthrop's speech provided the perfect mixture of apocalypse and jeremiad that Reagan was looking for. By the time he was elected president, Reagan was able to shift from a progressive jeremiad to a restorative jeremiad. Unlike the Hebrew prophets or Puritan preachers, he accused the leaders of the republic of "letting the soul of the nation rot" and exempted the people from God's wrath.

In the third, and final, phase of Reagan's rhetorical development, he developed a pastoral or priestly rhetoric in which he:

- Addressed abstract themes
- Relied on value-centered appeals
- Used narratives as the dominant argumentative form
- Populated the narratives with the heroic deeds of legendary figures and model citizens
- Spoke in the calm and confident manner of a clergyman

Reagan's pastoral persona also was enhanced by having his speeches designed with several features uniquely suited to television:

- He knew that television requires speeches that tell a story.
- He crafted a repeated and reassuring story of heroes who carried out the divine plan for the United States.
- He knew that an *oratorical* delivery style comes off badly on television and therefore developed a conversational, even intimate, mode of expression. Kathleen Jamieson (1988) describes this style as the "effeminate" rhetorical style (67–89); it is personal and self-disclosing, with a heavy emphasis on narrative.[2]
- He capitalized on television's capacity to enhance the visual dimension of his orations. He did not just tell a story about heroes, but rather he *showed* the story, sometimes even featuring the heroes in person.

William Lewis, in his classic essay "Telling America's Story" (1987), has provided a useful analysis of the role of narrative in Reagan's rhetoric. Lewis writes, "Reagan's message is a story. Reagan uses storytelling to direct his policies, ground his explanations, and inspire his audiences, and the dominance of narrative helps to account for the variety of reactions to his rhetoric" (295). Reagan uses two types of narrative: the quick anecdote (for example, schoolchildren forbidden from praying in the school cafeteria) and the myth (for example, a story of the United States origins and destiny). Reagan constructs a myth of "America as a chosen nation, grounded in its families and neighborhoods, and driven inevitably forward by its heroic working people toward a world of freedom and economic progress unless blocked by moral or military weakness" (Lewis 1987: 297).

In the Reaganesque myth, history is a struggle for progress against great obstacles and great villains: economic adversity, barbaric enemies, big government. The myth includes great heroes: Washington, Jefferson, Lincoln, Franklin Roosevelt. It also includes great villains: monarchs, the Great Depression, the communists, the "Democrat" Party. The myth's great theme is freedom and economic progress, sanctified by God and validated by the U.S. experience. The audience's role in the story is as "ordinary heroes," while Reagan's role is as the compassionate outsider who got there "just in time."

Lewis goes on to contend that the narrative form of Reagan's rhetoric helps to explain how he attained such high levels of personal support in national polls despite, in many cases, widespread opposition to his administration's policies. Facts alone were insufficient to refute Reagan's point of view; only Mario Cuomo, in his 1984 Democratic convention speech, attempted to meet Reagan head-on, on his chosen ground, with a counternarrative. The few occasions Reagan *did* get into trouble, for example during the Bitburg and Iran–contra controversies, were times when events and his rhetoric were inconsistent with his overall story of the United States as the Promised Land.

It is possible to build on the insights of Ritter, Henry, and Lewis to account for the ideological role of Reagan's rhetoric in defense of the free market. Although his economic advisers included disciples of Ayn Rand and Milton Friedman, Reagan for the most part avoided "free market" talk per se. He talked about the evils of government, the importance of freedom, and the nobility of the ordinary worker. Even the supply-side economics that he favored was a kind of antieconomics that required little technical skill to explain.

To understand Reagan's rhetoric as a narrative resolution of potentially conflicting ideological themes, we need to examine it at the point where it begins to fray at the edges. Isaac Kramnick (1988) has argued that the defenders of the U.S. Constitution skillfully deployed the four dominant "rhetorical idioms" of the U.S. political language: classical republicanism, Lockean liberalism, Protestantism, and national glory. As we saw in the scholarly accounts of Reagan's rhetoric, these four themes remain the central ones for Reagan (although in his version classical republicanism and Lockean liberalism have been synthesized in an artful way). As Daniel Bell (1976) has argued, however, capitalism itself creates a cultural contradiction. In order to survive as an economic system, capitalism requires self-discipline and the deferral of gratification (the so-called Protestant work ethic). Yet, it also requires massive consumption of commodities and the stimulation of desire for them, a process that tends to undermine the Protestant work ethic.

Another, more recent, contradiction has appeared: with the end of the Cold War, conservatives' automatic appeal to national glory as a proper norm for making judgments has eroded. With globalization, it becomes unclear whether national glory can best be maintained through efforts to enter (and dominate) the global economy or rather through a form of economic nationalism that will require increasing government intervention in the free market.

The major purpose of rhetorical practice is, through a sense of timing and taste, to make coherent the seemingly contradictory arguments, symbols, and narrative of a political tradition. Because the time for rhetoric is rather short these days, individual acts of "cut-and-paste" will tend to fall apart eventually under the weight of historical events. At less pressing times in the past, particularly strong rhetoric from individuals or collectivities served as relatively autonomous paradigms of discourse that remained more or less constant resources for political argument. Nowadays, however, rhetorical practice as a means of social integration of the lifeworld is constrained, however, by the overpowering logic of current system integration (in the form of global capitalism; see Habermas 1984 and 1987).

Ronald Reagan's great personal popularity and political success ultimately reflected his ability to paper over the contradictions in

Lockean liberalism, the Protestant ethic, and traditional conservatism, both through the force of his personality and through his use of the rhetorical idiom of national glory. The resulting ethos of the Reagan years is less the embodiment of a cultural tradition (as Aristotle saw it) than a masterful (though temporary) reconciliation or evasion of contradictions in that tradition.[3]

THE MARKET VERSUS NATIONAL GLORY

Now, what happens when the rhetorical idiom of national glory becomes so widespread that it can be turned upon its chief proponent? The rhetorical glue begins to melt, and the seams of the cut-and-paste job begin to show. This is precisely what happened during the 1988 congressional debate over the proper notice on plant closings. President Reagan, so fond of using historical narrative when discussing foreign policy or education, preferred to resort to an economic argument about global competitiveness when speaking about labor.

Until recently, the United States was the only Western industrialized nation without a law requiring some sort of advance notice to workers in the event of a plant closing. Senator Walter Mondale and Representative William Ford had originally introduced suggested remedies as early as 1973, but by 1988 legislation had still not been enacted. In fact, the bill being considered had lost former provisions requiring consultations between management and workers, compensation for communities hit by shutdowns, and mandatory short-term continuation of health coverage for displaced workers. The proposed legislation had been whittled down to simply a requirement that firms with more than 100 employees give them and the communities involved sixty days' notice in the event of a closing (or else pay workers for each day of notice missed). There were exemptions in cases of strikes or particularly precarious financial circumstances (see Wehr 1988).

Predictably, the Reagan administration came out against the legislation and on May 24, 1988, vetoed the trade bill to which it was attached. Also predictably, the U.S. Chamber of Commerce and the National Association of Manufacturers opposed it. Less predictably, James J. Kilpatrick, *The Wall Street Journal*, and Paul Weyrich's Institute for Cultural Conservatism (Weyrich was a founder of the Moral Majority) came out for it. Many Republican senators and representatives, as well as the Bush presidential campaign, urged President Reagan not to fight the bill, since public opinion polls indicated high public support (80–86 percent) for the legislation (including 70 percent support among Republican men). Articles in the conservative *American Spectator* ("Plant-Closing Bill" 1988a) and *National Review* ("An Opening Through Closing" 1988) supported the bill as well, although William F. Buckley, Jr. (1988a and 1988b) opposed it.[4]

After Reagan's veto, congressional supporters reintroduced the bill separately. The Senate approved the bill on July 6, 1988, by 72–23. The House approved it by 286–138 on July 13. On August 2, President Reagan sent a message to Congress in which he explained his decision to let the bill become law without his signature.

Reagan reminded his audience that his chief priority as president had been "to reduce the intrusion of the Federal government into the lives of all Americans." He first reviewed the economic accomplishments of his administration: "17 million new jobs—mostly high quality and full time," with the unemployment rate the lowest in fourteen years, and "more people . . . at work in America than ever before." Despite this record of success, Congress took "a step in the wrong direction by passing the plant closing legislation." The standard for judging such legislation is "flexibility": "If we are to be competitive, America must be able to adapt to changing conditions here and abroad. We cannot stand still. We must be flexible enough to meet the challenges of the future." He then characteristically appealed to the stories of ordinary workers and businesspeople in letters warning him against the legislation.

Arguing from analogy, he warned against going down the same slippery slope as the Western European countries:

> We should not go down the road of European labor policy—a policy that has resulted in no net job growth in the last decade. The European experience has proven that notification mandated by law does not create or save one job. Nor does it assist those who find themselves without work—it does just the opposite. Plant closing restrictions have resulted in fewer plant openings.

Finally, he explained the "real reason" why the legislation had been pushed through—namely, congressional Democrats' desire to score "political points with organized labor." Those in Congress who supported him were able to see beyond the "parochial interest" and vote for the "national interest." Yet, the national interest *also* dictated that the congressional majority (that is, the Democrats) be forced to stop playing politics; so, he said he would allow the bill to become law without his signature in order to put an end to Congress's "political shenanigans" (Reagan 1988: 2226).

The speech is interesting not so much for its effect on Congress or public opinion as for the way in which it reveals the tensions of conservative rhetoric under conditions of stress. All of Reagan's arguments unite his audiences across vast space, as part of a global economy with "competitors" rather than enemies. The only actual principle invoked in the speech is the rejection of government intrusiveness. This time it is not surrounded by images of national glory or the will of God. In other words, Reagan's rhetoric has been reduced to a pure rhetoric of the market.

One could argue a left-wing version of Hirschman's perversity thesis against Reagan. If Reagan's rhetoric worked because he was able to link the idioms of Lockean liberalism with those of national glory and Protestantism, it is no accident that Reagan's legacy should be most vulnerable where he was most effective in the short term. Reagan's own ethos helped gloss over contradictions, but with the recession of the late 1980s and increased racial tension, the antirhetorical presidency of George Bush was unable to keep Reaganism going. The only things that seemed to raise Bush to Reaganesque eloquence were the Gulf War, a capital-gains tax cut, and the free-trade agreement with Mexico. The rhetoric of the Gulf War revealed a deep-seated hunger in the United States, not so much for domination over others as for a renewal of national glory and a sense of community at home (see Berman 1991). That this quest for community was so powerful and yet so fleeting was perhaps at the root of Bush's political failure. He was never able to galvanize public opinion advantageously to support his domestic ends.

By the late 1990s the essential contradictions in U.S. free-market rhetoric had become far more apparent—such matters as:

1. The difficulty of criticizing the government while *being* the government.
2. The difficulty of reconciling popular democracy not only with corporate power but with an increasingly visible Federal Re-

serve chairman whose very words seem to have a magical hold on Wall Street and on financial markets throughout the world.

3. The difficulty of reconciling traditional family and neighborhood values with market values.
4. The difficulty of reconciling nationalism and patriotism with the increasing mobility of industry and capital across national borders.

It was easier to do all these things when the Soviet Union was the dialectical term defining the U.S. system by its opposite, and when the sheer rhetorical force of Reagan's ethos unified the libertarian, traditionalist, and neoconservative factions of the conservative coalition. But with the fall of communism and the emergence of anxiety over economic globalization, the conservative coalition split up. Both Newt Gingrich and Patrick Buchanan, for example, have been trying to inherit the Reagan mantle, Buchanan by invoking Reagan as more of a protectionist than he really was and Gingrich by trying to hold onto the social conservatives who feel betrayed by the Republican Party. Gingrich has left, in the wake of his quick exit, a Republican Party in utter disarray. Buchanan, perhaps because of continued strong economic growth, has thus far failed to attract a significantly broader audience than in 1992.

THE FREE MARKET VERSUS FREE TRADE

If globalization is the ultimate goal of capitalism, then capitalism is, finally, fatal to the conservative quest for order. The fusionism of Ronald Reagan and William F. Buckley, Jr., may have kept the unruly factions of the U.S. right together, but the disappearance of communism has unleashed long repressed political energies in the United States just as much as in Eastern Europe. The mainstream press treats Republican Party infighting as primarily a matter of abortion rights. Abortion rights, however, are a synecdoche for something much larger, namely, the triumph of an international elite seeking world domination.

Concern about an international elite was a major factor in the rise of Ronald Reagan. Phyllis Schlafly's *The Gravediggers* and *A Choice, Not an Echo* were widely distributed during the Goldwater campaign of

1964. Reagan was able to avoid using the more embarrassing conspiracy theories of the far right in his public rhetoric, but it was the mobilization of the right against the "elite" during the Panama Canal Treaty debate of 1976 that laid the foundation for both the Moral Majority and the Reagan campaign in 1980 (see Hogan 1986). Now that Reagan has departed from public life, the stranger features of far-right rhetoric have resurfaced, and they tap into the problem of globalization that Reagan had been unable to deal with toward the end of his presidency. Perhaps the strangest of all U.S. right-wing obsessions has been the "Federal Reserve Conspiracy."

THE FEDERAL RESERVE CONSPIRACY NARRATIVE

Despite the coverage of the Waco, Ruby Ridge, and Oklahoma City incidents, and occasional jokes about the UN's black helicopters on the popular television series *King of the Hill*, the mainstream press has been surprisingly silent about the revival of the Federal Reserve conspiracy thesis.

Right-wing conspiracy theory is a kind of postmodernism for the masses. Fredric Jameson (1991) has written, "It is safest to grasp the concept of the postmodern as an attempt to think the present historically in an age that has forgotten how to think historically in the first place" (ix). Whereas Jameson analyzes architecture, cyberpunk, and other forms of "art" to show how multinational capitalism has generated new kinds of superstructures, my purpose here is to show how the dynamic of globalization is explained in the narratives of the "new world order" and economic nationalism. In the absence of a credible counternarrative from the left, the combination of globalization with economic crisis has led to a revival of some fascistic, antisemitic narratives thought to have been vanquished with the close of World War II.

The following four narratives about globalization display a similar narrative structure and use similar symbols, although they use different characterizations for the main actors. The core narrative is the effort by an international elite to dominate the world. The most extreme version labels this international elite as a cabal of Jews; Pat Robertson's sanitized version uses the same antisemitic sources but prefers to link the cabal to the Illuminati and, ultimately, to Satan himself;

G. Edward Griffin eschews antisemitism entirely in his John Birch Society version of the conspiracy; finally, Patrick Buchanan uses the same arguments and appeals to similar audiences, but without the apparatus of conspiracy theory. It might seem to some that the conspiracy theories investigated here are both too far afield from the theme of the Reagan legacy and far too "fringe" to merit scholarly attention. My response is twofold. First, as I argued earlier, Reagan built his coalition on the skillful manipulation of apocalyptic religious themes, which have recently returned to public attention with the arrival of the new millennium. Second, given the continued growth of evangelical and fundamentalist Protestantism, efforts to explain political events in biblical terms are increasing. Anyone who lives and works in the Bible Belt knows that conspiracy narratives about globalization have gone mainstream, and the more extreme promoters of these narratives are just waiting to reap the whirlwind of the next economic downturn.

THE ELDERS OF ZION NARRATIVE

In its most unalloyed form the "globalization narrative" treats the Jewish people as the central characters. There are minor variants. Many writers make an effort to demonstrate that the Jews involved are not "real" Jews but descendants of Eastern European converts, the Khazars. Some, notably the poet Ezra Pound, draw a distinction between the "big Jews," such as the Rothschilds and the Warburgs, and ordinary Jews. Andrew Macdonald, the author of the *Turner Diaries* (1980), links African Americans and Jews together as "mud people." Despite differing emphases on economics, religion, and race, the pure globalization narrative posits that a group of Jewish leaders, the Elders of Zion, have conspired to do a variety of evil things, among them the following.

1. They have conspired to create money out of nothing, using the alchemy of fractional reserve banking (which allows banks to lend out money at interest without having 100% reserves of gold or silver to back up the money). The Bank of England was the first major international bank to use fractional reserve banking, and this fact has led to some interesting conspiracy theories centered on the Queen of England (most notably, theories expressed by Lyndon LaRouche).

2. Such a use of funds is quite literally an "unholy" procedure.

Christianity had always banned usury, the lending out of money at interest, period (not just exorbitant interest rates, as the term has come to be defined today). Enter the Jewish financiers who, banned from regular professions, became associated with banking early on.

3. Two prominent Jewish European investment banking families, the Rothschilds and the Warburgs, made a fortune through controlling central banks, especially by stirring up wars that would require national governments to go further into debt. (Much of the imagery surrounding the federal budget deficit in the United States seems to tap into some folk memory of the militaristic role of the deficit.)

4. Under the direct guidance of Rothschild and Warburg, U.S. banking interests (notably Jacob Schiff of Kuhn, Loeb and J. P. Morgan, Rothschild's U.S. stooge) were able to convince Congress to create the Federal Reserve System in 1913.

5. The Jewish bankers proceeded to finance the Bolshevik Revolution, and they supported Western political movements ostensibly opposed to communism: the Fabian socialists in England, the New Deal (Roosevelt's true name is "Rosenfeld"), the United Nations, and the Eisenhower wing of the Republican Party.

6. The bankers have conspired to drive up prices (inflation is the "hidden tax" paid to the Federal Reserve), drive out small farmers, ranchers, and businesspeople, and install a puppet regime in Washington, otherwise known as ZOG, "Zionist Occupied Government."

7. United Nations forces (the army of the one-world conspiracy) are already present in the United States, as evidenced by the sightings of sinister "black helicopters" frequently mentioned in Patriot literature and other paramilitary tracts. The actions of the Bureau of Alcohol, Tobacco, and Firearms (known as "BATFAG" in Patriot circles) at Ruby Ridge, Waco, and—some insist—the Oklahoma City Federal Building bombing are but the opening shots in the battle for the republic.

A representative and influential version of the antisemitic globalization narrative is Eustace Mullins's *The Federal Reserve Conspiracy*, first published in 1952 and still available today (even from Amazon Books). According to analyst Chip Berlet of Political Research Associates, Mullins is "the most vicious anti-Semite on the face of the planet." Readers of Ezra Pound are familiar with Mullins's biography of the poet and his efforts to free Pound from St. Elizabeth's Hospital in

Washington, DC. In his 1952 book, Mullins claimed that the Federal Reserve Act of 1913 put the nation's banking reserves in the hands of the "Jewish International Bankers." In a 1955 article titled "Jews Mass Poison American Children," posted on his website, Mullins claimed that the polio vaccine, invented by Jonas Salk, was a poison because it contains live polio germs. Mullins also has claimed that the greeting "have a nice day" is a code for Jews to begin killing Christians.[5] Apart from his literary connections, Mullins might appear to be yet another far-right conspiracy theorist, but it happens also that his version of the globalization narrative is the foundation of Pat Robertson's *The New World Order*.

THE NEW WORLD ORDER AND CHRISTIAN ECONOMICS

The second and by far most influential version of the globalization narrative is Pat Robertson's. His book *The New World Order*, a surprise *New York Times* best-seller, has sold millions of copies worldwide since 1991. I would hazard a guess that more people have read Robertson's book than the writings of Foucault, Derrida, and Baudrillard put together.

The New World Order begins, like all epics, *in medias res* ("in the middle of things"). Robertson tells us in the foreword that he was watching television coverage of the failed 1991 coup against Gorbachev and heard CNN reporter Mary Tillotson say that President Bush's "new world order is back on track, now stronger than ever" (Robertson 1991: xiii). The coup, and its failure, were one more part of a KGB plan "to lull the West with false 'liberalization,'" much as Lenin did with his 1921 New Economic Policy (xiv). The evidence? The coup leaders were part of a group that had engineered Gorbachev's rise to power, they failed to cut off communications to the West or to shut down the press, and they made no arrests: "In short, this 'coup' was programmed from the beginning to fail. So, if that is the case, why did it take place at all?" (xv). It was to persuade a suspicious West that "the hard-line reactionary communist elements of the 'military–industrial complex' have been banished from the land forever." With this sense of false security, the Western democracies can reduce their military arsenals and pump billions of dollars into the "Soviet economy to 'keep democracy alive'" (xv). In short, the events of 1989 were a total fraud.

But Robertson is not simply spinning a standard anticommunist tale—his story is much more complex. No summary can do justice to Robertson's narrative skill, especially his mastery of the rhetorical question as a device for instilling arguments in the reader's mind:

> Is George Bush merely an idealist or are there plans now under way to merge the interests of the United States and the Soviet Union in the United Nations—to substitute "world order" power for "balance of power," and install a socialist "world order" in place of a free market system? (58)

Is George Bush—scion of an old Connecticut family, a "Yalie, preppie, and a sissy" (as Ronald Reagan memorably called him in 1980), member of Skull and Bones, Texas oilman, head of the CIA—at best an idealist stooge and at worst a one-world socialist? If you believe that (as G. K. Chesterton said in another context), you will believe anything, and that is precisely what Robertson wants his readers to do.[6]

Robertson watchers should not have been surprised by *The New World Order*'s take on economics, since a current of heterodox free-market economics had run through Robertson's broadcasts and books throughout the 1980s. Prominent Christian economists include Gary North and Walter Nash. They consider themselves disciples of Ludwig von Mises, and the Mises Institute at Auburn University proudly publicizes its placement of recent Ph.D.s at evangelical and fundamentalist colleges. There is also a strain of antisemitic Federal Reserve conspiracy theory in right-wing Catholic circles. Christian economists are opposed to usury, the Federal Reserve, and the welfare state.

President Bush's unfortunate use of the phrase "new world order" in a key Gulf War speech in January 1991 marked the culmination of Robertson's suspicions:

> A single thread runs from the White House to the State Department to the Council on Foreign Relations to the Trilateral Commission to secret societies to extreme New Agers. There must be a new world order. It must eliminate national sovereignty. There must be world government, a world police force, world courts, world banking and currency, and a world elite in charge of it all. [6]

Robertson goes on to contend that there is an "Invisible Cord" that links:

- Cecil Rhodes, the English millionaire
- The Federal Reserve Board
- Colonel Edwin House, a (purportedly) sinister adviser to President Wilson
- The British Round Table (discussed later)
- The Morgan Bank (today known as J.P. Morgan and Co., Inc.)
- The Rockefellers, Chase Manhattan Bank, and the Council on Foreign Relations
- The Carnegie, Rockefeller, and Ford foundations (a Rockefeller Foundation treatise on abortion being "the only philosophical support" for Justice Harry Blackmun's (majority opinion in *Roe v. Wade* [190]).
- Henry Kissinger
- The Trilateral Commission
- Jimmy Carter
- George Bush

Robertson says that not all of these people were necessarily conscious of being part of a conspiracy. They may simply have been mouthing the phrases of "a tightly knit cabal whose goal is nothing less than a new order for the human race under the domination of Lucifer and his followers" (1991: 37). He goes on to ask such questions as: "Is it possible that the Gulf War was, in fact, a setup? What else explains the behavior of the Bush Administration prior to the Iraqi invasion of Kuwait?" (9–14). And why has the political left mounted a campaign to bring chaos to South Africa, the only healthy economy on the continent?

Robertson also draws our attention to the Great Seal of the United States, adopted by Congress in 1782. The designer of the seal, Charles Thompson, was a Mason who had served as secretary to the Continental Congress. The Great Seal's reverse depicts an unfinished pyramid, above which is set a shining eye. Below the pyramid is the Latin phrase *Novus Ordo Seclorum*, meaning "a new order of the ages," or, as Robertson puts it, in ominous italics: *a new world order*.[7] Thus, the Great Seal encodes, for those "in the know," this message: the unfinished pyramid represents the unfinished work of building a one-world government (the all-seeing eye being Osiris, the Egyptian deity featured in the secret ceremonies of the Masonic Order).

It thus becomes all the more significant that the Great Seal is featured prominently on dollar bills (the Federal Reserve System having been the instrument of the cabal since 1913). Paul Warburg, the *German* banker (Robertson is careful not to utter the words "Jewish Banker"), the Morgans, and the Rockefellers "custom designed" the Federal Reserve System and income tax to "force the American citizens to pay for the loans these bankers would make through the Federal Reserve Board to the treasury" (Robertson 1991: 65). Under the Rothschilds' influence, nearly a century earlier an attempt had been made to saddle the United States with a central bank, but this attempt had been foiled by President Andrew Jackson (123).

The Masons provide an early link to the real power behind the conspiracy: the Illuminati, formed on May 1 (still an important day for the left), 1776, by Adam Weishaupt, whose aims (according to Robertson) were to "establish a new world order based on the overthrow of civil governments, the church, and private property, and the elevation to world leadership of a group of hand-picked 'adepts' or 'illumined' ones" (Robertson 1991: 67). Weishaupt took over the Continental Order of Freemasons. In the only mention of Jews in the book, Robertson notes that Jews were admitted to the Masons in Frankfurt, Germany, in 1782. His Illuminati were instrumental in starting the French Revolution and, later, the international communist movement. Even today, Masons who reach the Thirty-Second Degree, Robertson writes, are told "that Hiram, the builder of Solomon's temple, was killed by three assassins. The candidate therefore must strike back at those assassins, which are, courtesy of the Illuminati, the government, organized religion, and private property" (185).

An important link between today's Council on Foreign Relations and Trilateral Commission and the overarching conspiracy is through Cecil Rhodes, who (with the help of the Rothschilds) founded the DeBeers Consolidated Mines and Consolidated Gold Fields. Rhodes, often castigated by the left as the archetypal British imperialist, was really a follower of John Ruskin, who persuaded Rhodes to create a *Republic*-style society for promoting rule by philosopher-kings, which became known as the British Round Table. Rhodes, of course, also funded the Rhodes Scholarships (thereby providing a direct link to President Clinton; I am not sure if Robertson has pursued this link further, although Clinton's 1992 praising of Carroll Quigley, an enigmatic Georgetown professor whose areas of expertise include the formation of international elites, probably provides sufficient grist for Robertson and other conservative mills (see Quigley [1966, 1981]).

Harvard, Yale, the University of Chicago, the mass media—including *The New York Times, Washington Post,* and the "Rothschild-owned" *Economist* magazine—Shirley MacLaine, John Dewey, Fritjof Capra, John Lennon, the Brussels supercomputer responsible for handling worldwide bank clearings (nicknamed "the Beast" [216]), and Margaret Sanger all are connected in a veritable witches' cauldron conspiracy.

But, at root, Robertson expresses an antielitist, populist thesis that could have been written by Christopher Lasch:

> [H]ow can a native-born American, educated at Groton, Harvard, and Oxford, who then goes to work on Wall Street, understand what goes on in the hearts of people in Iowa, Nebraska, Texas, or Florida? The Atlanticists on Wall Street may be willing to sell out America, but Main Street wants no part of their plan. It is these people who must hear what is being planned for their America. Then they must act to stop it. (259)

Robertson's book evoked something of a controversy, though one confined for the most part to those elite publications that were alleged to be part of the conspiracy. Michael Lind, erstwhile protégé of William F. Buckley, Jr., blew the whistle on Robertson in *The New Republic* in 1992, but his charges were ignored by the conservative establishment (including Irving Kristol, Lind's employer at the neoconservative policy journal *The National Interest,* and Buckley, who had nominated Lind for membership in the Council on Foreign Relations!). Lind's longer exposé, "Pat Robertson's Great Conspiracy Theory," on the cover of the February 2, 1995, issue of the *New York Review of Books,* received more attention. Lind pointed out that Robertson lifts passages of *The New World Order* (1991) almost word for word from the notoriously antisemitic writers Nesta H. Webster and Eustace Mullins, while carefully eliminating any references to Jews. Robertson later blamed the use of the Mullins and Webster materials on a research assistant's carelessness.

National Review accused Lind of being a tool of the liberal establishment, called out to "do a hit on Pat Robertson" in retaliation for the 1994 successes of the Christian Coalition in bringing a Republican majority to Congress. Midge Decter, who herself had "done a hit" on paleoconservatives M. E. Bradford (whose nomination as head of the National Endowment for the Humanities was derailed by controversy over his essays criticizing Abraham Lincoln) and Russell Kirk during the 1980s, along with her husband, Norman Podhoretz, absolved Robertson of antisemitism, citing his staunch Zionism. The neoconservatives have thus far been willing to tolerate Robertson's peculiar conspiracy theories; but, as Lind points out, Robertson's conspiracy theory is at times indistinguishable from that of Lyndon La Rouche. What would happen, he wonders, if it were discovered that Lyndon La Rouche's group controlled the Democratic Party in 18 states and was influential in 13 more, as Robertson's Christian Coalition is? Lind has demonstrated that the Christian Coalition promotes beliefs just as bizarre as Lyndon La Rouche's, but mainstream Republicans continue to look the other way, knowing how dependent they are on the organization's ability to mobilize voters at the local level.

Ralph Reed, the director of the Christian Coalition and generally perceived to be more moderate than Robertson, went to Robertson's defense before the Anti-Defamation League in April 1995. In a widely circulated speech, and later in his book *Active Faith*, Reed proclaimed Robertson's great love for Israel, describing firsthand Robertson's visible emotional upset when touring Yad Vashem, the Israeli Holocaust Memorial (Reed 1996: 208–209).

THE CREATURE FROM JEKYLL ISLAND

A slightly more responsible version of the globalization narrative appears in the self-published book *The Creature from Jekyll Island*, by G. Edward Griffin (1995), a longtime John Birch Society activist. ("The Creature from Jekyll Island" refers to the Federal Reserve System itself; "Jekyll Island" is a resort in Georgia where J. P. Morgan, Paul Warburg, and other bankers "secretly" met to draft the 1913 legislation establishing the central bank.) This book, now in its sixth printing, is widely distributed in John Birch Society outlets and by some right-wing Catholic groups. Griffin tells much the same story as Pat Robertson, although he eliminates any references to Jews, other than noting that Morgan was a useful cover for the Rothschilds because of pervasive antisemitism in the United States. The John Birch Society has had a history of avoiding antisemitism, preferring to concentrate on economic issues related to communist subversion. Griffin makes no mention of the Illuminati, the Masons, or other groups; however, like Robertson (although Robertson is not mentioned in Griffin's book), he does trace the Federal Reserve System back to the Ruskinian–Platonic fantasies of Cecil Rhodes. He also relies heavily on the work of Carroll Quigley. There is actually very little overtly outrageous conspiracy mongering in the book until page 123, when Griffin contends that the fall of communism itself was a charade.

Griffin relies heavily on Murray Rothbard's history of the United States, and on the general Austrian case for free banking (see Rothbard 1994). He provides some free investment advice along the way, and, by comparison with Eustace Mullins and Pat Robertson, comes off as eminently reasonable. Most interesting is that Griffin's book received the following political endorsements: from Ron Paul, the libertarian-turned-Republican congressman from Texas; and Mark Thornton, professor of economics at Auburn University, prominent disciple of Mises, and economic adviser to Governor Fob James of Alabama.

PAT BUCHANAN

A quick quiz: Who wrote the following?

> America is no longer one nation indivisible. We are now the 'two nations' predicted by the Kerner Commission thirty years ago. Only the dividing line is no longer just race; it is class.
>
> On one side is the new class, Third Wave America—the bankers, lawyers, diplomats, investors, lobbyists, academics, journalists, executives, professionals, high-tech entrepreneurs—prospering beyond their dreams. . . .
>
> On the other side of the national divide is Second Wave America, the forgotten Americans left behind. White-collar and blue-collar, they work for someone else, many with hands, tools, and machines in factories soon to be hoisted onto the chopping block of some corporate downsizer in some distant city or foreign country.

Is it: (a) John Sweeney, (b) Paul Wellstone, or (c) Pat Buchanan? The answer is (c) Pat Buchanan (1998: 7).

Pat Buchanan was the first U.S. politician to argue the problem of job losses. His 1998 book *The Great Betrayal* is a remarkably well written historical narrative about the U.S. economy and the threat of globalism to national sovereignty.[8] In the first part of the book, "A Tale of Two Nations," he crafts a powerful indictment of the impact of free trade on the U.S. economy. He describes his own personal epiphany (and I genuinely believe it is a sincere account) when he visited the James River paper mill in New Hampshire in 1991, while he was campaigning for President. On that very day, news of more layoffs had reached the workers, and he stood waiting to shake workers' hands as they stood in line to get their Christmas turkeys. Buchanan walked over to one "hard-looking worker about my own age who was staring at the plant floor. I grabbed his hand and told him who I was; he looked up, stared me in the eye, and said in an anguished voice, 'Save our jobs!' It went right through me." The next day Buchanan learned that the U.S. Export-Import Bank, a government agency, was financing a new paper mill—in Mexico. "*What are we doing to our own people? I asked myself*" (Buchanan 1998: 19).

Buchanan then reviews the history of U.S. trade policy from Bretton Woods down to NAFTA and GATT, concluding that a new "transnational elite" (including the Trilateral Commission and "Companies without a Country") has taken over the U.S. economy. Buchanan makes this argument without engaging in conspiracy theory.

The middle section of the book is a masterful historical narrative of trade and protectionism until the New Deal. Buchanan contends that George Washington, James Madison, and Alexander Hamilton all abhorred free trade and were instrumental in building a tariff wall that created economic independence for the United States. He calls Abraham Lincoln "America's Great Protectionist." He contends that until recently Republicans were economic nationalists and that the period during which Republican high tariffs prevailed (1865–1913) and the "roaring twenties" (when conservative Republican administrations manned the helm of state) were the times of greatest U.S. economic growth. He reverses his earlier belief that the Smoot–Hawley tariff was a cause of the Great Depression. And he amplifies his assertion that "free-trade policy is the legacy not of conservatives but of one-worlders and liberals like Woodrow Wilson" (Buchanan 1998: 114). He has a number of bad things to say about Adam Smith and David Hume and manages to turn the free traders into apostles of "atheism": "Born of rebellion against church and crown, free-trade ideology is a first cousin to Marxism, i.e., a secularist faith embraced by intellectuals in rejection of the world they lived in, the world of empires and nation-states" (175).

The last part of *The Great Betrayal* provides a blueprint for a "new nationalism" in which Buchanan attempts to marry "the patriotism of Theodore Roosevelt to the humane vision of Wilhelm Roepke," a disciple of Ludwig von Mises (but rather different from Rothbard!), who contended:

> The market is not everything. It must find its place in a higher order of things which is not ruled by supply and demand, free prices, and competition. It must be firmly contained within an all-embracing order of society in which the imperfections and harshness of economic freedom are corrected by law and in which man is not denied conditions of life appropriate to his nature. (Roepke 1960: 91; cited in Buchanan 1998: 288)

Buchanan proposes goals of full employment, high levels of worker compensation (refusing to put "U.S. free labor . . . into Darwinian competition with conscript labor"), high tariffs, a simpler and fairer tax code, and greater controls on the movement of capital across national boundaries (301). Buchanan goes to great lengths to show that Ronald Reagan would likely approve of these policies, given his strong emphasis on nationalism (1998: 258–259; 38–43). More accurately, Buchanan is seizing one part of Reagan's rhetorical idiom, as Reaganism itself comes increasingly under pressure at the hands of history.

CONCLUSION

The globalization narrative, almost from its inception, has been an effort to cope rhetorically with the contradictions of capitalism, most eloquently stated by Marx in 1848:

> Constant revolutionizing of production, uninterrupted disturbance of all social conditions, everlasting uncertainty and agitation, distinguish the bourgeois epoch from all earlier ones. All fixed, fast-frozen relations, with their train of ancient and venerable prejudices and opinions, are swept away, all new-formed ones become antiquated before they can ossify. All that is solid melts into air, all that is holy is profaned, and man is at last compelled to face, with

sober senses, his real conditions of life, and his relations with his
kind. (1848/1988: 58).

Marx was dead-on right in the first half of that last sentence but dread-
fully wrong in the second half. We are no closer to facing, with sober
senses, our real conditions of life and our relations with our kind than
we were in 1848.

What Marx (and Engels) did not understand, besides the possibility of Keynesian solutions to capitalist crises, was the ability of the
right to "steal the symbol" (as Burke put it) of class from the left.

Most important, the narrative ideological work of the right, in its
many guises, refigures, the very concept of the "free market" itself. The
right-wing critique of central banking—indeed, of finance capital in
general—permits a powerful rhetorical dissociation, in Perelman's
sense, of "free market" into "free market and free trade." Then, the rejection of the free-trade component enables one to reject as unacceptable (per Pat Buchanan) the negative consequences of downsizing,
deindustrialization, and other features of recent capitalist restructuring
of the global economy.

The rhetorical dissociation of "free market" provides a solution to
the slippery slope problem raised by the existence of the Federal Reserve. If a market in money is subject to recurring cycles of boom and
bust, and if government intervention in that market has a long history,
then the Federal Reserve's codified and ongoing intervention may be a
dangerous precedent, encouraging the government to step in and
resolve other alleged "market failures," ranging from providing environmental protection to public education to health care. The globalization narrative allows capitalists to eat their cake and have it, too—
especially since the likelihood of returning to free banking and a gold
standard is just about nil. In the absence of a truly free market, then,
radical capitalists need not be held responsible for the consequences of
the market. Whether it is Jewish bankers, the Illuminati, Satan, or a
cultural elite that is responsible for the current banking system, the
rhetorical-ideological uses to which the globalization narrative is put
in describing contemporary capitalism seem to account for its contin-
ual reinvention.

The ideological explanation for the persistency of the globalization narrative is, in many ways, too easy. Are we seeing the transition
from conspiracy theory to a reasoned opposition, sort of along the lines

noted by Gordon S. Wood (1982) in his essay on conspiracy theory in the early republic? Or have Griffin and Buchanan, at least, tapped into something that the left has failed to understand for at least a generation? Karl Marx praised free trade for bringing the inevitable showdown between the proletariat and the bourgeoisie that much closer to reality. The left has typically been internationalist and cosmopolitan (I cringe as Stalin's term for Jews—"rootless cosmopolitans"—comes to mind). U.S. leftists in the 1980s worried more about Managua, Nicaragua, than they did about Flint, Michigan. U.S. social democrats are split about whether to join hands with Pat Buchanan in promoting protectionism (and "saving jobs") or simply to insist upon raising the labor and environmental standards connected to NAFTA and GATT (see Galbraith 1998a).

The absence of a credible globalization narrative by the left (albeit a totally different one from those of the right) means that, depending on how far the stock market slides, the narratives offered up by the likes of Gingrich and Buchanan will remain the dominant efforts aimed at capturing the hearts and minds of Main Street citizens.

CHAPTER SEVEN

Newt Gingrich, Cyberpunk, and Globalization

Projecting the future has become a growth industry, both inside and outside of academe. Desire and anxiety about new communications technologies circulate in a steady flow from popular culture to government to big business to the university. Not coincidentally, the new world information order is an ideal site for the very different research strategies of rhetoric and cultural studies to meet. Each of these has its own concomitant skills and incapacities. The rhetorical tradition, adept at analyzing political strategy, has been less skillful in mapping the trajectories of popular desire, while the cultural studies tradition, rightly drawing attention to issues of gender, performance, and desire in popular media, has been less skillful in analyzing conventional political discourse.

Stephen Greenblatt's (1988) new historicist cultural poetics rejects a focus on single texts isolated from contemporary social practices and proposes instead that we ask "how collective beliefs and experiences [are] shaped, moved from one medium to another, concentrated in manageable aesthetic form, offered for consumption" (5). Greenblatt further attempts to determine how "social energy" such as pleasure, interest, and anxiety circulate among different cultural zones in a particular time period.

Tracing the circulation of this social energy—"power, charisma, sexual excitement, collective dreams, wonder, desire, anxiety, religious awe, free-floating intensities of experience" (Greenblatt 1988: 19)—provides important insights into the nature of *power-as-performance*, which I take to be the chief point of intersection between traditional rhetorical studies and the newer vocabularies of cultural studies. Yet, what both traditional rhetorical studies and cultural studies have tended to neglect is the way in which "power" is, in the last instance, *class* power. As Fredric Jameson tirelessly reminds his postmodern academic audience, all human cultural expressions are simultaneously utopian yearnings and attempts to manage the intolerable contradictions of a world in which, as always, "the underside of culture is blood, torture, death, and terror" (Jameson 1991: 5).

Following Greenblatt and Jameson, in my rhetorical-cultural analysis I compare differing forms of cultural and political discourse; that is, I examine how particular rhetorical forms (composed of stock arguments and narratives about globalization) interact with audience desire and anxiety. I analyze the more conventional political discourse of Alvin Toffler, George Gilder, and Newt Gingrich along with the cultural discourse of cyberpunk novelists William Gibson and Bruce Sterling and avant-garde communication scholar Roseanne Allucquére Stone.

In this case, the dominant discourse that circulates with surprising frequency among the various texts I examine is a libertarian ideological discourse that is at the same time a discourse of inevitability. The simultaneous celebration and denial of human agency in the face of "the Third Wave" is a theme shared by figures who would normally be viewed as occupying different sides in what has come to be called "the Culture War." This shared ideological theme serves as a point of condensation (and evasion) of social anxieties about the reconstitution of class boundaries in the late-twentieth-century industrialized world.

We thus have an opportunity, under the sign of an "articulated" rhetorical-cultural studies, to examine the interplay of division and mediation as political strategists and cultural workers attempt to understand the transition to an "information" economy. As we shall see, the very hypertrophy of "information" as a governing norm for ideal communication seems to generate anxiety about the nature and uses of the "body."

THE STRATEGIES OF CYBER-REPUBLICANS

While academic postmodernists were proclaiming the death of master narratives and neo-Marxists were arguing for a "Marxism without guarantees," the most influential theorists of the computer revolution ironically were reinventing the dialectical materialist view of history.

Shortly after the conservative Republican victory of 1994, Ted Turner published a short book by Alvin and Heidi Toffler (1995), with a foreword by Newt Gingrich, that summarized the Tofflers' three-stage theory of history. The Tofflers believe that we are experiencing a "system crisis," as the United States moves from a Second Wave industrial economy to a Third Wave information economy. As they see it, the "master conflict" of the industrial economy was the battle between agrarian interests defending the First Wave and industrial–commercial advocates of the Second Wave (a battle represented clearly by the War Between the States). The new master conflict will be between those (like Pat Buchanan on the right or the AFL-CIO on the left) who resist the transition to a global information economy and those who understand how the new system will work.

The Third Wave is marked by the following changes:

1. Knowledge becomes the chief factor in production.
2. Work, politics, and entertainment become less centralized, meaning that large organizations are doomed.
3. Work becomes more interesting and flexible.
4. Bureaucratic uniformity is replaced by sophisticated tools of system integration and information management.

These changes will require significant economic investments and political change. For the Tofflers, the United States, for example, should take the lead in developing the international information infrastructure. Further, alternative political institutions, based on the values of minority power and semidirect democracy will facilitate the peaceful transition to a Third Wave civilization.

The Tofflers lament, however, that our political imagination lags behind our technological imagination: traditional Republicans are still dreaming of "Ozzie and Harriet," while traditional Democrats are still dreaming of "River Rouge" (the giant auto plant in Dearborn) (Toffler and Toffler 1995: 77).

George Gilder (1994), the author of *Sexual Suicide* and *Wealth and Poverty*, two very influential books among conservatives, adopts a slightly different slant on the Third Wave in his *Life after Television*. While, like the Tofflers, Gilder contends that large organizations are in jeopardy, he also asserts that police states simply cannot work after computerization, since computers "increase the powers of the people far quicker than the powers of surveillance" (61). Gilder picks up the theme of cultural politics that entered mainstream Republican rhetoric after Dan Quayle's "Murphy Brown" speech of 1992: "the most dangerous threat to the U.S. economy and society is the breakdown of our cultural institutions" (56).

What will cure this breakdown? In Gilder's view it will be the death of television (caused by what media analysts call the "convergence of modes") and the accompanying restoration of the home and family as the center of society. Very soon, radio, television, the Internet, as well as books and newspapers will enter the home on a single cable and most telephones will be wireless. Then, a centralized media apparatus will no longer dictate tastes and values to a mass audience.

Gilder invites his audience to imagine creating "a school in your home that offers the nation's best teachers imparting the moral, cultural, and religious values you cherish" (55). Unlike the Tofflers, who are sympathetic to single-parent and gay families, Gilder argues that "The PC is a supply-side investment in the coming restoration of the home to a central role in the productive dynamics of capitalism, and the transformation of capitalism into a healing force in the present crisis of home and family, culture and community" (215). The computer makes possible both telecommuting and home schooling, and will no doubt restore the traditional division of labor between the sexes as well.

The Tofflers' historical dialectic and Gilder's concern for traditional values are merged in an important speech given by Newt Gingrich shortly after the 1994 elections. The speech, originally given to the Washington Research Group, has been widely circulated on the Internet by *Washington Weekly*, which appended this editorial comment: "[T]he following speech has been largely ignored by the media. You may find it a compelling vision for America's future. It may become a historic speech, setting a new course. Bypass the media by distributing the speech widely, and let an informed people decide."[1]

This call to bypass "the media" is a recurring theme in libertarian rhetoric about the Internet: one can now "pull" from many sources rather than having centralized media "push" information to passive audiences (see Negroponte 1995: 84).

Gingrich relies heavily on his credentials as an academic historian to tell his story about U.S. civilization. Gingrich first identifies what rhetoricians call *kairos*, a sense of speaking at the "right time," in this case on Veterans' Day. This day reminds us of the political failures of the Great War, which led to "Nazism and the Soviet Empire, the Gulag and Auschwitz," as well as of the sacrifice of "those who believed enough in freedom to have died for it."

The memory of wartime sacrifice also is appropriate because we are at another turning point in history comparable to the Great War. Our very civilization is at stake:

> I am a history teacher by background, and I would assert and defend on any campus in this country that it is impossible to maintain civilization with twelve-year-olds having babies, with fifteen-year-olds killing each other, with seventeen-year-olds dying of AIDS, and with eighteen- year-olds ending up with diplomas they can't even read. And that what is at issue is literally not Republican or Democrat or Liberal or Conservative, but the question of whether or not our civilization will survive.

Gingrich then notes the surprise felt by both Democrats and "the Washington elite" at the Republican victory, and compares it to the surprise felt by the Germans at D-day.

Gingrich, like the Tofflers and Gilder, next speaks within a rhetorical form that has exploded in popularity in recent years: an offshoot of the traditional advice manuals often associated with the rhetorical tradition. Gingrich first says that he follows the planning model used by Eisenhower, Marshall, and Roosevelt during World War II, "the most complex large human activity ever undertaken."

> This planning model consisted of a hierarchy of four layers: the top of it was vision, and after you understood your vision of what you are doing you design strategies, and once you had your vision and strategies square, you designed projects which were the building blocks of your strategies, and inside the context of those projects, you delegated dramatically, an entrepreneurial model in which a project was a definable, delegatable achievement. . . . At the bottom of the model is tactics, what you do everyday.

Gingrich then combines this planning model with a leadership model ("listen, learn, help, and lead") and explains how the "Washington elite" cannot understand the 1994 Republican revolution because they have ceased to listen to the people.

Somewhat abruptly, Gingrich then characterizes himself as a "conservative futurist," something that "obviously doesn't fit anybody's current word processor." His canon of recommended works on planning and leadership are the Tofflers' works, Peter Drucker's "Effective Executive," W. Edwards Deming's "Concepts of Quality," the *Federalist Papers*, and Alexis de Tocqueville's *Democracy in America*.

Gingrich's study of these works led him to conclude that there were five large changes "we have to go through" in order to get to the twenty-first century.

First, "we have to accelerate the transition from a Second Wave mechanical bureaucratic society to a Third Wave information society." Gingrich contrasts the speed and ease of using an ATM card with the process of communicating with the federal government. He proposes that government should update its information systems and help develop distance medicine, distance learning, and distance work, which could "revolutionize" the rural U. S. Government should provide access to all of its documents on the Internet so that the ordinary citizen has the same access to them that "the highest paid Washington lobbyist" has.

Second, we have to recognize the reality of the coming global market, yet commit ourselves to creating highly paid and productive jobs for all U.S. citizens. Such a world market requires rethinking our current view of "litigation, taxation, regulation, welfare, education, the very structure of government, the structure of health." An important step toward coming to terms with the world market is "that every child in America should be required to do at least two hours of homework every night"—required not by government but as a result of "a level of civic responsibility we are not used to."

Third, "we have to replace the welfare state with the opportunity society," eliminating the culture of poverty created by the Great Society.

Fourth, we have to reassert "the deeper, underlying cultural meanings of being American" and say to "the counter-culture: nice try, you failed, you're wrong."

Fifth, citizens have to exercise more individual and civic responsibility to ensure that downsizing the federal government will work.

Gingrich here cites historian Gordon S. Wood to demonstrate that Jefferson's great insight was "that you had to have limited but effective government in order to liberate people to engage in civic responsibility."

The rhetorical structure of Gingrich's address thus includes a mythic narrative of a transition from feudalism to industrial capitalism to information-based capitalism; a stock set of characters—Washington elites, counterculture types, pregnant teens, wise military and business leaders, the Founding Fathers, and the ideographs of "government," "civic responsibility," "happiness," and "information."

Since Gorgias, rhetoricians have taught that persuasion is accomplished when audiences hear messages at the right time and are enabled to forget about the contradictory aspects of political practice. The rhetorician promotes an illusion of harmony until the rhetorical situation matures and dies; some illusions persist and become recognizable "ideologies," or what Pocock (1975) and others (see Fallon 1989) call "political languages." As Michael Calvin McGee (1980) has taught us, the power and vulnerability of a given rhetorical practice often can be located in the peculiarly nonreferential characteristics of ideographs.

The contradictions in Gingrich's rhetoric are not difficult to locate. How can we promote civic responsibility while proclaiming that government is evil? How can we promote the work ethic while maintaining that consumption and "lifestyle choice" represent happiness? How can we promote individual liberty while constrained by world-historical shifts in the mode of production? How can we make government more local without a corresponding shift in business and financial organizations? How can we proclaim U.S. exceptionalism while committing ourselves to a global economy and the rule of multinational corporations? How can we commit ourselves to unlimited access to "information," when information includes words and images that are destructive of civic responsibility?

It is not surprising, really, that the Gingrich coalition of 1994 should have fallen apart so swiftly, since the forces concerned with the restoration of family, local government, and traditional values inevitably conflict with the forces committed to a world market, unlimited access to information, and increased consumption. As Jefferson and de Tocqueville themselves recognized, there is an inherent tension between civic virtue and the demands of commerce, a tension that their "biggest fan," Professor Gingrich, seems to have forgotten. The Republicans came to power in 1994 largely by redefining popular economic anxiety as created by excessive government control and by the decline in traditional values; as economic anxiety declined and as President Clinton skillfully co-opted Republican symbols, the Republican redefinition seemed incoherent at best, or mean and backward-looking at worst.

Perhaps most important, Gingrich's speech ignores the body-based so-called social issues that had energized participation by the Christian Right in the 1994 elections. When pressed on issues such as abortion and homosexuality, at least among elite audiences, Gingrich typically echoes the argument of his friends the Tofflers that the Third Wave will radically restructure family life, sexual attitudes, and personal morality (Toffler and Toffler 1995: 9, 25). The freedom of the unattached self in the global marketplace overrides traditional moral concerns, as Gingrich's opposition to the Communications Decency Act demonstrates. The journalistic revelations during Gingrich's divorce from his second wife in the summer of 1999 underscore the difficulties created by playing the "morality card" too frequently.

The old split between traditionalists and libertarians in the Republican Party, temporarily healed by Ronald Reagan's powerful ethos, has reopened as Reagan's heirs compete for legitimacy. The anxious concern for personal morality and religious transcendence, which tend to increase in times of rapid economic change (see Harvey 1990), is reflected in popular and journalistic anxiety about pornography on the Internet. It is an anxiety easily channeled against economic elites as well as against so-called cultural elites, as the success of Patrick Buchanan with some traditional Democratic constituencies suggests. Under pressure, cyber-Republicans like Gingrich propose to salve popular anxiety with appeals to the historical dialectic and the invisible hand of the market. Such appeals, however, are ideally better suited to audiences of intellectuals than to mass audiences.

ARISTOCRATS SLUMMING IN THE CYBERCULTURE

Around the time that Professor Gingrich was lecturing his comrades, the counterculture he demonized in those lectures was discovering the Internet as well. It was as if poststructuralist French theorists—with their arguments about the priority of writing over speech, the body-without-organs, the decentered subject, the simulacrum, the Panopticon, and the floating signifier—had called a whole material infrastructure into being that verified their most far-out theories.

The personal computer and the Internet revolution also proved to be a cure for a certain exhaustion in the academic practice of the humanities. Soon scholars were designing their own Web pages, literary research centers were using hypertext to integrate the study of text production with traditional literacy criticism, and technologues and computer geeks of all sorts were following the pronouncements of Baudrillard, Foucault, and Derrida. After 1994, job announcements in "computer-mediated communication" or "new technologies" began to appear. Students who for years had avoided library research found it easier to locate and read rhetorical documents on the Web. I, like many of my colleagues, suddenly found it easier to "keep in touch" via e-mail, and my sense of community often extended further in cyberspace than within my own academic institution.

Shortly after my introduction to e-mail, USENET (the Internet news groups), and later IRC (Internet Relay Chat) and MUDs (Multiple User Dungeons), I felt as if the texture of my everyday life had changed. For Raymond Williams, one of the tasks of cultural studies is to understand "a felt sense of the quality of life at a particular place and time: a sense of the ways in which the particular activities combined into a way of thinking and living"—what Williams (1961) called a "structure of feeling" (48).

Williams's analysis of the communicative forms and narratives of 1840s England in The Long Revolution (1961) is instructive for the present analysis. According to Williams, by the 1840s the dominant social character included

> [T]he belief in the value of work, and this is seen in relation to individual effort, with a strong attachment to success gained in these terms. A class society is assumed, but social position is increasingly defined by actual status rather than by birth. The poor are seen as the victims of their own failings, and it is strongly held that the best among them will climb out of their class. A punitive Poor Law is necessary in order to stimulate effort. . . . Thrift, sobriety, and piety are the principal virtues, and the family is their central institution. The sanctity of marriage is absolute, and adultery and fornication are unpardonable. (61)

These views made up the "dominant social character" of the dominant group of the time: the industrial and commercial middle class. Williams points out, however, that there was also a residual aristocratic social character that believed "birth mattered more than money; that work was not the sole social value and that civilization involved play; that sobriety and chastity, at least in young men, were not cardinal virtues but might even be a sign of meanness and dullness" (61–62).

It is interesting that many of the major reforms of the period were accomplished by Disraeli's successful rhetorical strategy of using aristocratic ideals to temper middle-class ideals. Class anxiety was often expressed in the literature of the period, as Williams writes, as "a pervasive atmosphere of instability and debt," with characters being rescued by an unexpected legacy or by emigration (1961: 65).

The structure of feeling of the late 1980s and 1990s in academe consists of another sort of anxiety: a sense that knowledge has in fact become capital, but that knowledge workers remain doomed to enjoy the fruits of their knowledge in "psychic" rather than real income. This anxiety has also resulted in a valorization of the "body" as a theme in cultural and literary analysis and in a turn toward the popular as revenge against the holders of capital.

Among the best conveyors of this structure of feeling are Roseanne Allucquére Stone, Bruce Sterling, and William Gibson, who combine an ecstatic sense of language and performance, an emotional undertone of body anxiety and sexual transgression, and a critique of corporate capitalism that ends in a defense of radical libertarianism.

The genre that came to be known as "cyberpunk" fiction began with the 1984 publication of William Gibson's *Neuromancer*, a novel that coined the term "cyberspace" and contributed a number of terms that recur in the discourse of cyberculture, including "jacking in" (connecting to the Net) and "the meat" (to refer to the body).

Cyberpunk had its own literary precursors, notably William S. Burroughs (whose description of "the Interzone" in *Naked Lunch* bears an uncanny resemblance to some aspects of today's Internet); Thomas Pynchon, with his black-comedic blending of high science and low popular culture; and Samuel R. Delaney, author of poststructuralist science fiction, notably in the Neveryön tales.

What is distinctive about cyberpunk, however, is its ability to continue the modernist project of representing "the city in crisis."

Gibson's Sprawl is as much a depiction of present-day Houston or Los Angeles as it is of a future dystopia: a city of rampant crime, widespread drug use, medical experimentation, governmental collapse, and corporate control.[2] Unlike the modernist hero of hard-boiled fiction— say, Sam Spade or Philip Marlowe—Gibson's heroes possess no fundamental moral code that can serve as a basis for opposition to the existing order. Plot movement takes the form of a quest, but it is a quest driven more by addiction to information—or, better, to the act of being "jacked in" to acquire information—than by a search for truth.

Later incarnations of cyberpunk try to address the problem of human agency, which had been termed inadequate in the earliest novels. For example, in *Snow Crash* (1992) and *The Diamond Age* (1995), Neal Stephenson creates plucky, street-smart young women who learn to use technology effectively and seem to possess a Marlowe-like moral code. Still, as David Brande (1996) has noted, the achievement of cyberpunk in general lies in its having already established a symbiotic or even "parasitic" relationship to the post-Fordist, globalized capitalist economy (99).

But what of the general political stance of cyberculture and its inhabitants? Gibson and Sterling's coauthored novel *The Difference Engine* (1991) seems to provide an ideological underpinning for the Third Wave that rests on a return to nineteenth-century radicalism (see Sussman 1994). Gibson and Sterling invite us to imagine Victorian England as it might have developed had Charles Babbage's plan for a "Difference Engine," or computer, been realized. The Difference Engine makes possible immense economic productivity—but at the cost of increased air pollution ("the Stink") and extensive invasion of privacy. The ideological basis of this society is "Radicalism," in which knowledge alone serves as the basis of social mobility and entry into the aristocracy. The Radical Lords (successful scientists and engineers) are also allied with the working class, which is organized into guildlike unions.

Although at one level *The Difference Engine* reads as though the story were set in a dystopia, Gibson and Sterling have clearly captured the political utopian fantasies of the professional-computing class. The novel, like other cultural representations of new communications technology, serves an invaluable cognitive function. The reason popular narratives should be studied side by side with conventional political rhetoric is, as Fredric Jameson (1979) writes, following Althusser, that ideologies inevitably take the form of narratives that invent a place for the subject in history, and that artistically interesting or successful narratives inevitably bring ideological contradictions to the surface: "What art makes us *see*, and therefore gives us in the form of '*seeing*,' '*perceiving*,' and '*feeling*' (which is not a form of *knowing*) is the ideology from which it is born, in which it bathes, from which it detaches itself as art, and to which it alludes" (21).

The core political narrative being revised in *The Difference Engine* is Disraeli's (1980) Victorian novel *Sybil: Or The Two Nations* (from which several of the characters' names are derived), which proposed an alliance between the aristocracy and the working class to solve the political problems of England. The negative elements of the new Victorian England notwithstanding, the implied reader of *The Difference Engine*, like the implied reader of Gibson's Sprawl trilogy or Sterling's *Islands in the Net*, is one who possesses knowledge or computer expertise as his only capital and feels caught between the older ruling class and the working class into which he fears he may fall.

A recurring theme in political, journalistic, and fictional representations of the Third Wave is a heightened awareness of the importance of play. What members of the older working class, like the backward-looking parts of the capitalist class, do not understand is that *work* and *play*, rather than being the antinomies they are in the old capitalist work ethic, have now been brought together by the new technologies. Anyone who spends some time MUDing or IRCing can confirm the observation that work and play appear to constitute a continuum for the digerati. A fascination with role-playing games such as Dungeons and Dragons, with the novels of Anne Rice, and an interest in sex-magick, wicca, sadomasochism, gender-bending, and the like are common cultural characteristics of these avid Internet users.

Roseanne Allucquére Stone, a transgendered former audio engineer for Jimi Hendrix and now professor and director of the Interactive Multimedia Laboratory at the University of Texas at Austin, accurately reflects the cultural sensibility of the technical avant-garde. Stone's *The War of Desire and Technology at the Close of the Mechanical Age* (1995) emphasizes the element of play in human–computer interaction and the role of the computer as an arena for social experience rather than a "medium" or "tool." Stone is absorbed in the fantasy of escaping the body and reinventing one's identity—in the form of the cyborg or the vampire—and she places at the center of her cultural criticism the social behavior on the Internet that has occasioned so much puzzlement, namely, the chat rooms of IRC and the role-playing MUDs that have occasioned anxious discussions of computer addiction by college administrators.

Stone artfully weaves together chapters on multiple-personality disorder, the oft-told tale of the cross-dressing psychiatrist on CompuServe, phone sex, the vampire Lestat, and corporate crisis at Atari. The recurring image in her writing is boundary crossing:

> We are no longer unproblematically secure within the nest of our location technologies, whose function for us (as opposed to for our political apparatus) is to constantly reassure us that we are without question ourselves, singular, bounded, conscious, rational; the end product of hundreds of years of societal evolution in complex dialogue with technology as Other and with gender as an othering machine. (1995: 182)

Stone urges us to go beyond the disruption of current body definitions by androgyny and cross-dressing. In a performance titled "What Vampires Know: Transsubjection and Transgender in Cyberspace" (1997) she holds up the image of Fakir Musafar hanging by ropes entwined through slits in his pectorals as having real potential for disrupting our gender structures.

The sadistic hunger of the vampire Lestat gives him a perspective on human bodies that others lack:

> He sees people trapped, stuck in their particular gender positions, in their particular subjectivities, not able to make the jump to seeing subject position as a boat that's momentarily at anchor, but that can actually move through a sea of possible subject positions. The vampire would like to make more of that visible. He talks about it in terms of the Dark Gift that turns one into a vampire. (Stone 1997)

Stone (1997) is concerned that "power is most powerful when it's invisible, and in the new social spaces of communication technology is as yet quite invisible." The radicalism of the privileged-spectator position of the vampire Lestat and of the practices of sexual role-playing and sadomasochism consists in a willingness to make the process of power exchange visible rather than invisible. It is one thing when people play at dominance and submission games as consenting adults, with clearly defined rules and "safewords," but quite another when the participants are, say, students at the Citadel. Gender-bending, consensual sadomasochism, and role-playing are, in Stone's terms, political acts because they make structures of power visible.

Now, all of this is fine as far as it goes. Transgender liberation may be one of the last steps in the fulfillment of the liberal project: the removal of all artificial barriers to participation in the public world. On the other hand, the seemingly boundless variety of "lifestyle choices" and the seemingly boundless plasticity of the human body itself are but variations on the traditional libertarian capitalist theme of the individual being left free to maximize utility in any way that does not infringe on other individuals' comparable freedom. The message of the transgendered cultural radical Sandy Stone is essentially the same as that of the conservative economists Milton Friedman and Deirdre McCloskey: liberty means unlimited self-expression in rhetoric and other forms of cultural performance. The new technologies liberate the self, not the community.

And in this respect, at least, Newt Gingrich and the cyberpunk cultural radicals strangely share the same political imagination: detached from the production of anything real, detached from any location in traditional communities or cultural practices (other than occasional nods to the Framers), the liberated subject is free to commune with like-minded subjects on a Net that exists in "real time," but not in space. And if you do not happen to like what you see rolling across your screen, you can always log off—and then even log on again, with a new identity.

While the cyber-Republicans and the cultural radicals have thought that they are discovering the new country of the Third Wave, they have instead reinvented the mythology of the frontier, where unlimited extension in space is the basis of the freedom to invent oneself. That such freedom should be the cause of tremendous anxiety among Rust Belt workers, inner-city youth, or newly divorced mothers is but a sign of their failure of imagination, presumably curable with the distribution of free laptops or subscriptions to *Wired*.

As Christopher Lasch (1995), whose untimely death came just as the ideology of the Third Wave was consolidating its successes, wrote in his last work:

> The thinking classes . . . live in a world of abstractions and images, a simulated world that consists of computerized models of reality— "hyperreality," as it has been called—as distinguished from the palpable, immediate, physical reality inhabited by ordinary men and women. Their belief in the "social construction of reality"—the central dogma of postmodernist thought— reflects the experience of living in an artificial environment from which everything that resists human control . . . has been rigorously excluded. (20)

But the reinvention of the three-stage dialectical theory of history (which, to borrow a phrase from Marx, has now occurred twice—the first time as tragedy, the second time as farce), however reassuring to nervous academics, computer professionals, and capitalist entrepreneurs, cannot wish away the Second Wave-like effects of a computerized economy. What of Superfund environmental disaster cleanup sites in Silicon Valley (belying the myth that computing is somehow a "clean" industry), the dramatic increase in repetitive stress disorders and other computer-related illnesses, the exploitation of Third World women and children in computer manufacturing, computerization, huge displacement of middle-management jobs, the role of investments in computer equipment in inflating educational and business costs (without corresponding increases in productivity), and the coming crash in overinflated technology stocks? For all the energy, desire, and anxiety expended on promoting fantasies of the Third Wave, the real world appears to be founded on much the same class divisions, regimentation, and environmental degradation as characterized by the Second Wave.

BRINGING "CLASS" BACK IN

Two features of the Third Wave represent positive opportunities for political organizing and rhetorical mediation of the contradiction between information and body. The first lies in the role of what can only be called the "proletarianization" of the professional-managerial class under the impact of computerization of information (see Aronowitz and DiFazio 1994). Physicians subjected to "medicine by the numbers" in health maintenance organizations, managers faced with downsizing, and professors threatened with the loss of tenure are now facing the same kind of economic restructuring and anxiety that blue-collar workers experienced during the early 1980s.

The second positive feature of the Third Wave lies in the ideology of "information" itself, which in the "hacker ethic" serves to reinforce the individualism of the capitalist order but in turn undercuts the ability of capitalism to enforce privacy and property rights (see Levy 1984: 26–36). Critical social scientists have had trouble understanding what the late Alvin Gouldner meant in *Against Fragmentation* when he proposed that the "New Class" of humanistic intellectuals and technical intelligentsia represents a potential "universal class" in the way that the working class was for Marxism (see Gouldner 1985). The positive moment in the Third Wave lies in its creation of technical opportunities for bridging the "two cultures" gap as well as in uniting the "New Class" against the old capitalist elite.

CONCLUSION

The rhetoric of cyberculture does not yet know itself as a class-based rhetoric. It has so far proceeded by reaching out to two of the available "languages": the rhetoric of the sixties counterculture and sexual revolution, with its valorization of the desiring body and its complicity with the commodification of that desiring body by the culture industry; and the rhetoric of liberty and the free market, the capitalist ideology most congenial to the financial wing of the ruling class. If my analysis in this chapter is correct, the avant-garde of the technical intelligentsia and cultural critics share the following characteristics.

First, they share a rejection of tradition, whether modernist narratives of liberalism, social democracy, or communism, or even older religious or classical humanist narratives. Second, they share a sense of distance both from the working class and from the capitalist class, and a conviction that "information," whether defined in technical or cultural terms, is the fundamental resource of the new world order rather than land, capital, or labor power. Third, they both valorize cultural "play" as a quasi-utopian fusion of technology, labor, and the arts. Fourth, they share a sense of blocked ascendancy, in part because of the de-funding of higher education and of basic scientific research, and also in part because of the instability of employment in the new-technologies sector. Fifth, they both lack any genuine *politics*, in the sense either of a political party or a social movement (although the environmental movement remains the one site of potential unification of the two halves of the New Class). Even the politician most savvy about the political hopes of the technical intelligentsia, namely Newt Gingrich, has been unable to provide an effective voice for them, given his dependence on the highly moralistic Christian Right for part of his power base.

If it is true, then, that a way into reading the cultural narratives about the Internet revolution is through understanding them as expressing class anxieties and utopian fantasies, as well as enacting the contradictions of a split New Class, what political alternatives remain? Is the New Class potentially an agent of liberation, whose essential libertarianism could be turned as easily against big business as it has against big government, and thus preparing the way for "the withering away of the State" that Marx had sought? Or does the proletarianization of scientists, engineers, and college professors under the constraints of capitalist globalization represent an opportunity for a new alliance with the working class in a new configuration of the traditional socialist or social-democratic project? The solution to the New Class's thus-far limited bid for hegemony is either, like Christopher Lasch, to launch a neopopulist critique of the revolt of the elites, or, like Alvin Gouldner, to help the information class develop a sense of its possibilities as a universal class.

My chief concern in this chapter has been to identify some contradictory moments in the discourse about the Internet. George Gilder, Newt Gingrich, and the Tofflers simultaneously defend laissez-faire economics while affirming the inevitability of a new stage of history. They defend traditional values while celebrating technologies that erode traditional communities. Although at first sight the cyberpunk writers create dystopias critical of late capitalism, they end up creating libertarian heroes worthy of Ayn Rand. In any case, the new technologies of communications represent sites of class struggle as real and significant as the dark satanic mills of "the Second Wave." According to Karl Marx, the primary reason epochal social change occurs is that the promise of new technologies is hampered by existing relations of production (see Cohen 1978: 206). If personal computing and the Internet promise individual empowerment, more meaningful work, and greater democracy, these promises are unlikely to be fulfilled fully under capitalism as we know it.

Conclusion

The Market and Human Happiness

The 1997 Nobel Prize for Economics was awarded to Robert C. Merton of Harvard University and Myron S. Scholes of Stanford University. Merton and Scholes, with their now deceased colleague Fischer Black, provided a new means of dealing with financial risk, specifically by showing how to determine the value of "derivatives."

"Derivatives" is short for "derivative securities"—the market in options and futures. Options give the right—not the obligation—to buy or sell something in the future at a predetermined price. Futures contracts promise future delivery of an item at a fixed price. These derivatives allow firms to shift risks to others more capable of assuming them.

Despite the importance of risk management in the modern economy, there had been no agreed-upon way to calculate the value of derivatives. Then Black and Scholes (1973) provided a formula for pricing options. This formula led to a tremendous expansion in the market for derivatives and, in addition, laid the foundation for a unified theory of corporate liabilities generally. Nowadays, portfolio managers, companies, and banks use the option-pricing formula on a daily basis to reduce risk and to value stock options.[1]

Merton and Scholes hit the headlines again in 1998, not because of some new academic discovery but because of their role in a multibillion-dollar fiasco. By late September 1998, Long-Term Capital, a Greenwich, Connecticut, "hedge" fund, had lost more than $4 billion in placing its bets on various interest-rate movements through various derivative securities.[2] Merton and Scholes were among the firm's most prestigious advisers. The firm was extraordinarily successful over a four-year period, at times achieving a 43% annual return on investments, but its complicated computer models failed to predict the instability that beset the global economy and its markets in 1998. Estimates of the firm's potential exposure to losses ranged from $80 billion to $1 trillion.

When the peak of the crisis hit, the firm approached some major financial leaders for hoped-for assistance; among those approached were George Soros and Warren Buffett. They declined. At that point the head of the New York Federal Reserve Bank, William McDonough, stepped in to urge Merrill Lynch, Goldman Sachs, and twelve other top financial institutions to meet with Long-Term Capital. The fourteen institutions ultimately agreed to invest about $3.5 billion in return for 90 percent of the investment fund. As *Newsweek* pointed out, these new investors agreed to pay the managers of the fund 1 percent of the assets for a year, and 12.5 percent of any profits, in effect for the right to rescue the fund. These transactions enabled the original investors in the fund to cap their losses at about 90 percent of their money.

The spokesman for the New York Fed argued that this was no bailout, because no government money was involved. But even such stalwart capitalists as Paul Volcker, former chairman of the Fed, Laurence Tisch of the Loew's insurance and tobacco conglomerate, and Llewellyn Rockwell of the Mises Institute, contended that the New York Fed's behavior was disastrous, not just in terms of public relations but also because it created a dangerous precedent in which *some* firms are identified as "too big to fail."[3]

The Long-Term Capital hedge fund crisis encapsulates in many ways the tale of economics and the free market that I have been trying to tell in this book: (1) it demonstrates the use—until it no longer works—of quasi-scientific rhetoric as an ethos-enhancing device; (2) it proves that economic science can accurately predict the future *only part of the time*; and (3) it points out the unfair demand that farmers, workers, and small-business owners submit to the "discipline" of the market completely even if the very wealthy are given an occasional break.

During the same week that the New York Fed twisted the arms of the major financial firms, the U.S. Senate radically changed existing bankruptcy laws. Credit card companies, which had been aggressively pushing their cards on "subprime" borrowers, lobbied for the creation of a "means test" for families declaring bankruptcy. Families earning over $51,000 a year would have to file under Chapter 13 instead of Chapter 7, thus forcing them to pay off at least a portion of their debt (Ivins 1998).

The bailout of Long-Term Capital (however informally accomplished) is a case of flagrant injustice in that a financial safety net was rapidly deployed (thanks to the Fed) that benefited mainly the very rich. That case study also points out a fundamental problem with the free-market rhetoric that I have been examining in this volume, namely, *no one wants to live in a totally unregulated marketplace.* And without government regulation that is responsive to the needs of ordinary people who lack the clout of a Long-Term Capital, free markets are led—as if by an invisible hand—to concentrate power among a very rich few. Committed libertarians, especially scholars of public choice, will object to my argument by saying that they want to eliminate "corporate welfare" and any other government handouts to "special interests." While the critique of corporate welfare has been a major contribution of libertarian scholars, the simple elimination of all government aid cannot solve the problem. Imagine if the United States were to adopt a constitutional amendment of the sort proposed by libertarian economists James M. Buchanan and R. D. Congleton (1998); namely, a "generality constraint" on the political process would prohibit congressional majorities from treating various persons and groups differently. In the absence of any compensation to the public for past inequities, the libertarian reform would simply leave the present set of power relations in the economy intact. Corporate farmers would cease to receive price supports, but they would already have driven small farmers off the land. The managers of the Long-Term Capital hedge fund will already have been bailed out, and the disabled on SSI will already have had their purchasing power halved since 1970. In the absence of campaign finance reform (opposed by libertarians on the grounds that money is "speech" under the First Amendment), there are strong incentives for the rich and powerful to reconstitute corporate welfare in new forms. The economic analysis of special-interest groups (like so much else in the economic theory of human behavior) turns out to be relevant only at the "constitutional" moment of human action; that is, the "original position" in which a group of people creates a set of guidelines for their common life. At any other point, the economic analysis can only justify the status quo.

THE POLITICAL LESSONS OF SELLING THE FREE MARKET

I hope that I have successfully substantiated the following claims:

- Communication cannot be reduced to the exchange of "information" without radically limiting the possibilities for humans to flourish—not just economically but also socially, culturally, and in every other way.
- The ideological rhetoric of "the market" refuses to acknowledge itself as a rhetoric, and the identification of "rhetoricity" can be seen as a vital first step in radical critique.
- The attempt by Deirdre McCloskey to preempt an assault on the rhetoric of the market by redefining "rhetoric" as the conditions of "good talk" and "effective scholarly conversation" ignores the agonistic nature of rhetoric and the political implications of scholarly economic argument.
- The classical economists crafted a "realist style" in which the economic and the social displaced the political dimension of human action.
- The modern-day heirs of the classical economists, Mises and Hayek, Friedman and Posner, reduce both rhetoric and politics to economic calculation in the name of "liberty" and/or "efficiency."
- The political disciples of the radical free-marketeers—Thatcher, Reagan, Objectivists, and libertarians—paradoxically seek to eliminate political communication entirely, replacing it with the pure logic of exchange.
- No human being can for long live solely as *Homo economicus*, so all free-marketeers end up with elements of irrationality in their systems: disciples of Mises become radical neo-Confederates; Randians become love junkies; Republicans become Cold Warriors or find Jesus; and libertarians become racists or gun fanatics.

- The globalization of capitalism, the collapse of socialism and social democracy, and the rise of the Internet have all facilitated the convergence of the ideologies of information and of the market.
- The free market and free trade have a contradictory relationship to each other and to the nationalism that has provided the main rhetorical resource for U.S. conservatism.

More concretely, I want the reader of this volume who may participate in policy debates with free-marketeers not to be cowed by the claimed "scientific" arguments of their opponents. Time and again free-marketeers assert as truth methodological statements and effects of policy that are either plainly wrong or are more controversial than they claim. Foremost among these assertions are:

Rational choice—that is, the application of cost–benefit, economic "reasoning"—is the best possible mechanism in the human sciences for explaining and predicting human behavior. In fact, rational choice theory lacks empirical verification; rhetorical and communication theory explains the emergence of social norms far better than rational choice theory does.

Government intervention in the marketplace is always bad. The fall of communism has settled once and for all the question of the superiority of the free market to any form of government intervention. Market ideology relies on a radical dissociation between "government" and "people." Marketization seeks to place political decisions about education, welfare, and even foreign policy beyond the reach of democratic publics.

Labor is a commodity like everything else; prounion or minimum-wage legislation is an unwarranted interference with the labor market. Once labor is defined as a commodity, there is no brake on the slippery slope to cultural destruction.

The Internet will ensure the triumph of the free market worldwide by reducing information costs and transaction costs, thus ensuring "frictionless capitalism." It also shows how individual initiative and free markets develop unexpected solutions to old problems. The Internet is the product of the greatest single government expenditure outside of Cold War military spending in general (see Borsook, *Cyberselfish* [2000]). It is the product of planning, just as much as any democratic future for communication technology must be.

But, above all, the political message of this book is optimistic. Although libertarianism has captured many minds among the technical intelligentsia and has established beachheads in the universities, it is inherently incapable of motivating the public, which may explain the hostility of free-marketeers to majoritarian democracy.

It is only recently (since the triumph of the market between 1975 and 1989) that the mass democratic public has tended to vote against its own economic interest. The reduction of everything to the "cash nexus" in the wake of globalization provides a significant opportunity for the left and center-left. However successful the disciples of Hayek, Mises, Friedman, and Posner may have been in the academic fields of economics, law, and political science, they possess an inherent inability to persuade a democratic public. Only the external threat of communism and, in its absence, the merging of free-market arguments with nationalist appeals have made radical marketization attractive to voters. A new political program for a global, democratic left must emphasize the importance of the welfare state, strong unions, and regulation of the financial markets *for the preservation of traditional communities.*

The classical theorists of rhetoric and their twentieth-century successors knew that human beings are a composite of appetite, spiritedness (*thymos*), and reason. Free-market economists are at a loss to explain the development of social norms. Only epideictic discourse, or the kind of craft knowledge—practical wisdom—that transcends the calculation of costs and benefits, can explain their development. The triumph of a one-dimensional *Homo economicus* occurs at the expense of family, work, neighborhood, freedom, and faith—the *topoi* of conservatism at its best.

The late Russell Kirk, the great conservative, saw the limitations of the market better even than most radicals, and I will give him the last word. In one of his last speeches, Kirk (1989) told the story of an encounter between Wilhelm Roepke and Ludwig von Mises:

> Roepke told me once, apropos such alternative means of subsistence in industrial society, of an amusing exchange between himself and Ludwig von Mises—who, though agreeing with Roepke in a good many matters, was a disciple of Jeremy Bentham in his utilitarianism. During the Second World War, the city of Geneva had made available to its citizens plots of ground along the ring around the city where the ancient walls had stood. On these allotments, in time of

scarcity of food, the people of Geneva, particularly the laboring folk, could cultivate vegetables for themselves. These allotments turned out to be so popular, both as recreation and as a source of supplementary food, that the city continued to make this land available to applicants after the war was over. Now Mises, who had been professor years before at the Geneva Institute of International Affairs, came to visit Roepke in Geneva, about 1947. Happy at the success of these garden allotments, Roepke took his guest to see Genevan working people digging and hoeing in their gardens. But Mises shook his head sadly: "A very inefficient way of producing foodstuffs!" he lamented. "Perhaps so," Roepke replied, "But perhaps a very efficient way of producing human happiness."

An Appendix for Academics
Deirdre McCloskey's Rhetoric of Economics

Given that twentieth-century rhetorical scholars wrote extensively in attempting to explain the downfall of the rhetorical tradition, it probably becomes all the more daunting a task to explain why the study of rhetoric suddenly revived in the last twenty years of the twentieth century. Any history of the rhetorical revival will need to begin in the amiable atmosphere of the University of Iowa, where in 1980 John Nelson (a political scientist), Allan Megill (an intellectual historian), then Donald McCloskey (an economic historian and economist), and several rhetoricians in the communication department (John Lyne, Bruce Gronbeck, and Michael Calvin McGee) began a colloquium on rhetoric that has since been expanded into a full-blown academic program—the Project on the Rhetoric of Inquiry (POROI, or "ways and means" in Greek). POROI established two important book series, one at the University of Wisconsin and the other at the University of Chicago Press. It has come to involve now hundreds of Iowa faculty in "improving the conversations of scholarship by listening to the 'rhetoric' of a paper in mathematics, law, or economics" (McCloskey 1998: xv). An important offshoot of the group has been the Rhetoric of Science and Technology, represented by a journal, *Social Epistemology*, and several university programs, the most important of which is at the University of Pittsburgh. Although in the second edition of *Rhetoric of Economics* McCloskey bemoans the limited impact her work has had in her chosen discipline, it may actually have had a larger impact in legal studies, where economic analysis has become such a powerful intellectual (and ideological) tool in recent years (xiii).

The impact of the rhetoric of economics upon the community of rhetorical scholars, however, has been remarkably limited. There is now a critical mass of rhetoricians of science, both in Rhetoric and Composition programs and in speech communication departments, but there has been only a very small handful of rhetoricians studying economic discourse (see Kiewe and Houck 1991; Bazerman 1993; Conti 1998). Even in economics itself, the number of practitioners of rhetorical analysis has been small, with many, notably Jack Amariglio (1998, 1990), taking the analysis of economic discourse in an essentially postmodern and, I would argue, ultimately antirhetorical Foucauldian direction.[1]

I cannot speak for the field of economics, but my observation of the community of rhetorical scholars suggests two explanations for the limited impact of McCloskey's work. First, most rhetoricians became rhetoricians in part because of math phobia, and even the most user-friendly economics texts—my favorite is David Colander (1995)—have the dreaded x and y axes in them. Second, and more seriously, rhetoricians spend most of their time analyzing practical discourse; while practitioners of litcrit exhausted their "canon" long ago, the canon of British and U.S. political oratory alone has scarcely been touched. So it is not surprising that the first book-length studies of economic discourse in the field of speech communication have been of presidential rhetoric about the economy. The rhetoricians have proceeded on the assumption that the "value added" to public life by rhetorical criticism is the improved teaching of advocacy skills to college students and the improved scholarly understanding of public communications. For all her protestations of being against the "coasties"—the elitists on both coasts who ignore virtuous Midwesterners—McCloskey really appears to be interested only in academic communication.

In this appendix I present McCloskey's contribution to a rhetoric of economics, emphasizing her contributions to epistemology, her unique framing of the concept of rhetoric and its methods, her close reading of economic texts, and, most important, her encomium to the "bourgeois virtues."

REFRAMING THE RHETORICAL TRADITION

Here are some of the definitions of "rhetoric" McCloskey uses. Keep in mind, though, that she frequently uses the term "rhetoric" interchangeably with "literary analysis"—the study of figures of speech and narratives—especially in *If You're So Smart* (1990).

- "Rhetoric is an anti-epistemology epistemology that breaks down the barriers to trade among disciplines" (1994: 84).
- "Rhetoric is an economics of language, the study of how scarce means are allocated to the insatiable desires of people to be heard" (1998: xx).
- "Rhetoric is the art of a democracy and the science of a liberal education, the art and science of good people speaking well" (1990: ix).
- "[Rhetoric] is the river of discourse, the thought sprung from the sophist Protagoras of Abdera concerning orations, persuasion, poetry, symbolism, storytelling, and literature in general" (Klamer and McCloskey 1988: 10).

As McCloskey's framework developed, she advanced the concept of the Rhetorical Tetrad, consisting of: *fact*, based on the reasoning faculty of induction; *logic*, based on deduction; *story*, or metonymic representation, from understanding; and *metaphor*, from abduction (McCloskey 1994b: 62; 1998: 19).

Deduction and induction are familiar terms, but metonymy and abduction may require further explanation. "Metonymy," in classical rhetoric, is a figure of speech, or trope—a deviation from normal meaning at the level of the word—in which something intangible or incorporeal is represented by something tangible or corporeal. As Kenneth Burke (1969) argued, certain fields of inquiry engage in metonymic and synecdochic processes of reduction in order to create "representative anecdotes" for human action (59–61; 323–325); for example, behavioral psychology "reduces" human action to an organism seeking reinforcement and avoiding punishment.

"Abduction" is a term developed by American philosopher C. S. Peirce to describe the nature of inquiry. Abduction extracts meaning from ambiguous or indeterminate fields of data. Abduction, then, is a *selection* of reality intended to be a reflection of reality, although, as Kenneth Burke (1966) puts it, it runs the risk of being a "deflection" of reality, too (45).

The reaction of most economists to McCloskey's arguments has centered on the relationship between rhetoric and science. In the introduction to *Consequences of Economic Rhetoric* (1988), Klamer and McCloskey identify five recurring themes in their opponents' arguments:

1. *The chaos argument*: "If we abandon all standards and deny the existence of any criterion of truth, anything goes. And anything will."

2. *The Hitler-and-other-irrationalists argument*: "According to the rhetorical approach, everything is relative, so Hitler would be irrefutable."

3. *The fallacy argument*: rhetorical methods are mere fallacies.

4. *The reactionary plot argument*: the rhetoric of economics is just another defense of neoclassical economics.

5. *The antieconomics argument*: "Rhetoric is an attack on economics, undermining the claims of economics to be a scientific discipline" (16–18).

Although McCloskey usually practices her version of *Sprachethik* (ethics of controversy), her testy response to Philip Mirowski's assault on the politics of economic theory is revealing. An essay by Philip Mirowski with the rather extraordinary title "Shall I compare thee to a Minkowski–Ricardo–Leontief–Metzler matrix of the Mosak–Hicks type? Or, Rhetoric, mathematics, and the nature of neoclassical economic theory" takes McCloskey's politics on directly:

> I believe that McCloskey understood that the implicit theory of social order in classical rhetoric is diametrically opposed to the atemporal existence of the neoclassical *Homo economicus*, and therefore a full rhetorical analysis would be congenitally critical of neoclassical economic theory. Of course, this would never do for his purposes, so in order to restrain and repress this tendency, McCloskey tried to restrict his definition of rhetoric to an atemporal consideration of the style of argumentation of economists independent of all historical context. (1988: 123)

Mirowski goes on to contend that rhetorical analysis can provide valuable insights, but only when it is "diachronic as well as synchronic." Mirowski's own remarkable analysis of the rhetoric of classical economics provides a diachronic alternative. He asks the fundamental question, Where did the metaphors *come from? The classical economists*

> appropriated a mathematical model lock, stock, and barrel from somewhere else, in the guise of a metaphor. In particular, the early neoclassicals took the model of "energy" from physics, changed the names of all the variables, postulated that "utility" acted like energy, and then flogged the package wholesale as economics. (1988: 130)

Mirowski then identifies the political interests behind the appropriation of the physics metaphors in a passage worthy of Karl Marx's own "rhetorical criticism" of the classical economists:

> The physics metaphor implies that economics is a science and deserves all the legitimacy that is granted to physics itself because there exists no great

difference between the two modes of inquiry. The economy is portrayed as a self-contained and separable subset of social life, and as such has the character of a stable natural process. "Capitalism" as a natural entity is implied to be timeless; that is, it has always existed and will always continue to exist. . . . The "individual" is taken to be more real than any other social formation, be it the family, the firm, the nation-state, and so on. (141)[2]

McCloskey's (1988a) response to Mirowski's critique is remarkable, not only because it evades the problem of ideology and economic interests, but also because it seems to violate her own principles of "good conversation." She writes that neoclassical economics has done a good job of explaining lots of things, such as the rise of real wages since 1840 and the difficulties of big bankers in the 1980s. Then she wonders

> if the critics of neoclassicism know what they are talking about, literally. They seem to identify neoclassical economics with Paul Samuelson's youthful enthusiasm for identifying economics with constrained maximization, embodied now in dozens of intermediate and graduate texts. I wonder if the critics have read enough real price theory from the hands of the masters, such as Armen Alchian or Ronald Coase. I wonder if they could handle the end-chapter questions in Economic Theory, Price Theory, the Theory of Price, or The Applied Theory of Price. (291)

McCloskey thus engages in a testy, *ad hominem* attack on Mirowski and anyone who would deign to criticize neoclassical economics, charging them with math inadequacy. She neglects Mirowski's (and my) fundamental point: there is nothing wrong with the neoclassical theory of price. *The problem arises when the neoclassical theory of price takes over the entire social and political world, displacing all alternative accounts of human motivation.*

Another useful criticism of the politics and rhetoric of neoclassical economics comes from feminist economists Nancy Folbre and Heidi Hartmann, who charge that the economic individualism of neoclassical theory would be better termed "male individualism." Our view of politics and the economy would be very different if we saw the relationship between mother and child as the fundamental form of social interaction rather than the market. In the famous statement by Adam Smith (at the beginning of Chapter 2) about not owing one's dinner to the virtues of the butcher and baker who provided it, "Smith never pointed out that these purveyors do not in fact make dinner. Nor did he consider that wives might prepare dinner for their husbands out of regard for their self-interest" (187). It is instructive that the great apostle of laissez-faire Herbert Spencer counseled against women's participation in politics, because it would lead to a welfare state. Women's natural altruism might run amok (cited in Folbre and Hartmann 1988: 188).

THE LIMITS OF RATIONAL CHOICE?

Besides questioning the gendered nature of the rational actor, Mirowski, Folbre, and Hartmann ask another radical question, namely, What are the limits of the "market" and "rational choice" metaphors and abductions? Or, in Burkeian terms, is utility maximizing truly a "representative anecdote" for human interaction? Perhaps one way to begin answering the question about the limits of the rational choice perspective is to ask: Can rhetorical choice be redescribed as a form of rational choice? Shall we model the inventional process as if the rhetor weighs the costs and benefits of particular strategies? Does the explanation of rhetorical craft rely on a principle of methodological individualism? McCloskey appears to believe so, although the links in the argument are never clearly spelled out.

Elster (1985) and other rational choice Marxists have developed useful correctives to the purely functionalist forms of social explanation that have been popular on the left. Resolving these methodological disputes is considerably beyond my expertise, but the tension between methodological individualism and methodological collectivism has interesting implications for the study of rhetoric. Although you may explain the selection of rhetorical strategies on the basis of weighing costs and benefits, it seems impossible to account for the interaction of rhetor and audience in totally individualistic terms, because you will inevitably run aground on the problem of social norms. Rhetorical practice is fundamentally an *emergent* phenomenon, not reducible to individual steps. The only extended effort to discuss rhetoric in rational choice terms is Richard Posner's, as presented in Chapter 2.

It is difficult to read McCloskey's account of rational choice without arriving at Mirowski's conclusion that it is an effort to inoculate rational choice against criticism. McCloskey writes, "Rational choice is a master metaphor among mainstream economists, and it has disciplined them considerably" (1994b: 48). A recurring *topos*[3] in McCloskey's writings says, "Now I agree with everything Richard Posner, Ronald Coase, or Gary Becker say; I just don't like the scientistic rhetoric they use."

At a more practical level, the neglect of social and institutional constraints on rhetorical invention is a major failing of McCloskey's theory. This neglect is part of the larger promotion of economic correctness. Now,

McCloskey has sat at the feet of the great rhetorician Wayne Booth, and Booth (1974) has taught her to shout "motivism"[4] whenever arguments such as the one I have just made rear their ugly heads.

Here is my response:

1. It would be nice if the whole world were like a good graduate seminar, with no one jockeying for position and everyone willing to abide by the force of the better argument, without reference to the personality of the speaker. But the real world of controversy is not like that (rhetoricians may note both the "realist" and "dissociative" strategies I have quietly used in the first part of this sentence). As long as people make arguments, their motives will be questioned.

2. Questioning motives not only is part of "real-world" argument but also it is rational. If the credit card companies fund a study of consumer bankruptcy, "proving" that bankruptcy laws need reform, someone should question the motives of the study before voting on new laws.[5]

3. McCloskey's consistent failure to *argue* for Chicago-school positions, while consistently taking oblique shots at other schools of economics, at least raises a question of fundamental motive in the skeptical reader. For example, she talks about Massachusetts Marxist economists watching the 1989 events in China's Tiananmen Square in a state of confusion, needing to wait for the editorials in left publications to make up their minds about what happened. No particular economist is identified, but the underlying major premise is evident: we Chicago school folks are partisans of liberty, and those Massachusetts Marxists are still sliding down the slippery slope to serfdom (McCloskey 1998: 187).

Further, defining rhetoric as "the anti-foundational foundation" that enables good conversation in the human sciences is a way of smuggling Austrian subjectivism into rhetorical studies. In *Knowledge and Persuasion in Economics* (1994b), the most complete response to her critics, McCloskey writes that "rhetoric" is a characterization of economics favoring Austrian over conventional neoclassicism (313). For readers unfamiliar with Austrian economics, what McCloskey is referring to here is the Austrian "subjectivist" theory of value. In classical economics—Smith, Ricardo—value is based on resource costs, with individual economists differing on the relative importance of land, labor, and capital in creating value. Neoclassical economics introduced the notion of marginal utility—value as defined by the utility of the last, least-wanted of a set of goods. Carl Menger, the father of Austrian economics, argued that the only value a good has is its importance for an individual. The Austrians were thus antifoundationalists before their time (see Vaughn 1994; and Chapter 5 in this volume). McCloskey is far more willing to let rhetoric trump the scientific pretensions of rational choice theory than to let any doubt be cast on the virtues of the free market.

THE BOURGEOIS VIRTUES

In her work on rhetoric, McCloskey usually simply asserted in a self-effacing manner her belief in Chicago-school economics. More recent work, notably the essay "Bourgeois Virtue" (1994a) and the book *The Vices of the Economists; the Virtues of the Bourgeoisie* (1997), takes on the direct defense of free-market capitalism. In an audacious move, McCloskey creates a capitalist apologia within a framework of virtue ethics, using three main strategies: (1) redefine the audience of educated readers as "bourgeois"; (2) avoid the word "capitalism," thus emphasizing the character of persons, not of a system; and (3) emphasize the communicative functions of the bourgeois virtues in ways that parallel academic virtues.

Previous accounts of the "virtues" have relied either on the patrician ones (prudence, temperance, justice, and courage) or the Christian "plebeian" ones (faith, hope, and charity). Neither group is satisfactory for the bourgeois life of the town. The bourgeois virtues are integrity, honesty, trustworthiness, enterprise, humor, respect, modesty, consideration, responsibility, prudence, thrift, affection, and self-possession (McCloskey 1994a: 180). The bourgeoisie put a premium on discourse, emphasize cooperation, and avoid violence. Academic intellectuals have simply failed to appreciate the virtues of the bourgeoisie.

McCloskey has a point: academics at times exhibit an aristocratic disdain for ordinary Main Street commerce. Yet, her picture of the virtuous small-town shopkeeper ignores the way that bourgeois virtues have been systematically subordinated by the advent of the multinational corporation. She ignores the way in which the values of hard work and craftsmanship have been eroded by the increased use of technology, as if it were inevitable that it occur in a particular way. As historian David Noble (1977) has demonstrated, U.S. managers invariably choose new technologies based on their ability to enhance managerial rather than worker control.

In McCloskey's world, the workers are disappearing through the magic of economic growth. Her examples of the virtuous include the aristocracy, the peasantry, and the bourgeoisie—but not the proletariat, who are presumed to be devoid of virtue. But what a remarkable approach that would strive to include Goldman Sachs, Donald Trump, Lee Iacocca, my local tobacconist, and Frank Lorenzo all under the same virtuous heading!

CONCLUSION

I want to conclude with a different account of virtue. The General Motors strike in the summer of 1998 was about job security. GM, unlike Ford and Chrysler, had failed to downsize its workforce aggressively in the face of increased global competition. *The Economist* magazine—no particular friend of the labor movement, to put it mildly—published an interesting piece during the strike about a GM electrician in Flint, Michigan, named (improbably) Dwight BoBo (1998: 79). The article illustrates an aspect of the language of virtues that was neglected by McCloskey.

Mr. BoBo, fifty-four years old, had worked for GM since high school. His only break was two years of military service in Vietnam. His father, his brother, and most of his wife's family had also worked for GM as well. "It is tempting," the author of the article writes, "to assume that Mr. BoBo is an industrial brontosaurus, prepared—thrilled, even—to hold his employer to ransom." But Mr. BoBo was not opposed to managers being paid well, nor even to replacing workers with machines. What troubled him was the tremendous gulf in values between the boardroom and the shopfloor: "I think about how things will be when I'm dead; the guys in the boardroom don't. I'm worried about our children's jobs—and the towns around here. They just care about bonuses." Mr. BoBo had never even met the current head of his factory.

Not only did GM break its promise to invest $300 million to upgrade the Flint factory, it also failed to communicate with its workers: "Mr. BoBo admits that change is necessary, but has never heard managers set out an honest vision for GM's future; just a succession of unrealistic promises that have since been broken, with an undertone of ugly rumours about closures that have since come true."

GM also failed to make use of the "tacit knowledge" that Mr. BoBo and "his kind" have about manufacturing cars. He developed a new way of using welding wire, for example, that saved the company thousands of dollars, but he was barely compensated for it: "It wasn't so much the money as the principle. . . . It's like we are the peasants and they are the kings."

Surely Mr. BoBo exhibited the virtues of hard work, honesty, and crafts-manship. What virtues, "bourgeois" or not, have his bosses exhibited?

It is difficult to critique the work of Deirdre McCloskey. Her own stead-fast commitment to *Sprachethik* and her own personal courage in promoting public understanding of the transgendered are both commendable. But this chapter has been based on my perception that the rhetoric of economics has reached something of a conceptual dead end. By emphasizing the institu-tional context of economic arguments and by emphasizing economic rhetoric in the public, rather than academic, realm, perhaps the "conversation" can be advanced a bit. McCloskey's rhetorical tetrad of fact, logic, metaphor, and story is a persuasive account of how rhetorical invention works. It remains for scholars of rhetoric to promote more widespread understanding of the strate-gic and agonistic dimensions of public debate over the economy.

Notes

INTRODUCTION

1. "Whatever it might be suitable to state about philosophy in a preface—say, an historical sketch of the main drift and point of view, the general content and results, a string of desultory assertions and assurance about the truth—this cannot be accepted as the form and manner in which to expound philosophical truth" (Hegel 1967: 67).
2. "Writing is an unfortunate necessity; what is really wanted is to show, to demonstrate, to point out, to exhibit, to make one's interlocutor stand and gaze before the world. . . . In a mature science, the words in which the investigator 'writes up' his results should be as few and as transparent as possible" (Rorty 1982: 94).
3. The first person to use the phrase appears to be Alice Amsden, a professor of economics at the New School for Social Research, in a 1993 *New York Times* article.
4. Personal communications with Conrad Martin, March 18, 1998.
5. For a moving narrative of Douglass's discovery of the art of oratory, through *The Columbian Orator*, see Lampe (1998).
6. The rationale for selling rights to pollute begins with Coase (1960). A surprisingly balanced account of the free-market approach to regulating pollution is in Posner (1992a: 375–380). The proposal to sell body parts comes from Epstein (1997). The proposal to sell babies comes from Posner (1992a: 150–154).

CHAPTER ONE

1. Smith's lectures on rhetoric were not discovered until 1958; they are now available in an inexpensive reprint edition from Liberty Fund (Adam Smith 1983). Perhaps the best recent discussion of Smith that takes his rhetorical theory seriously is Muller (1993). A recent discussion of his rhetorical theory is Spano (1993).
2. For summaries of Ricardo's speeches from contemporary newspaper accounts, see Ricardo (1952).
3. De Quincey (1950: 230–231). For his economic writings, see De Quincey (1968).
4. See Richard Whately, *Introductory Lectures on Political Economy* (1832). His *Elements of Rhetoric* was perhaps the last important and influential treatise on rhetoric published in the nineteenth century; the Ehninger edited volume in the Southern Illinois University Press Landmarks in Rhetoric and Public Address series (1963) is a reprint of the seventh British edition of 1846 (originally published in 1828).
5. For a discussion of the emergence of economics out of the Moral Sciences Tripos at Cambridge, see Skidelsky (1986: 26–50).
6. See also the 1999 follow-up report, *$1 Billion for Ideas: Conservative Think Tanks in the 1990s*, which received much less press coverage; see the website, www.ncrp.org, for ordering information for the 1999 and 1997 reports.
7. The conservative think tanks target the op-ed pages of local newspapers, populate the talk shows, supply quick "research" to politicians, and provide internship opportunities to oppressed conservative undergraduates. A recent study of think tank citations in the news media found that the Heritage Foundation, Cato Institute, and American Enterprise Institute received 46 percent of the citations, *and* they were less likely to have their ideological character identified than the other think tanks that were cited (Paget 1998: 90).
8. See www.tamu.edu/perc. See also Soley (1995: 116–118).
9. "Draft Curriculum for the Master's in Public Administration," Bush School Advisory Committee, February 1996, Appendix D.
10. On the NLRB during the 1980s, see Geoghegan (1992).
11. This note is probably a good place to confront more fully the puzzlement some readers may be experiencing when I cite both a Donald and a Deirdre McCloskey. They are one and the same person, a professor of economics and history at the University of Illinois, Chicago. Donald became Deirdre in 1995–1996 and has become an outspoken and courageous defender of the rights of the transgendered. See Polanyi (1997) for an interview with McCloskey.

12. For another example of this sort of rhetorical analysis, see George (1990).
13. Such an uncomplimentary assessment makes one wonder whether or not the Friedmans spoke from firsthand knowledge or experience—or precisely how they arrived at their overall assessment.

CHAPTER TWO

1. For one example, see Colander (1995: 9). As far as I know, the phrase became popular through its use in Robert Heinlein's libertarian science fiction utopia, *The Moon Is a Harsh Mistress*.
2. For a balanced introduction to the public choice literature, see Farber and Frickey (1991). I recognize that there is a distinction between Arrow's "social choice" theory and the more radical "public choice" theory of Buchanan and Tullock. I also know it is inaccurate to label Arrow and Olson as conservatives. I am constructing here an "ideal type" of public choice theory that, I believe, captures fairly the ideological uses to which it is usually put in academe, law, and politics.
3. But surely there must be a middle ground between purely positive and purely advocacy scholarship. Posner's insistence on cabining off rhetoric from other aspects of the law seems to shift a bit in *Problems of Jurisprudence* (1990b): he analyzes the Hart–Fuller debate on natural law in terms of their disagreement over the "rhetoric" in which to express their shared values (238), and seems to move closer to McCloskey's position when he writes, "Persuasion and reason tend to merge in a pragmatist view of truth" (151). Such merging tends to be more evident during "seismic changes" in the law (151). Posner here appears to be close to the sophistic notion of "possibility" as a dimension of rhetoric (see 1983: 44–46).
4. See Heinrichs (1995) on "How Harvard destroyed rhetoric." True to the Ivy League tradition, however, Heinrich neglects the fact that the Midwest and South did preserve the rhetorical tradition (heavily filtered through the philosophy of John Dewey).

CHAPTER THREE

1. People continue to mispronounce Rand's first name; a good mnemonic device is to note that it rhymes with "mine"!
2. I have collated the lists in Sciabarra (1995: 1–2); and in Barbara Branden (1986: 400, 410, 419, 420, 422).
3. On self-esteem see Nathaniel Branden (1994). The six pillars are: the practice of living consciously; the practice of self-acceptance; the practice

of self-responsibility; the practice of self-assertiveness; the practice of living purposefully; and the practice of personal integrity. For Branden's account of his affair with Rand and her later purge of him from the
Objectivist movement, see Nathaniel Branden (1989).

4. The "orthodox" Ayn Rand Institute is at http://www.aynrand.org. The Institute for Objectivist Studies is at http://ios.org.

5. For this insight, I am indebted to Edwin Black's analysis of the sentimental
   style of the nineteenth century in Black (1992: 97–112).

6. Burke (1968): "Form in literature is an arousing and fulfillment of desires.
   A work has form in so far as one part of it leads a reader to anticipate another part, to be gratified by the sequence" (124).

7. Whittaker Chambers (1990) also notes the childless aspect of Rand's preferred universe in his 1957 review of *Atlas Shrugged*.

CHAPTER FOUR

1. The bee analogy is appropriate here, since one of the first defenses of the
   "virtue of selfishness" was Bernard Mandeville's *Fable of the Bees* (1729).

2. For a start, see Hauerwas (1994).

3. I recognize that G. A. Cohen has contended that Nozick posed more of a
   problem for Marxists than he did for traditional welfare state liberals,
   mainly because the Marxian imagery of the capitalist seizing the surplus
   value created by the worker is similar to the Lockean–Nozickian view of
   property rights. See Cohen (1995), especially chs. 1 and 6. My point here
   is simply that, as a matter of persuasion (as opposed to setting up a technical problem for philosophers to solve), Nozick's account of Marxism is extraordinarily sketchy. He cites only Marx and Ernest Mandel as representatives of the socialist view, and does so very briefly. I agree with Alasdair
   MacIntyre (1984) that Marxists and classical liberals such as Nozick share
   a common set of problems that stem from their refusal to engage the Aristotelian and Thomist traditions.

4. For a fascinating study of the ideological function of the exemplum, see
   Lyons (1989). Lyons observes that example is often labeled as such. Texts
   do not announce, here is a metaphor, but they *do* say "for example . . . "

   > Yet once the text has advertised an example, the complexity, not to say trick-
   > iness, of the relationships established is often completely unperceived by the
   > reader. Perhaps this is because example is so central to systems of belief that
   > we occasionally think of it as the direct manifestation of reality when, in fact,
   > example is a way of taking our beliefs about reality and reframing them into
   > something that suits the direction of a text. Example may therefore qualify as
   > the most ideological of figures, in the sense of being the figure that is most in-

timately bound to a representation of the world and that most serves as a veil for the mechanics of that representation. (ix)

CHAPTER FIVE

1. In structural-Marxist terms, one would say that an ideology "interpellates" or "hails" a certain kind of "subject." See Althusser (1984: 49). I discuss Althusser in more detail in Aune (1994: 108–112).
2. See Ludwig von Mises (1949). Mises makes an interesting comment in the introduction: " It must be emphasized that the destiny of modern civilization as developed by the white peoples in the last two hundred years is inseparably linked with the fate of economic science" (10). Mises is the favorite economist of the far right. The copy of *Human Action* I checked out from the Texas A&M University Library was donated to the university by a segregationist group in Dallas.
3. To my knowledge, Rothbard does not address Aristotle's notorious concept of the "natural slave" (*Politics* 1254a). A strong sense of property rights and individual liberty can be consistent with the practice of slavery. The trick, as with Aristotle or southern slave owners, is to define the human nature of one's slave (or one's women) away.
4. To trace affiliations, simply explore the Internet links among Samuel Francis, fired from the conservative *Washington Times* for affiliation with racist groups (http://www.samfrancis.net); Joseph Sobran—who left *National Review* after allegations of antisemitism (http://www.sobran.com); American Renaissance, an organization opposing immigration and devoted to the promotion of "scientific" racism (http://www.amren.org); the Mises Institute at Auburn University (http://www.mises.org); and the Committee on Documentation of the Holocaust (CODOH), a Holocaust revisionist website that includes an article by Rothbard on "the importance of revisionism for our time" (http://www.codoh.com).
5. Rothbard was an activist against the Vietnam War. His writings on foreign policy are indistinguishable from those of Noam Chomsky. See Ronald Radosh (1975) on the old right–new left coalition against the Vietnam War.
6. See the League's website (http://www.dixienet.org) for a number of interesting documents, including the *Dixie Manifesto*. The League strongly distances itself from white supremacist movements, although the interrelationships among members of the Mises Institute, American Renaissance, and some Holocaust revisionists make one skeptical.
7. At least *Forbes* magazine is honest about these things—see Huber (1996); the globalization of capital means that governments cannot "ignore eco-

nomic realities" when providing welfare, since it is comparatively easy for business to pick up and leave heavily taxed communities.

8. See Peterson (1995: 109–114). Peterson is no "liberal" ideologue; he is a strong supporter of vouchers and of returning many economic functions to state and local government.

CHAPTER SIX

1. For an exception, see Hall (1988). One significant limitation of my analysis in this volume is the neglect of free-market arguments in other countries, especially the United Kingdom. Arguably, though, British Prime Minister Tony Blair's successful use of U.S. public relations techniques and his attempt to articulate a "third way" between libertarianism and communism represents a corrective to the left's antirhetorical stance. Whether it remains meaningful to speak of Blair (much less Clinton) as a true member of the left is, of course, another question.

2. For a recent extension of the notion, see Campbell (1998). Jamieson uses the term "effeminate," while Campbell prefers "feminine."

3. As in my discussion of Rand in Chapter 3, I rely here on Jameson's notion of the narrative form as a system for the resolution of contradictions: "Any 'story,' whether literary or philosophical, can be described as a narrative system of characters or agents" that is then transformed into "an exchange mechanism by which some final illusion of harmony, some final 'imaginary' solution of the contradiction it articulates, can be generated" (Jameson 1979: 99).

4. The following historical narrative draws on *The New York Times*, July 2, 1988, I:1:6; July 7, IV:13:1; July 12, I:24:1; July 14, I:1:1, and IV:1:3; on the Bush campaign, see July 27, I:1:1 and August 2, II:4:3.

5. I have constructed this narrative from a number of sources on the Internet and from my own collection of far-right documents. For Mullins's website, see http://home.increach.com/dov/mullins.htm; for the best site on antisemitic groups, see http://www2.ca.nizkor.org; for overviews of antisemitic conspiracy theories, see the site of the indispensable Political Research Associates: http://www.publiceye.org. A particularly good book on the subject is Ridgeway (1991).

6. To be fair—although the hedging seems such a consistent part of Robertson's overall strategy—he says later: "I know George Bush. I have met with him in the White House, and I personally believe that President Bush is an honorable man and a man of integrity. Nevertheless, I believe that he has become convinced, as Woodrow Wilson was before him, of the idealistic possibilities of a world at peace under the benign leadership of a forum for all nations" (92).

7. "Novus ordo seclorum" is a line from Virgil's "Fourth Eclogue," previously believed by Christians to have foretold the birth of Jesus.
8. Buchanan develops the themes of globalism and elite betrayal in his *A Republic, Not an Empire* (1999). He constructs a revisionist history of World War II, trying to rehabilitate the isolationist ideology of Charles Lindbergh and the "America First" movement's opposition to the war. As I write, Buchanan's peculiar vision of U.S. history is being widely discussed in the press for the first time; see, for example, the discussion of the book in the neoconservative *The Weekly Standard*, September 27, 1999. First, editor William Kristol compares Buchanan to (of all people) Henry Wallace ("Pat the Bunny" 9); then Robert G. Kaufman analyzes Buchanan's historical claims ("Wrong from the Beginning: Pat Buchanan as Historian" 29). Kaufman discusses Buchanan's recent proposal to adopt a maximum quota system for Jews and Asians at elite universities, thus effectively implementing "affirmative action" for "European-Americans."

CHAPTER SEVEN

1. Newt Gingrich, "Speech given to the Washington Research Group: 11 November 1994." Online. Internet. 15 April 1997. Available at http://dolphin.gulf.net/Gingrich.html. For a more extended discussion, see Gingrich (1995), especially 51–62: "America and the Third Wave Information Age."
2. For a different take on the politics of cyberpunk, see Goodwin and Rogers (1997). They discuss the role of the cyberpunk dystopias in influencing Clinton administration rhetoric about the National Information Superstructure (54). They also contend that the purpose of cyberpunk is to "cast doubt on the extravagant promises of the 'neoliberal' thesis of their time" (49), namely, that technology plus an unfettered market will create utopia.

CONCLUSION

1. For an accessible introduction to derivatives and other current financial issues, see Martin Mayer (1998), especially ch. 10.
2. A "hedge" fund is simply a mutual fund that accepts 499 or fewer rich investors. Long-Term Capital accepted no investment under $10 million. James K. Galbraith (1998b) describes hedging as like "making money on a rounding error: you only earn a little on each sale, but make up for it with volume." See also "Riding for a Fall," *Newsweek* (1998). The funds have had no government regulation, because firms under 500 investors are exempt; see Ivins (1998).

3. See "Riding for a Fall," *Newsweek* (1998) for comments by Volcker and Tisch; see http://www.mises.org (downloaded 9/25/98) for Rockwell's comments.

APPENDIX

1. What I mean is that, for better or for worse, the tradition of rhetorical inquiry in Western culture is heavily invested in the notion that human agents are capable of using language effectively to alter their political and social environments. Postmodernists are skeptical about the very notion of human agency. A. W. Coats (1988) makes an interesting distinction between two different attitudes toward discourse: *Anglo-Saxon*, in which "discourse is epiphenomenal and clearly distinguishable from actual scientific practice"; and *French*, in which discourse is constitutive of action and the distinction between language and action can be dissolved (66). Coats opts for "the so-called Anglo-Saxon approach . . . , according to which there is a clear and essential distinction between content and discourse (or form), although the interrelationships between these elements are subtle, varied, and changing over time" (78). I confess to sympathy for the Anglo-Saxon approach.

2. For a thorough discussion of the physics metaphors in economics, see Mirowski (1989). See also Goodwin's (1988) essay in *Consequences* (207–220). Goodwin identifies three personae assumed by economists: scholar (philosopher), practitioner (priest), and interpreter (hired gun) (209). Alfred Kahn moved from philosopher (microeconomist at Cornell), to priest (member of the Civil Aeronautics Board), to hired gun (economic consultant to regulated industries) (210). Goodwin notes that after the Marginal Revolution of the 1870s (when the theory of marginal utility replaced the labor theory of value) the virtues of free trade were mainly explained with terminology borrowed from physics and engineering: the market economy as a "system" wherein "forces" led to "outcomes" in equilibrium. Money was treated as the "wheel" or "lubricant" of commerce and traveled through the system at a certain velocity. Alfred Marshall depicted the economy as a battleship, the ultimate engineering accomplishment of his day (211). He also makes the interesting observation, "When attempting to persuade laypersons, economists abandon to some degree the physical and mechanical metaphors they employ so widely in their own research and either pick the forbidden fruit of biology and medicine or move into realms one might think they were well equipped to understand, such as the analysis of human conflict" (218).

3. In classical rhetoric, a topos is a "place" for locating arguments, or, in Richard Lanham's happy comparison, that repository of ways of making and framing arguments that the skilled rhetor carries around as if on a computer clipboard, ready to be cut and pasted at the appropriate moment.

4. Booth defines "motivism" this way: "What we call reasons can always be seen through as rationalizations or superstructures or disguises or wishful thinking: our minds are really determined, in all of our values, either by nonrational conditioning in the past, or by present motives or drives, many of them lying so deep that we can never find them out" (24).

5. "America Goes Bust" (1998: 78). The only studies that show abuse of bankruptcy laws have been funded by credit card companies (see Warren 1998). Both houses of Congress have voted to tighten bankruptcy restrictions, after heavy lobbying by credit card companies, but the final version of the bill has not yet been passed (see Caher 2000: 5).

References

$1 Billion for Ideas: Conservative Think Tanks in the 1990s. 1999. Washington, DC: National Committee for Responsive Philanthropy.

Ackerman, Bruce. 1991. *We the People: Foundations.* Cambridge, MA: Harvard University Press.

Alston, William. 1993. "American Farming: If It's Broke, Why Can't We Fix It?" In Donald N. McCloskey, ed., *Second Thoughts: Myths and Morals of U.S. Economic History.* New York: Oxford University Press. 50–56.

Althusser, Louis. 1984. "Ideology and Ideological State Apparatuses." In *Essays on Ideology.* London: Verso. 1–60.

Amariglio, Jack. 1988. "The Body, Economic Discourse, and Power: An Economist's Introduction to Foucault." *History of Political Economy* 20: 583–613.

Amariglio, Jack, Stephen Resnick, and Richard Wolff. 1990. "Division and Difference in the 'Discipline' of Economics." *Critical Inquiry* 17: 108–137.

"America Goes Bust." 1998. *The Economist,* July 4: 78

Amsden, Alice. 1993. "From P.C. to E.C." *The New York Times,* January 12: A15.

Aronowitz, Stanley, and William DiFazio. 1994. *The Jobless Future: Sci-Tech and the Dogma of Work.* Minneapolis: University of Minnesota Press.

Arrow, Joseph Kenneth. 1951. *Social Choice and Individual Values.* New York: Wiley.

Aune, James Arnt. 1994. *Rhetoric and Marxism.* Boulder, CO: Westview.

Aune, James Arnt. 1996. "Reinhold Niebuhr and the Rhetoric of Christian Realism." In Francis A. Beer and Robert Hariman, eds., *Post-Realism: The Rhetorical Turn in International Relations.* East Lansing: Michigan State University Press. 75–93.

Bailyn, Bernard. 1967. *The Ideological Origins of the American Revolution*. Cambridge, MA: Harvard University Press.

Bazerman, Charles. 1993. "Money Talks: The Rhetorical Project of *The Wealth of Nations*." In Willie Henderson, Tony Dudley-Evans, and Roger Backhouse, eds., *Economics and Language*. London: Routledge. 173–199.

Becker, Gary S. 1976. *The Economic Approach to Human Behavior*. Chicago: University of Chicago Press.

Becker, Gary S., and George Stigler. 1996. "De Gustibus Non Est Disputandum." In Gary S. Becker, *Accounting for Tastes*. Cambridge, MA: Harvard University Press. 24–49.

Bedau, Hugo Adam. 1982. *The Death Penalty in America*. New York: Oxford University Press.

Beer, Francis A., and Robert Hariman. Eds. 1996a. *Post-Realism: The Rhetorical Turn in International Relations*. East Lansing: Michigan State University Press.

Beer, Francis A., and Robert Hariman. 1996b. "Realism and Rhetoric in International Relations." In Francis A. Beer and Robert Hariman, eds., *Post-Realism: The Rhetorical Turn in International Relations*. East Lansing: Michigan State University Press. 1–30.

Bell, Daniel. 1976. *The Cultural Contradictions of Capitalism*. New York: Basic Books.

Berger, Peter L., and Richard John Neuhaus. 1977. *To Empower People: The Role of Mediating Structures in Social Policy*. Washington, DC: American Enterprise Institute.

Black, Edwin. 1970. "The Second Persona." *Quarterly Journal of Speech* 56: 109–119.

Black, Edwin. 1992. "The Sentimental Style as Escapism." In *Rhetorical Questions: Studies of Public Discourse*. Chicago: University of Chicago Press. 97–112.

Black, F., and M. Scholes. 1973. "The Pricing of Options and Corporate Liabilities." *Journal of Political Economy* 81: 637–654.

The Book of Common Prayer. 1948. Greenwich, CT: Seabury Press.

Booth, Wayne. 1974. *Modern Dogma and the Rhetoric of Assent*. Notre Dame, IN: University of Notre Dame Press.

Borsook, Paulina. 2000. *Cyberselfish: A Critical Romp Through the Terribly Libertarian Culture of High Tech*. New York: Public Affairs Press.

Brande, David. 1996. "The Business of Cyberpunk: Symbolic Economy and Ideology in William Gibson." In Robert Markley, ed., *Virtual Realities and Their Discontents*. Baltimore: Johns Hopkins University Press. 79–106.

Branden, Barbara. 1986. *The Passion of Ayn Rand*. Garden City, New York: Doubleday.

Branden, Nathaniel. 1989. *Judgment Day: My Years with Ayn Rand*. Boston: Houghton Mifflin.

Branden, Nathaniel. 1994. *The Six Pillars of Self-Esteem*. New York: Bantam Books.

Brimelow, Peter. 1996. *Alien Nation: Common Sense About America's Immigration Disaster*. New York: Harper Perennial.

Buchanan, James M., and Roger D. Congleton. 1998. *Politics by Principle, Not Interest: Toward Nondiscriminatory Democracy*. Cambridge, UK: Cambridge University Press.

Buchanan, James M., Robert D. Tollison, and Gordon Tullock, eds. 1980. *Toward a Theory of the Rent-Seeking Society*. College Station: Texas A&M University Press.

Buchanan, James M., and Gordon Tullock. 1962. *The Calculus of Consent: Logical Foundations of Constitutional Democracy*. Ann Arbor: University of Michigan Press.

Buchanan, Patrick J. 1998. *The Great Betrayal: How American Sovereignty and Social Justice Are Being Sacrificed to the Gods of the Global Economy*. Boston: Little, Brown.

Buchanan, Patrick J. 1999. *A Republic, Not an Empire: Reclaiming America's Destiny*. Washington, DC: Regnery.

Buckley, Jr., William F. 1988a. "On the Right." *National Review*, August 19: 61

Buckley, Jr., William F. 1988b. "On the Right." *National Review*, September 16: 64.

Buckley, Jr., William F. 1995. "Murray Rothbard RIP." *National Review*, February 6: 19–20.

Burke, Kenneth. 1966. *Language as Symbolic Action*. Berkeley: University of California Press.

Burke, Kenneth. 1968. *Counter-Statement*. Berkeley: University of California Press.

Burke, Kenneth. 1969. *A Grammar of Motives*. Berkeley: University of California Press.

Caher, John. 2000. "Bankruptcy Reform." *New York Law Journal*, June 1: 5.

Cairns, John W. 1991. "Rhetoric, Language, and Roman Law: Legal Education and Improvement in Eighteenth-Century Scotland." *Law and History Review* 9: 30–58.

Campbell, Karlyn Kohrs. 1998. "The Discursive Performance of Femininity: Hating Hillary." *Rhetoric and Public Affairs* 1, 1: 1–19.

Card, David, and Alan B. Krueger. 1995. *Myth and Measurement: The New Economics of the Minimum Wage*. Princeton, NJ: Princeton University Press.

Chambers, Whittaker. 1990. Review of *Atlas Shrugged*. *National Review*, November 5: 120–122; originally published 1957.

Coase, R. H. 1960. "The Problem of Social Cost." *Journal of Law and Economics* 3: 1–44.

Coats, A. W. 1988. "Economic Rhetoric: The Social and Historical Context." In Arjo Klamer, Donald N. McCloskey, and Robert M. Solow, eds., *Consequences of Economic Rhetoric*. New York: Cambridge University Press. 64–84.

Cohen, G. A. 1978. *Marx's Theory of History: A Defence*. Princeton, NJ: Princeton University Press.

Cohen, G. A. 1995. *Self-Ownership, Freedom, and Equality*. Cambridge, UK: Cambridge University Press.

Cohen, David. 1997. "Pseuds in a Corner." *The Guardian*, May 27, Higher Education Supplement: 2.

Colander, David. 1995. *Economics*. 2nd ed. Chicago: Irwin.

Conti, Delia. 1998. *Reconciling Free Trade, Fair Trade, and Interdependence*. New York: Praeger.

Coryman, Marjorie. 1996. "Who Should Decide on a Minimum Wage Hike?" *Restaurant Business*, March 20: 16.

"The Crunch Comes for Welfare Reform." 1999. *The Economist*, March 20: 29.

Cultural Conservatism: Toward a National Agenda. 1988. Washington, DC: Institute for Cultural Conservatism/Free Congress Research and Educational Foundation.

De Quincey, Thomas. 1950. *The Confessions of an English Opium-Eater*. New York: Heritage Press; originally published 1866.

De Quincey, Thomas. 1968. *The Collected Writings of De Quincey*, ed. David Masson, Vol. 9: *Political Economy and Politics*. Edinburgh: Adam and Charles Black; originally published 1890.

Diamond, Sara. 1995. *Roads to Dominion: Right-Wing Movements and Political Power in the United States*. New York: Guilford Press.

Disraeli, Benjamin. 1980. *Sybil: Or, The Two Nations*. Harmondsworth, UK: Penguin.

Downs, Anthony. 1957. *An Economic Theory of Democracy*. New York: Harper & Row.

Dworkin, Ronald. 1977. *Taking Rights Seriously*. Cambridge, MA: Harvard University Press.

Ehninger, Douglas. 1970. "Argument as Method: Its Nature, Its Limitations, and Its Uses." *Speech Monographs* 37: 101–110.

Ehrenreich, Barbara. 1989. *Fear of Falling: The Inner Life of the Middle Class*. New York: Pantheon.

Ehrlich, Isaac. 1975. "The Deterrent Effect of Capital Punishment." *American Economic Review* 65: 397–417.

Ellis, Richard E. 1971. *The Jeffersonian Crisis: Courts and Politics in the Young Republic*. New York: Knopf.

Elster, Jon. 1985. *Making Sense of Marx*. Cambridge, UK: Cambridge University Press.

Epstein, Richard. 1995. *Simple Rules for a Complex World*. Cambridge, MA: Harvard University Press.

Epstein, Richard A. 1997. *Mortal Peril: Our Inalienable Right to Health Care?* Reading, MA: Addison-Wesley.

Fallon, Jr., Richard H. 1989. "What Is Republicanism and Is It Worth Reviving?" *Harvard Law Review* 102: 1695–1735.

Farber, Daniel A., and Philip P. Frickey. 1991. *Law and Public Choice: A Critical Introduction*. Chicago: University of Chicago Press.

Fish, Stanley. 1988. "Comments from Outside Economics." In Arjo Klamer, Donald N. McCloskey, and Robert M. Solow, eds., *Consequences of Economic Rhetoric*. New York: Cambridge University Press. 21–31.

Folbre, Nancy, and Heidi Hartmann. 1988. "The Rhetoric of Self-Interest: Ideology and Gender in Economic Theory." In Arjo Klamer, Donald N. McCloskey, and Robert M. Solow, eds., *Consequences of Economic Rhetoric*. New York: Cambridge University Press. 184–206.

Francis, Samuel. 1995. "The Legacy of Murray Rothbard." *The Washington Times*, January 16: A30.

Freeman, Richard B., and James L. Medoff. 1984. *What Do Unions Do?* New York: Basic Books.

Friedman, Milton. 1968. "The Role of Monetary Policy." *American Economic Review*, March: 1–17.

Friedman, Milton. 1982. *Capitalism and Freedom*. 2nd ed. Chicago: University of Chicago Press.

Friedman, Milton, and Rose Friedman. 1980. *Free to Choose: A Personal Statement*. New York: Harcourt Brace Jovanovich.

Gadamer, Hans-Georg. 1975. *Truth and Method*, tr. Garrett Barden and John Cumming. London: Sheed & Ward.

Galbraith, James K. 1998a. *Created Unequal: The Crisis in American Pay*. New York: Free Press.

Galbraith, James K. 1998b. "The Sorcerer's Apprentice." *Texas Observer*, October 9: 20.

Geoghegan, Thomas. 1992. *Which Side Are You On? Trying to Be for Labor When It's Flat on Its Back*. New York: Penguin Books.

George, David. 1990. "The Rhetoric of Economics Texts." *Journal of Economic Issues* 24: 861–878.

Gilder, George. 1994. *Life after Television: The Coming Transformation of Media and American Life*. Rev. ed. New York: Norton.

Gibson, William, and Bruce Sterling. 1991. *The Difference Engine*. New York: Bantam Books.

Gibson, William. 1984. *Neuromancer*. New York: Ace Books.

Gingrich, Newt. 1994. "Speech given to the Washington Research Group: 11 November 1994." Online. 15 April 1997. Available: http://dolphin.gulf. net/Gingrich.html.

Gingrich, Newt. 1995. *To Renew America*. New York: HarperCollins.

Gladstein, Mimi. 1984. *The Ayn Rand Companion*. Westport, CT: Greenwood Press.

Glendon, Mary Ann. 1994. *A Nation Under Lawyers: How the Crisis in the Legal Profession Is Transforming American Society*. New York: Farrar, Straus, and Giroux.

Glendon, Mary Ann, and David Blankenhorn. Eds. 1995. *Seedbeds of Virtue: Sources of Competence, Character, and Citizenship*. Lanham, MD: Madison Books.

Goodwin, Craufurd D. 1988. "The Heterogeneity of the Economists' Discourse." In Arjo Klamer, Donald N. McCloskey, and Robert M. Solow, eds., *Consequences of Economic Rhetoric*. New York: Cambridge University Press. 207–220.

Goodwin, Craufurd D., and Alex Rogers. 1997. "Cyberpunk and Chicago." In James P. Henderson, ed., *The State of the History of Economics*. London: Routledge. 39–55.

Gottfried, Paul, and Thomas Fleming. 1988. *The Conservative Movement*. Boston: Twayne.

Gouldner, Alvin W. 1985. *Against Fragmentation: The Origins of Marxism and the Sociology of Intellectuals*. New York: Oxford University Press.

Greeley, Andrew. 1976. *The Communal Catholic: A Personal Manifesto*. New York: Seabury.

Green, Donald P., and Ian Shapiro. 1994. *Pathologies of Rational Choice Theory: A Critique of Applications in Political Science*. New Haven, CT: Yale University Press.

Greenblatt, Stephen. 1988. *Shakespearean Negotiations: The Circulation of Social Energy in Renaissance England*. Berkeley: University of California Press.

Greve, Michael S. 1999. *Real Federalism: Why It Matters, How It Could Happen*. Washington, DC: American Enterprise Institute Press.

Griffin, G. Edward. 1995. *The Creature from Jekyll Island*. 2nd ed. Westlake Village, CA: American Media.

Habermas, Jürgen. 1979. *Communication and the Evolution of Society*, tr. Thomas McCarthy. Boston: Beacon Press.

Habermas, Jürgen. 1984 and 1987. *The Theory of Communicative Action*, Vols. I and II, tr. Thomas McCarthy. Boston: Beacon Press.

Habermas, Jürgen. 1991. "What Does Socialism Mean Today? The Revolutions of Recuperation and the Need for New Thinking." In Robin Blackburn, ed., *After the Fall: The Failure of Communism and the Future of Socialism.* London: Verso. 25–46.

Hall, Stuart. 1988. "The Toad in the Garden: Thatcherism among the Theorists." In Cary Nelson and Lawrence Grossberg, eds., *Marxism and the Interpretation of Culture.* Urbana: University of Illinois Press. 35–74.

Hariman, Robert. 1995. *Political Style: The Artistry of Power.* Chicago: University of Chicago Press.

Hariman, Robert. 1996. "Henry Kissinger: Realism's Rational Actor." In Beer and Hariman, *Post-Realism.* 35–53.

Harrison, Bennett, and Barry Bluestone. 1991. *The Great U-Turn: Corporate Restructuring and the Polarizing of America.* New York: Basic Books.

Harvey, David. 1990. *The Condition of Postmodernity: An Inquiry Into the Origins of Cultural Change.* Oxford: Blackwell.

Hauerwas, Stanley. 1994. "The Church and the Mentally Handicapped: A Continuing Challenge to the Imagination." In *Dispatches from the Front: Theological Engagements with the Secular.* Durham, NC: Duke University Press. 177–186.

Haworth, Alan. 1994. *Anti-Libertarianism: Markets, Philosophy, and Myth.* London: Routledge.

Hayek, Friedrich. 1944. *The Road to Serfdom.* Chicago: University of Chicago Press.

Hayek, Friedrich. 1960. *The Constitution of Liberty.* Chicago: University of Chicago Press.

Hegel, G. W. F. 1967. *The Phenomenology of Mind,* tr. J. B. Baillie. New York: Harper & Row.

Heilbroner, Robert. 1988. "Rhetoric and Ideology." In Arjo Klamer, Donald N. McCloskey, and Robert M. Solow, eds., *Consequences of Economic Rhetoric.* New York: Cambridge University Press. 38–46.

Heinrichs, Jay. "How Harvard Destroyed Rhetoric." *Harvard Magazine,* July–August 1995, 37–42.

Hempel, Carl, G. 1965. *Aspects of Scientific Explanation.* New York: Free Press.

Henning, Douglas. 1998. *Wall Street.* 2nd ed. London: Verso.

Herrnstein, Richard J., and Charles Murray. 1994. *The Bell Curve: Intelligence and Class Structure in American Life.* New York: Free Press.

Hirschman, Albert O. 1970. *Exit, Voice, and Loyalty: Responses to Decline in Firms, Organizations, and States.* Cambridge, MA: Harvard University Press.

Hirschman, Albert O. 1991. *The Rhetoric of Reaction: Perversity, Futility, Jeopardy.* Cambridge, MA: Belknap Press.

Hogan, J. Michael. 1986. *The Panama Canal in American Politics: Domestic Advocacy and the Evolution of Policy.* Carbondale, IL: Southern Illinois University Press.

Horwitz, Morton J. 1977. *The Transformation of American Law, 1780–1860*. New York: Oxford University Press.

Huber, Peter. 1996. "Cyber-Power." *Forbes*, December 2: 142–147.

Ivins, Molly. 1998. "Helping the Rich, Punishing the Rest." *Bryan-College Station Eagle*, September 30: A10.

Jameson, Fredric. 1979. *Wyndham Lewis, The Modernist as Fascist*. Berkeley: University of California Press.

Jameson, Fredric. 1981. *The Political Unconscious: Narrative as a Socially Symbolic Act*. Ithaca, NY: Cornell University Press.

Jameson, Fredric. 1991. *Postmodernism, Or The Cultural Logic of Late Capitalism*. Durham, NC: Duke University Press.

Jamieson, Kathleen Hall. 1988. *Eloquence in an Electronic Age: The Transformation of Political Speechmaking*. New York: Oxford University Press.

Johnstone, Henry L. 1966. "The Relevance of Rhetoric and Philosophy and Rhetoric." *Quarterly Journal of Speech* 52: 41–46.

Kant, Immanuel. 1951. *Critique of Judgment*, tr. J. H. Bernard. New York: Macmillan.

Kaufman, Robert G. 1999. "Wrong from the Beginning: Pat Buchanan as Historian." *The Weekly Standard*, September 27: 29.

Kenney, Tom. 1995. " 'Business as Usual' Shouldn't Include Politics." *Nation's Restaurant News*, June 19: 28.

Kiewe, Amos, and Davis Houck. 1991. *A Shining City on a Hill: Ronald Reagan's Economic Rhetoric, 1951–1989*. New York: Praeger.

Kirk, Russell. 1989. "A Conservative Program for a Kinder, Gentler America." Heritage Foundation lecture, April 27 (Lecture #198).

Klamer, Arjo, and Donald N. McCloskey. 1988. "Economics in the Human Conversation." In Arjo Klamer, Donald N. McCloskey, and Robert M. Solow, eds., *Consequences of Economic Rhetoric*. New York: Cambridge University Press. 3–20.

Klamer, Arjo, Donald N. McCloskey, and Robert M. Solow, eds. 1988. *Consequences of Economic Rhetoric*. New York: Cambridge University Press.

Kramnick, Isaac. 1988. "The 'Great National Discussion': The Discourse of Politics in 1787." *William and Mary Quarterly* 45: 3–32.

Kristol, William. 1999. "Pat the Bunny." *The Weekly Standard*, September 27: 9.

Krugman, Paul. 1994. *Peddling Prosperity: Economic Sense and Nonsense in the Age of Diminished Expectations*. New York: Norton.

Lampe, Gregory P. 1998. *Frederick Douglass, Freedom's Voice, 1818–1845*. East Lansing: Michigan State University Press.

Lasch, Christopher. 1995. *The Revolt of the Elites and the Betrayal of Democracy*. New York: Norton.

Levy, Steven. 1984. *Hackers*. Garden City, NY: Anchor Press/Doubleday.

Lewis, William F. 1987. "Telling America's Story: Narrative Form and the Reagan Presidency." *Quarterly Journal of Speech* 73: 267–279.

Liebowitz, S. J., and Stephen E. Margolis. 1990. "The Fable of the Keys." *Journal of Law and Economics* 31, 1: 1–25.

Lind, Michael. 1996. "No Enemies to the Right: The Pat Robertson Scandal and What It Means." In *Up from Conservatism*. New York: Free Press. 97–120.

Lynd, Staughton P. 1982. *The Fight against Closings: Youngstown's Steel Mill Closings*. San Pedro, CA: Singlejack Books.

Lyons, David. 1989. *Exemplum: The Rhetoric of Example in Early Modern France and Italy*. Princeton, NJ: Princeton University Press.

Macdonald, Andrew. 1980. *The Turner Diaries*. Washington, DC: National Alliance.

MacIntyre, Alasdair. 1984. *After Virtue*. 2nd ed. Notre Dame, IN: University of Notre Dame Press.

"A Man of Flint." 1998. *The Economist*, June 20: 79.

Mandeville, Bernard. 1729. *The Fable of the Bees*. London: J. Roberts.

Marshall, Alfred. 1997. *Principles of Economics*. 8th ed. Buffalo, NY: Prometheus Books; originally published 1920.

Marx, Karl. 1988. *The Communist Manifesto*, ed. Frederic L. Bender. New York: Norton; originally published 1848.

Mayer, Martin. 1998. *The Bankers: The Next Generation*. New York: Truman Talley Books/Plume.

McCloskey, Deirdre N. 1997. *The Vices of Economists, the Virtues of the Bourgeoisie*. Amsterdam: University of Amsterdam Press.

McCloskey, Deirdre N. 1998. *The Rhetoric of Economics*. 2nd ed. Madison: University of Wisconsin Press.

McCloskey, Donald N. 1983. "The Rhetoric of Economics." *Journal of Economic Literature* 31: 434–461.

McCloskey, Donald N. 1984. "The Literary Character of Economics." *Daedalus*, Summer: 97–119.

McCloskey, Donald N. 1985. *The Rhetoric of Economics*. Madison: University of Wisconsin Press.

McCloskey, Donald N. 1988a. "The Consequences of Rhetoric." In Arjo Klamer, Donald N. McCloskey, and Robert M. Solow, eds., *Consequences of Economic Rhetoric*. New York: Cambridge University Press. 280–294.

McCloskey, Donald N. 1988a. "The Rhetoric of Law and Economics." *Michigan Law Review* 86: 752–767.

McCloskey, Donald N. 1990. *If You're So Smart: The Narrative of Economic Expertise*. Chicago: University of Chicago Press.

McCloskey, Donald N. 1991. "The Essential Rhetoric of Law, Literature, and Liberty." *Critical Review* 5: 209.

McCloskey, Donald N. 1994a. "Bourgeois Virtue." *The American Scholar*, Spring: 177–191.

McCloskey, Donald N. 1994b. *Knowledge and Persuasion in Economics*. Cambridge, UK: Cambridge University Press.

McGee, Michael Calvin. 1980. "The 'Ideograph': A Link Between Rhetoric and Ideology." *Quarterly Journal of Speech* 66: 1–16.

Mirowski, Philip. 1988. "Shall I Compare Thee to a Minkowski-Ricardo-Leontief-Metzler Matrix of the Mosak-Hicks Type?" In Arjo Klamer, Donald N. McCloskey, and Robert M. Solow, eds., *Consequences of Economic Rhetoric*. New York: Cambridge University Press. 117–145.

Mirowski, Philip. 1989. *More Heat than Light: Economics as Social Physics, Physics as Nature's Economics*. Cambridge, UK: Cambridge University Press.

Moore, Mark P. 1993. "Constructing Irreconcilable Conflict: The Function of Synecdoche in the Spotted Owl Controversy." *Communication Monographs* 60: 258–274.

Moving a Public Policy Agenda: The Strategic Philanthropy of Conservative Foundations. 1997. Washington, DC: National Committee for Responsive Philanthropy.

Muller, Jerry Z. 1993. *Adam Smith in His Time and Hours: Designing the Decent Society*. Princeton, NJ: Princeton University Press.

Mullins, Eustace. 2000. *Jews Mass Poison American Children*. Online. Available: http://increach.com/dov/mullins.htm

Murray, Charles. 1994. *Losing Ground: American Social Policy, 1950–1980*. 10th anniversary edition. New York: Basic Books.

Murray, Charles. 1997. *What It Means to Be a Libertarian*. New York: Broadway Books.

Nash, George. 1976. *The Conservative Intellectual Movement in America*. New York: Basic Books.

Negroponte, Nicholas. 1995. *Being Digital*. New York: Knopf.

Nelson, John S. 1989. "Political Mythmaking for Post-Moderns." In Bruce E. Gronbeck, ed., *Spheres of Argument*. Annandale, VA: Speech Communication Association. 175–183.

Newman, Roger K. 1994. *Hugo Black: A Biography*. New York: Pantheon.

Niskanen, William A. 1995. "More on the Minimum Wage." *Regulation* 18: 9–11.

Noble, David. 1977. *America By Design: Science, Technology, and the Rise of Corporate Capitalism*. New York: Knopf.

Norquist, Grover. 1996. "Republicans and Democrats." *The American Enterprise*, January–February: 24.

Norton, Rob. 1996. "The Minimum Wage Is Unfair." *Fortune*, May 27: 53.

"Novelist Ayn Rand." 1998. *Investor's Business Daily*, June 25: A1.

Nozar, Robert A. 1996. "Don't Bump the Minimum Wage—Dump It." *Hotel and Motel Management*, June 3: 12.

Nozick, Robert. 1974. *Anarchy, State, and Utopia*. New York: Free Press.

Nozick, Robert. 1981. "On the Randian Argument." In Jeffrey Paul, ed., *Reading Nozick: Essays on Anarchy, State, and Utopia*. Totowa, NJ: Rowman & Littlefield. 206–231.

Oakeshott, Michael. 1962. *Rationalism in Politics and Other Essays*. London: Methuen.

Olson, Mancur. 1971. *The Logic of Collective Action: Public Goods and the Theory of Groups*. Cambridge, MA: Harvard University Press.

"An Opening Through Closing." 1988. *National Review*, August 5: 18.

Paget, Karen M. 1998. "Lessons of Right Wing Philanthropy." *The American Prospect* 40: 90.

Perelman, Chaim. 1982. *The Realm of Rhetoric*. Notre Dame, IN: University of Notre Dame Press.

Perelman, Chaim, and L. Olbrechts-Tyteca. 1969. *The New Rhetoric: A Treatise on Argumentation*, tr. John Wilkinson. Notre Dame, IN: University of Notre Dame Press.

Peterson, Paul E. 1995. *The Price of Federalism*. Washington, DC: Brookings Institution.

Phillips, Kevin. 1990. *The Politics of Rich and Poor: Wealth and the American Electorate in the Reagan Aftermath*. New York: Random House.

"Plant-Closing Bill." 1988. *The American Spectator*, July: 29–30.

Pocock, J. G. A. 1975. *The Machiavellian Moment: Florentine Political Thought and the Atlantic Republican Tradition*. Princeton, NJ: Princeton University Press.

Polanyi, Livia. 1997. "Interview with Deirdre McCloskey." *Challenge* 40, 1 (January–February): 16–29.

Pollak, Richard A. 1997. *The Creation of Dr. B: A Biography of Bruno Bettelheim*. New York: Simon and Schuster.

Posner, Richard A. 1981. *The Economics of Justice*. Cambridge, MA: Harvard University Press.

Posner, Richard A. 1988. *Law and Literature: A Misunderstood Relation*. Cambridge, MA: Harvard University Press.

Posner, Richard A. 1990a. *Cardozo: A Study in Reputation*. Chicago: University of Chicago Press.

Posner, Richard A. 1990b. *The Problems of Jurisprudence*. Cambridge, MA: Harvard University Press.

Posner, Richard A. 1992a. *The Economic Analysis of Law*. 4th ed. Boston: Little, Brown.

Posner, Richard A. 1992b. *The Essential Holmes*. Chicago: University of Chicago Press.

Posner, Richard A. 1995. "Rhetoric, Legal Advocacy, and Legal Reasoning." In *Overcoming Law*. Cambridge, MA: Harvard University Press. 498–530.

Posner, Richard A. 1999. *The Problematics of Moral and Legal Theory*. Cambridge, MA: Belknap Press of Harvard University Press.

Quigley, Carroll. 1966. *Tragedy and Hope: A History of the World in Our Own Time*. New York: Macmillan.

Quigley, Carroll. 1981. *The Anglo-American Establishment: From Rhodes to Cliveden*. New York: Books in Focus.

Radosh, Ronald. 1975. *Prophets on the Right: Profiles of Conservative Critics of American Globalism*. New York: Simon and Schuster.

Rakove, Jack N. 1996. *Original Meanings: Politics and Ideas in the Making of the Constitution*. New York: Alfred A. Knopf.

Rand, Ayn. 1957. *Atlas Shrugged*. New York: New American Library.

Rawls, John. 1971. *A Theory of Justice*. Cambridge, MA: Belknap Press of Harvard University Press.

Reagan, Ronald. 1988. "Statement." *Congressional Quarterly Weekly Report*, August 6: 2226.

Reed, Ralph. 1996. *Active Faith: How Christians are Changing the Soul of American Politics*. New York: Free Press.

Ricardo, David. 1952. *The Works and Correspondence of David Ricardo*. Vol 5, *Speeches and Evidence*, ed. Piero Sraffa. Cambridge: Cambridge University Press.

Ricardo, David. 1996. *Principles of Political Economy and Taxation*. Buffalo, NY: Prometheus Books; originally published 1817.

Ridgeway, James. 1991. *Blood in the Face: The Klu Klux Klan, Aryan Nations, Nazi Skinheads, and the Rise of a New White Culture*. New York: Thunder's Mouth Press.

"Riding for a Fall." 1998. *Newsweek*, October 5, 56–58.

Riggenbach, Jeff. 1982. "The Disowned Children of Ayn Rand." *Reason*, December: 57–59.

Riley, Sid. 1996. "Our Politicians Are Playing Economic Craps." *Bobbin*, April: 76–79.

Ritter, Kurt W., and David Henry. 1992. *Ronald Reagan: The Great Communicator*. Westport, CT: Greenwood.

Robertson, Pat. 1991. *The New World Order*. Dallas: Word Publishing.

Rockwell, Llewellyn. 1998. "Mises and Liberty." Keynote address at the Ludwig von Mises Institute, Auburn University, Auburn, Alabama, June 5. Online. Available: http://www.mises.org.

Roepke, Wilhelm. 1960. *A Humane Economy: The Social Framework of the Free Market*. Chicago: Henry Regnery.

Rorty, Richard. 1982. *Consequences of Pragmatism: Essays, 1972–1980*. Minneapolis: University of Minnesota Press.

Rothbard, Murray N. 1994. *The Case Against the Fed*. Auburn, AL: Ludwig von Mises Institute.

Rothbard, Murray N. 1978. *For a New Liberty: The Libertarian Manifesto*. Rev. ed. New York: Collier Books.

Rust, Michael. 1999. "Rand's Story." *Insight on the News*, May 31: 10.

Schwartz, Nancy L. 1988. *The Blue Guitar: Political Representation and Community*. Chicago: University of Chicago Press.

Schiappa, Edward. 1991. *Protagoras and Logos: A Study in Greek Philosophy and Rhetoric*. Columbia: University of South Carolina Press.

Sciabarra, Chris Matthew. 1995. *Ayn Rand: The Russian Radical*. University Park: Pennsylvania State University Press.

Sharlet, Jeff. 1999. "Ayn Rand Finally Caught the Attention of Scholars." *Chronicle of Higher Education*, April 9: A17.

Skidelsky, Robert. 1986. *John Maynard Keynes: Hopes Betrayed, 1883–1920*. New York: Viking Press.

Smith, Adam. 1976. *The Wealth of Nations*, ed. Edwin Cannan. Chicago: University of Chicago Press; originally published 1776.

Smith, Adam. 1983. *Lectures on Rhetoric and Belles Lettres*. New York: Oxford University Press.

Soley, Lawrence. 1995. *Leasing the Ivory Tower: The Corporate Takeover of Academia*. Boston: South End Press.

Soskis, Benjamin. 2000. "Bush Family Values." *Lingua Franca*, March: 6–8.

Sowell, Thomas. 1995. "Repealing the Law of Gravity." *Forbes*, May 22: 82.

Spriggs, William, and Bruce Klein. 1994. *Raising the Floor: The Effects of the Minimum Wage on Low-Wage Workers*. Washington, DC: Economic Policy Institute.

Stephenson, Neal. 1992. *Snow Crash*. New York: Bantam Books.

Stephenson, Neal. 1995. *The Diamond Age, or, A Young Lady's Illustrated Primer*. New York: Bantam.

Stone, Allucquére Roseanne. 1995. *The War of Desire and Technology at the Close of the Mechanical Age*. Cambridge, MA: MIT Press.

Stone, Allucquére Roseanne. 1997. "What Vampires Know: Transsubjection and Transgender in Cyberspace." Online. 15 April 1997. Available: http://www.actlab.utexas.edu/~sandy.

Summers, Christina Hoff. 1994. *Who Stole Feminism?: How Women Have Betrayed Women*. New York: Simon & Schuster.

Sunstein, Cass. 1997. *Free Markets and Social Justice*. New York: Oxford University Press.

Sussman, Herbert. 1994. "Cyberpunk Meets Charles Babbage: *The Difference Engine* as Alternative Victorian History." *Victorian Studies* 38: 1–23.

Tackett, Michael. 1998. "Campaign for Righteousness." *Chicago Tribune*, May 25: A1.

Toffler, Alvin, and Heidi Toffler. 1995. *Creating a New Civilization: The Politics of the Third Wave*. Atlanta: Turner Publishing.

Van Warner, Rick. 1996. "Foodservice Industry Walks Fine Line in Minimum Wage Debate." *Nation's Restaurant News*, May 27: 21.

Vaughn, Karen. 1994. *Austrian Economics in America: The Migration of a Tradition*. Cambridge, UK: Cambridge University Press.

Verdisco, Robert J., and Morrison G. Cain. 1996. "Maximum Confusion over the Minimum Wage." *Discount Merchandiser* 36 (June): 8.

Von Mises, Ludwig. 1949. *Human Action*. 1st ed. New Haven, CT: Yale University Press.

Walton, Douglas. 1992. *Slippery Slope Arguments*. Cambridge, UK: Cambridge University Press.

Walzer, Michael. 1983. *Spheres of Justice: A Defense of Pluralism and Equality*. Oxford: Basil Blackwell.

Warren, Elizabeth. 1998. The Bankruptcy Crisis, *Indiana Law Journal*, 73 (Summer): 1079–1110.

Weaver, Richard M. 1953. "The Spaciousness of Old Rhetoric." In *The Ethics of Rhetoric*. Chicago: Regnery. 164–185.

Weaver, Richard M. 1964. *Visions of Order*. Baton Rouge: Louisiana State University Press.

Wehr, Elizabeth. 1988. "Trade, Plant-Closing Bills Win Strong House Backing." *Congressional Quarterly Weekly Report*, July 16: 1991.

Whately, Richard. 1832. *Introductory Lectures on Political Economy*. 2nd ed. London: B. Fellowes.

Whately, Richard. 1963. *Elements of Rhetoric*, ed. Douglas Ehninger. Carbondale: Southern Illinois University Press; originally published 1828.

"Who Pays for Unions?" 1998. *The Economist*, July 11: 75.

Wiethoff, William. 1996. *A Peculiar Humanism: The Judicial Advocacy of Slavery in High Courts of the Old South, 1820–1850*. Athens: University of Georgia Press.

Williams, Raymond. 1961. *The Long Revolution*. New York: Columbia University Press.

Wilson, John K. 1995. *The Myth of Political Correctness: The Conservative Attack on Higher Education*. Durham, NC: Duke University Press.

Winthrop, John. 1995. "A Model of Christian Charity." In Ronald F. Reid, ed., *American Rhetorical Discourse*. 2nd ed. Prospect Heights, IL: Waveland Press. 23–35.

Wolff, Jonathan. 1991. *Robert Nozick: Property, Justice, and the Minimal State*. Stanford, CA: Stanford University Press.

Wolff, Robert Paul. 1981. "Robert Nozick's Derivation of the Minimal State." In Jeffrey Paul, ed., *Reading Nozick: Essays on Anarchy, State, and Utopia*. Totowa, NJ: Rowman & Littlefield. 77–104.

Wolin, Sheldon S. 1960. *Politics and Vision*. Boston: Little, Brown.

Wolin, Sheldon S. 1989. *The Presence of the Past: Essays on the State and the Constitution*. Baltimore: Johns Hopkins University Press.

Wood, Gordon S. 1972. *Creation of the American Republic, 1776–1787*. New York: Norton.

Wood, Gordon S. 1982. "Conspiracy and the Paranoid Style: Causality and Deceit in the Eighteenth Century." *William and Mary Quarterly* 39: 401–441.

Woodward, Bob. 1994. *The Agenda*. New York: Simon & Schuster.

Wright, Erik Olin. 1985. *Classes*. London: Verso.

Zarefsky, David. 1995. "Coherence in Argumentation Studies: Can the Center Hold?" In Sally Jackson, ed., *Argumentation and Values*. Annandale, VA: Speech Communication Association. 54–59.

Index

About the Author

James Arnt Aune is Associate Professor of Speech Communication at Penn State University. He received his BA from St. Olaf College in 1975 and his PhD from Northwestern University in 1980. He has taught at Tulane University, the University of Virginia, the University of St. Thomas, and Texas A&M University. Professor Aune is also the author of *Rhetoric and Marxism* (Westview Press, 1994).

① a metaphorical precursor to the
rational choice model / master metaphor (?)

② perversity thesis (25 - Hirschman) and
early tariff debates

③ getting people to adopt "long term" perspective (28)

④ recurrent problem of meta communication - Alt.
(42)   conclusion ??

⑤ rent-seeking behavior — pursuit of special favors / protection
(46)   benefits

                                    (73)
⑥ conservative theme in A Rand - gov't function is to
protect (preserve) what exists (hence locus)

└ vs a more liberal mission to promote the Possible
                                    └ (what GB does
                                         capture)

⑦ conservative's appeal to
       victimhood (91)

                        ̶ "Social Darwin"

⑧ market - evolution (95)